A long and winding road

A *long and winding road*

XAVIER HERBERT'S LITERARY JOURNEY

SEAN MONAHAN

University of Western Australia Press

First published in 2003 by
University of Western Australia Press
Crawley, Western Australia 6009
www.uwapress.uwa.edu.au

 The State of Western Australia has made an investment in
this project through ArtsWA in association with the
artswa Lotteries Commission.

 Western Australia

Publication of this book was also made possible with funding assistance from
the Australian Academy of the Humanities.

National Library of Australia
Cataloguing-in-Publication entry:

Monahan, Sean.
    A long and winding road: Xavier Herbert's literary journey.

    Bibliography.
    Includes index.
    ISBN 1 876268 93 X.

    1. Herbert, Xavier, 1901–1984—Criticism and interpretation. 2. Herbert,
    Xavier, 1901–1984. Poor fellow my country. I. Title.

A823.2

Produced by Benchmark Publications, Melbourne
Consultant editor Amanda Curtin, Curtin Communications, Perth
Series design by Robyn Mundy Design, Perth
Cover design by Ron Hampton, Pages in Action, Melbourne
Typeset in 9½pt Garamond Light by Lasertype, Perth
Printed by BPA Print Group

For dearest Suss

We shared this project as
we've shared everything else

CONTENTS

ACKNOWLEDGMENTS

To Van Ikin of The University of Western Australia for his unfailing encouragement and perceptive advice during the writing of this book.

To Janet and Bill Grono, Suss and Niels Monahan and Barbara Harris for constructive criticism at the revision stage.

To Northrop Frye for his amazing *Anatomy of Criticism*. How much I owe to this ground-breaking work of criticism will very quickly become apparent.

To Frances de Groen for her superb biography *Xavier Herbert*. Its timely appearance in 1999 helped me sort out the fact from the fiction in Herbert's own accounts of his life.

To Russell McDougall for finding and collecting into one volume all Herbert's early stories. Without his *South of Capricornia* I could not have written Chapter 1.

To Amanda Curtin for her superb editing.

To Robyn Pill, heir to the Xavier Herbert literary estate and copyright holder, and to Curtis Brown (Aust.) Pty Ltd, for permission to quote from the works of Xavier Herbert.

CHRONOLOGY

1901	Born Geraldton, Western Australia.	
1904	Moves with family to Perth.	
1922	Qualifies as pharmacist.	
1923	Moves to Melbourne.	
1925	Enrols at Melbourne University.	First story published: 'North of Capricorn'.
1926	Moves to Sydney.	Two stories published.
1927	Journeys north, first to Queensland, then to Darwin.	Five stories published including: 'The Atheist', 'The Coming of Ezekiel Mort', 'The Way of a Man'. Two novellas written. One published: 'The Sea Vultures'.
1928	Takes hospital job in British Solomons. Leaves after three months. Back to Sydney.	Seven stories published including: 'The Medicine', 'The Rainmaker', 'When an Irresistible Force', 'The Beauty of Barbara'. One novella written. Not published.
1929	Returns to Darwin. Gets job as Government Pharmacist.	First novel started: 'Black Velvet'.
1930	Sails for London. Meets Sadie Norden on the boat.	'Black Velvet' completed.
1931	Living in London.	'Black Velvet' rejected by British publishers. *Capricornia* started.
1932	Living in London. Returns to Australia.	*Capricornia* completed. *Capricornia* rejected by British publishers.

1933	Living in Sydney. Writing stories to finance Sadie's return. Sadie arrives back in Australia.	Fourteen stories written. Thirteen published. Stephensen advises changes to *Capricornia*.
1934	Living in Sydney.	*Capricornia* revised in the light of Stephensen's advice.
1935	Moves to Darwin. Gets job as Relieving Superintendent, Kahlin Aboriginal Compound.	
1936	Temporary job at Kahlin finishes.	'Yellow Fellow' started.
1937	Pharmacy work and prospecting.	
1938	Moves back to Sydney.	*Capricornia* published.*
1939–40	Involved with Stephensen's Australia First movement.	Having difficulties with 'Yellow Fellow'.
1941		'Yellow Fellow' abandoned. *Seven Emus* (first version, 30,000 words) written.
1942–43	Army service in North Australia Observer Unit under W. E. H. Stanner.	
1943	In Sydney on leave without pay.	*Soldiers' Women* started.
1944	Army service in Sydney.	
1945–47	Living in Sydney.	Having difficulties with *Soldiers' Women*.
1948	Travels to Daintree, Cairns region.	Having difficulties with *Soldiers' Women*.
1949–50	Living in Daintree.	Having difficulties with *Soldiers' Women*.
1951	Buys house at Redlynch, near Cairns. Living at Redlynch from now on.	Writing *Soldiers' Women*.
1952–55		Writing *Soldiers' Women*.

1955		*Soldiers' Women* completed.
1956		*Soldiers' Women* rejected by Angus & Robertson. Substantial revision asked for.
1957		*Seven Emus* rewritten (final version, 60,000 words). 'The Little Widow' started.
1958		'The Little Widow' completed.
1959		'The Little Widow' rejected by Angus & Robertson. *Seven Emus* published.
1959–60		*Soldiers' Women* revised.
1961		*Soldiers' Women* published.
1962		*Disturbing Element* written. 'A Town Like Elliott' (essay) published.
1963		*Disturbing Element* published. *Larger than Life* (short stories) published.†
1964		Planning *Poor Fellow My Country*.
1965–67		Writing *Poor Fellow My Country*.
1968	Relieving pharmacist at Innisfail Hospital.	Writing *Poor Fellow My Country*.
1969–72		Writing *Poor Fellow My Country*.
1973		*Poor Fellow My Country* finished.
1974		*Poor Fellow My Country* published.

* Stephensen had intended to publish *Capricornia* much earlier than this, but the collapse of his publishing business in 1935 prevented him doing so. In 1937, he persuaded W. J. Miles to approve its publication by the Publicist Press.

† He wrote thirteen stories between 1933 and 1963. I have not listed the years in which each was first published. In 1963 they were included in *Larger than Life*.

A PARTISAN INTRODUCTION

I FIRST discovered Xavier Herbert in 1978, a year after my arrival in Australia. Recruited to teach English, and knowing next to nothing about Australian literature, I had embarked, during my first year, on a somewhat chaotic form of self-education. Seeking guidance from no-one, I simply picked Australian books at random off the library shelves and read as many as I had time for. Thus it was that I came to *Poor Fellow My Country* with no preconceptions at all. I had, to that point, read nothing else by Herbert. I knew nothing at all about the author or the reception his books had received and, after my year's reading of Australian novels, I certainly wasn't expecting a momentous experience. I had found plenty of interest and much pleasure in reading the work of writers like Richardson and Clarke, Prichard and Franklin, White and Stow, but nothing up to that point had affected me very profoundly. Thus it was that I opened *Poor Fellow My Country* with no very great expectations—and was bowled over!

I was caught from the first page: that marvellous scene by the waterhole. It was magical. It was exhilarating. It had, for me, a quality different from any other Australian book I had read. The characters and themes seemed to be working on a richer level of creative complexity. My reading till then had, to some extent, been duty. This was obsession. This was a book I could not put down. I loved its size. The longer, the better, as far as I was concerned. I enjoyed it all: the melodrama and Delacy's pontificating as much as the numinous scenes involving Prindy and the Australian bush. I knew this was a book I would read again and again, whatever its length. I had never read a novel quite like it, one that, as well as telling a great story, caught within its pages so full, so complex and so illuminating a picture of a whole culture. The novels it brought to mind were Tolstoy's *War and Peace* and Hugo's *Les Miserables* and it bore comparison with both.

Its capacity to illuminate the culture was, perhaps, even more evident to a newcomer than it might have been to Australians of longer standing. It is Alice, the recent arrival, who sees the strangeness of Wonderland. For those who have always lived there, the strange has become normal, as indeed it has for me after twenty-five years in Australia. I no longer see things with the fresh eyes of an immigrant. Back in the seventies I did, and there were many things I found hard to understand until the day I started reading *Poor Fellow My Country*. To give just one example, at first sight the Australian approach to life seemed attractively tough and independent-minded, and the cheerfully aggressive attitude to 'bloody poms' seemed to indicate a belligerent rejection of the former colonial master. Gradually, though, I began to notice perplexing anomalies. I followed a debate in the letters pages of the local paper over proposals for an Australian flag minus the Union Jack, and was mystified to find dyed-in-the-wool patriots supporting retention of the British symbol, those who wanted a wholly Australian flag stigmatised as unpatriotic. I went to an international hockey tournament and watched in disbelief as an Australian audience rose for the British national anthem. Involved in helping to plan conferences, I found it hard to understand why third-rate British and American academics were routinely preferred as keynote speakers to first-rate locals. Turning to party politics, my confusion grew. How to understand the veneration of Menzies, with his unabashed preference for England over Australia? How to explain the rejection of Whitlam, with his confident assertion of Australian independence? How to comprehend the deep-rooted assumption that Australia could not survive if it did anything to irritate its 'great and powerful friends'? Those brought up in the country seemed to find none of this strange. To an outsider it was like straying through the looking glass. There were, and still are, strange contradictions here whose nature, causes and effects are expressed and explored as well through the narrative of *Poor Fellow My Country* as in anything I have since read.

Impressed as I was by the novel, it came as a surprise to discover how mixed a response it had received. Highly praised by a few, it was mercilessly treated by others: a 'botch' according to one academic[1], a 'literary brontosaurus, Poor Bugger My Book' according to another.[2] Puzzled by what seemed an inexplicable injustice, I began reading the rest of Herbert's work and soon had something else to puzzle over—its strangely mixed quality. It was strange for two reasons: first, because the variations were so extreme, from very good to embarrassingly bad; second, because the movement was up and down, not, as one would expect in a developing writer, up and up. It was hard to understand how the man whose early short stories were crudely stereotypical tales written for popular magazines suddenly produced, in his first published novel, something of the calibre of *Capricornia*. It was even harder to understand how, having written something as good as *Capricornia*, he followed it up with two novels as bad as *Soldiers' Women* and 'The Little Widow'. Why was it that, instead of steady development of the talent evident in *Capricornia*, the next thirty years produced nothing but regression? And how was it that, after thirty years of failure, he finally moved forward again and produced *Poor Fellow My Country*?

The impetus for this book, then, was twofold. The primary motivation was a desire to enter the lists on behalf of *Poor Fellow My Country*. The secondary motivation was an interest in finding explanations for the strangeness of Herbert's total output. The result, many years later, is a book with three aims. The first is to explore the nature of Herbert's achievements in *Capricornia* and *Poor Fellow My Country*. The second is to examine Herbert's oeuvre as a series of steps along the road to *Poor Fellow My Country*, seeing how in writing each of the earlier books he developed practices that had significant effects, some good and some bad, on the form of his final novel. The third aim is to attempt to find explanations for what happened to Herbert's writing in the second half of his career—why it took the direction it did, why that direction caused him problems in the fifties and how he overcame those problems in the sixties.

In pursuit of the third aim, I soon found myself considering the relationship between Herbert's personality and his writing. While any conclusions drawn could only be speculative, the more I read the biographical evidence, the more it seemed that such speculation would, at the least, be interesting, and at best might provide useful insights into why Herbert's writing developed as it did. One question, for instance, that began to fascinate me as I learned more and more about Herbert was the fundamental question of how he ever managed to become as good as he did, since he seemed, in a number of ways, temperamentally unsuited to novel writing. For one thing, he was utterly self-absorbed and showed little interest in anyone else. On at least one occasion he admitted he found other people boring, and while renowned for his habit of talking relentlessly and endlessly to anyone willing to listen, he was not himself a good listener.[3] He liked conversations—but only if he could monopolise them. In the second half of his life, even one-sided conversations must have become few and far between, since he opted, more and more, to live in solitary fashion with few social contacts. All this helps to explain why the dialogue is often bad and the characterisation often weak in the books of the fifties. What is harder to fathom is how Herbert ever managed to create the successful characters of *Capricornia* and *Poor Fellow My Country*.

Another obvious handicap was that Herbert was a limited thinker, with an inflated view of the importance of his ideas, and a more and more insistent urge to use fiction for didactic purposes. It was a dangerous combination. Even when the ideas are profound, didacticism rarely produces good novels. Since Herbert's thinking was anything but profound, the failures of the didactic novels of the fifties are easy to understand. The difficulty is to explain the success of the equally didactic *Poor Fellow My Country*.

A further handicap was the fallibility of Herbert's taste. He thought everything he wrote superb—the stereotypical short stories, the seriously flawed *Soldiers' Women* and the mercifully unpublished 'The Little Widow' as much as *Capricornia* and *Poor Fellow My Country*. The mannered and cumbersome new style he 'invented' in the fifties in a foolish attempt to prove his 'originality' provides a good illustration of the fallibility of his taste.[4] The style he fondly believed would prove his 'mastery' of the novel was, in fact, an unmitigated disaster, as his editor, Beatrice Davis, did her best to make him see. She had no success, however, since, as well as finding it impossible to judge the quality of his own work accurately, Herbert also found it impossible to respond sensibly to criticism, however friendly and constructive. It was, again, a dangerous mix for an author.

Given his handicaps, it is all too easy to understand why Herbert sometimes wrote bad books. What is harder to understand is how he ever wrote good ones. How can that be explained? How did a man of very average intelligence and very real weaknesses as a writer manage to write a book as ambitious, original and successful as *Poor Fellow My Country*? Partly, I think, by sheer persistence. William Blake once wrote, 'If the fool would persist in his folly he would become wise'[5], and Herbert was proof of that dictum. Despite his less than obvious qualifications for the task, he managed in the end to write a great novel simply by keeping at it until he found the way to do so. And he kept at it because he had what Arthur Miller, in a different context, once described as 'a fanatic insistence on his self-conceived role'.[6] In Herbert's case, the role he conceived was to be the writer of great novels. *Soldiers' Women*, he believed, would 'have as great an effect upon mankind as had "The Origin of the Species"'.[7] As for *Poor Fellow My Country*, in that book, he said, 'I am building a monument out of the truths I have collected. [...][8] I can smile when I die looking up at that monument, knowing that I have contributed to the advancement of my species'.[9]

As he believed it was his destiny to write great novels, so he believed he had the talent to fulfil that destiny. Though the critical establishment's refusal to acknowledge the fact always bothered him, he persisted in regarding himself as one of the giants of literature. Among modern Australian writers only Patrick White, he said, could 'truly claim to be my equal'.[10] Nor did he hesitate to match himself with older masters. As he worked on one scene from *Poor Fellow My*

Country, he said to his wife, 'Shakespeare made a masterpiece of the "Rape of Lucrece"—I've got to make a better one'.[11] As he worked on another, he mused, 'Am I a squib that I will avoid difficulties like Tolstoy in *Anna Karenina?*' He continued with sublime certainty, 'This piece is a superb one. Imagine me trying to squib it! [...] I can't help but do it superbly. It is my existence, my purpose'.[12]

All this explains why Herbert persevered. It does not explain why he succeeded. A clue to that is found in something Gore Vidal once wrote:

> Dostoevsky, Conrad and Tolstoy [...] were not much con-
> cerned with laboratory experiments. Their interest was in
> what Miss Sontag calls 'The subject'; and though it is true
> they did not leave the form of the novel as they found it,
> their art was not the product of calculated experiments
> with form so much as it was the result of their ability, by
> virtue of what they were, to transmute the familiar and
> make it rare. They were men of genius unobsessed by
> what Goethe once referred to as 'an eccentric desire for
> originality'. Or as Saul Bellow puts it: 'Genius is always,
> without strain, avant-garde. Its departure from tradition is
> not the result of caprice or of policy but of an inner
> necessity.' Absorbed by his subject, the genius is a natural
> innovator—a fact which must be maddening to the ordi-
> nary writer.[13]

In Herbert's career we find evidence of both kinds of writing. It was a thoroughly 'eccentric desire for originality' that led Herbert in the fifties to embark on the calculated experiment with style whose unhappy results can be seen in *Soldiers' Women* and 'The Little Widow'. In contrast, the writer of *Capricornia*, unconcerned with originality and so absorbed in his subject that he wrote in a kind of 'trance'[14], produced a novel whose genuine originality the author himself never properly recognised. In *Poor Fellow My Country* the natural innovation of a writer absorbed in his subject becomes even more evident. It is in that book that he demonstrates most clearly the ability to 'transmute the familiar and make it rare' by virtue simply of the kind of man he was—a dreamer, a romancer, a symbol thinker, a natural allegorist. These are not qualities commonly associated with Herbert, but they are qualities he reveals again and again in his letters and novels, and they were central to his success as a writer. Also important to his success was the one subject that always brought out the best in him—Australia. It was the only subject he ever dealt with effectively. When, in the fifties, he attempted others, he failed. But, absorbed in writing about Australia, he did indeed become 'a natural innovator', unfettered by the constraints of tradition and driven by some 'inner necessity' to find new ways to express all he wanted to say.

It is, I believe, because Herbert *was* an innovator, particularly in his use of genre, that his achievements have still not been properly recognised. Northrop Frye, in his *Anatomy of Criticism*, explains why generic experiments of the kind found in Herbert's novels are often poorly understood. The root of the problem, he suggests, is 'the sloppy habit of identifying fiction with [...] the novel'. The term 'novel', he argues, which 'up to about 1900 was still the name of a more or less recognizable form, has since expanded into a catchall term which can be applied to practically any prose book that is not "on" something'. We must, he says, 'start to think seriously about the novel, not as fiction, but as a form of fiction' and recognise that there are other forms, equally valid, with their own features and conventions.[15] In place of the catch-all term 'novel', Frye proposed a division of prose fiction into four genres, which he called 'anatomy', 'confession', 'romance' and 'novel'. Three of these will already be familiar to readers. Frye's more narrowly and precisely defined 'novel' is the genre found in the work of writers like Jane Austen and Henry James. His 'romance' includes both the popular romance of modern thrillers, adventures and love stories and the high romance of classical and medieval periods. His 'confession' is the genre more commonly called 'autobiography'. His fourth genre, 'anatomy', is a genre that is less often recognised. Books in which this genre plays a major part include *Gargantua and Pantagruel*, *The Anatomy of Melancholy*, *The Compleat Angler*, *Gulliver's Travels*, *Erewhon*, *The Water Babies*, *Les Miserables*, *Brave New World* and *Such is Life*. Distinguishing features of the genre are its didacticism, its lengthy intellectual discussions, its willingness to digress from the narrative in order to explore ideas, and its connection with satire and the comedy of humours.

Frye's taxonomy is particularly useful in studying the achievement of writers who make extensive use of genres that are unfashionable or unrecognised. 'In nearly every period of literature', Frye points out, 'there are many romances, confessions, and anatomies that are neglected only because the categories to which they belong are unrecognised'.[16] Nor is it only neglect writers of such books suffer. They also tend to be unfairly criticised not for doing badly what they have set out to do but for not doing what they never intended to do in the first place. They are blamed, as Herbert has all too often been blamed, for offending against the conventions of the 'novel'[17], rather than judged on the effectiveness of their use of the conventions of romance, confession and anatomy.

It is in *Poor Fellow My Country* that Herbert's use of genre is most original and most successful, and it is *Poor Fellow My Country* that suffers most when criticism fails to understand quite what is going on generically. One problem is that the book's central genre, romance, tends to be undervalued nowadays in comparison with 'novel'. It was predictable, for instance, that early criticism paid so much attention to Delacy, the 'novel' anti-hero, and so little to Prindy, the romance hero. Many commentators found it hard to see past the voluble, opinionated, active white male to the passive, silent Aboriginal boy. They found it hard to understand that Prindy is at least as important as Delacy. Concentrating not on the symbol and allegory of romance but on the social history and psychology of 'novel', they sometimes failed even to recognise, let alone explore, Prindy's complexity.

A second problem is that the anatomy elements in *Poor Fellow My Country* are rarely recognised as the conventions of a perfectly valid prose fiction genre, and are therefore almost never judged on their own terms. Instead of being examined for what they achieve and how well they achieve it, the anatomy elements are more often seen as failed attempts to utilise 'novel' conventions and criticised accordingly. The *Oxford History of Australian Literature*'s criticism is typical. 'Too much of the narration', it complains, 'is flat dialogue or prosy exposition. The social anthropology is explained, not dramatised'.[18] The problem with this is that the standards applied are inappropriate to anatomy. It is the 'novel' in which the convention of 'naturalistic dialogue' is preferred to the flatter sounding, didactic dialogue of anatomy. And it is the 'novel' in which, as Frye says, an 'interest in ideas and theoretical statements is alien' and the 'technical problem is to dissolve all theory into personal relationships'.[19] To criticise *Poor Fellow My Country* for explaining rather than dramatising ideas is, in effect, to criticise it for selecting the conventions of anatomy over those of 'novel'. It is only when the genre of anatomy is recognised for what it is, and when its conventions are accepted as perfectly appropriate for use in prose fiction, that it becomes possible to see how well Herbert uses those conventions and how effectively they achieve his purposes.

I began writing this book in the belief that Herbert deserved better than he had received in the way of critical acknowledgment. Nothing I have learned during the course of studying his work has changed that view. Flawed though he was even in his best books, capable though he was of serious errors of judgment and very bad writing, at his best he wrote with a power matched by few, and an originality that is startling. *Poor Fellow My Country* is, I believe, one of the great novels of world literature, and the relative neglect it has suffered in recent years will not, I hope, continue for much longer. Describing similar cases of neglect, Frye comments:

> A great romancer should be examined in terms of the conventions he chose. William Morris should not be left on the side lines of prose fiction merely because the critic has not learned to take the romance form seriously. [...] If Scott has any claims to be a romancer, it is not good criticism to deal only with his defects as a novelist.[20]

For 'Scott' and 'Morris' read 'Herbert', and to 'romance' add 'anatomy'. It was as romancer and anatomist that, against the odds, and from the least promising of beginnings, Herbert achieved greatness.

PART I

THE SHORT STORIES

CHAPTER 1

An Apprenticeship in
Popular Romance

ERBERT'S first short story was published in 1925. In the years leading up to the writing of *Capricornia*, he wrote fourteen more stories and three novellas[1], most of them for the *Australian Journal*, a popular magazine offering its readers stereotypical tales of adventure and romance. None of Herbert's early stories rose significantly above that level, and were it not for his later achievements, there would be no reason to give them a second glance. Intrinsically they are of minuscule interest. The interest comes from their relationship to the novels that followed. It is interesting to see how the lessons he internalised as a writer of popular romance influenced the way he plotted his novels later. And, since the leap from the hackneyed cliché of the stories to the assured ironies of *Capricornia* seems at first inexplicable, it is interesting to search for clues to the mystery of where Herbert learned skills that no-one reading his early stories would have dreamed he possessed.

Herbert's first attempts at writing were not promising. His own taste at the time was for popular adventure and romance[2], and it was, he later said, because he was so powerfully affected by stories of 'innocence cruelly besmirched by libertines' that he decided to try writing one himself.[3] The result was his first published story, 'North of Capricorn'. Its quality can be seen from the following:

> She rushed into the man's arms, and clung to him, fiercely. 'Fred, oh Fred, you came!' she sobbed, hysterically as she buried her head on his great chest. But in a moment she had regained herself, and slipping from his protection, cried, 'Oh, Fred...Rossell!'
> Even as she uttered his name the man sprang to the deck. He stopped as he saw Carter, his face demoniac and flushed, his heavy lips sagging horribly in a bestial leer. 'Stay where you are, Rossell,' warned Fred.
> 'Ho, Mr. Blooming Engineer, so yer follered me. I see all through yer little game now [...] Yer after my girl, yer— swine, but it's hands off. Understand? Hands off, she's my girl. Mine! See?' snarled Rossell. The man was beside himself with an insane lust, his eyes searching the figure of the girl maniacal.
> 'I'm not yours, you dog!' cried Olive. A moment ago she was a sobbing, terrorized little animal, and now, her head was erect, and her dark eyes flashed the fury which she felt.
> Fred bunched up two huge fists, and his jaw snapped shut.
> 'Not mine, eh? You minx. I'll show yer!' Rossell jumped forward quickly and grasped the slender waist of the girl, and pulling her to him, bent his leering mouth close to her lips.
> Like a shot Fred sprang. He tore the girl away, and then, with the full weight of his body behind it, his iron fist crashed into the face of Rossell. The man staggered and fell, pressed his hand to his face, then slowly rose. Diabolical passion lusted in his eyes, the passion to kill. His lips twisted in a snarl.[4]

It's hard to see in this welter of stereotype and cliché any hint of a major Australian novelist in the making. But it wasn't a major novelist the editor of the *Australian Journal* was looking for. His readers, he once said, wouldn't 'have recognised a cliché if they had stubbed their toes on one'.[5] Nor were they interested in development of character or exploration of issues. What they wanted was what Herbert gave them: noble heroes, dastardly villains, beautiful heroines and plenty of action. Herbert's other audience at this time, the readers of boys' magazines, wanted much the same. The quality of the stories Herbert wrote for them can be seen in the following extract from 'The Sea Vultures', a novella he wrote for *PALS* magazine:

> 'I have got you at last, you dog!' he hissed, his snake-like lips writhing in a grin that was horrible to see. 'You thought to frustrate Ling Siang Mei, prince of the great Kia Yoh! Bah! But Ling Siang Mei and his Sea Vultures are as old as the great Yangtse River, and as relentless and irresistible as its flood. You will pay, Harry Quaile, you white faced dog—pay!'
> The claws of the Vulture beat hideously against the boy's defenceless face. Harry, powerless in the grim paralysis of the Living Death, stared at his captor, chilled with horror.[6]

In terms of sheer quality, the gulf between these early stories and the novels that came later is obvious. There are, however, similarities in their plotting. In both the stories and the novels, Herbert gravitated naturally towards the genre of romance and often employed plot conventions Frye describes as follows:

> The essential element of plot in romance is adventure [...] and as soon as romance achieves a literary form, it tends to limit itself to a sequence of minor adventures leading up to a major or climacteric adventure, usually announced from the beginning, the completion of which rounds off the story. We may call this major adventure [...] the quest.[7]

Of the eighteen stories Herbert wrote prior to 1930, all but three[8] involve the romance plot as here defined. In the boys' adventure stories, the quest element is always central. 'The Sea Vultures', for instance, follows the quest of a schoolboy hero to solve the mystery of his father's disappearance. In pursuit of that quest, the hero tumbles in and out of a succession of unlikely and exotic adventures. The love stories, too, are built around a quest, in this case the quest of the hero to overcome the obstacles in his path and win, finally, the heroine. To increase the adventure element in these love quests, a favourite plot, used in six of the love stories[9], involves either the hero or heroine taking on a contract and struggling to fulfil it in the teeth of fierce opposition from powerful enemies and/or the forces of nature.

Given the nature of this apprenticeship, it comes as no surprise to find a strong element of quest romance in the plotting of Herbert's novels. In *Capricornia* the central plot element is Norman's quest to achieve success and respect in Capricornian society. In *Poor Fellow My Country* the central element is Prindy's quest to find his 'own road' and achieve initiation into the Snake Cult. In both, as in the stories, the quest involves a series of adventures, one of whose aims is simply to catch and hold the reader's interest.

An important lesson Herbert learned from writing the short stories, he later said, was the need to give readers 'a thrill in every line. If there's not a thrill, they won't want to read it'.[10] It was a lesson he never forgot. In the novels, too, he always sought to hold the reader's interest by filling the plot with exciting incident. In just two chapters of *Capricornia*, for instance, he gives us a man-hunt, a wife stealing, a caricature wedding, a trial, two beatings, two attempted murders, a riotous party, a natural disaster, a fight and three railway accidents.[11] 'My stories', he said, 'were always dramatic. There are nearly 1500 pages in [*Poor Fellow My Country*] and every one of them has got to tell a story, so that people do not put it down'.[12] Thus it was that he structured *Poor Fellow My Country*, on one level, as a succession of adventures. No sooner does one end than the next begins. In one section, for instance, Nell and Prindy escape from custody. They flee in a small boat with George and Queeny. They are shipwrecked. They fall into the hands of the nightcart men, who rob them and rape Nell. They escape again. Prindy has an accident. They are helped by Nugget Knowles, who falls in love with Nell. Nugget's brother rapes Nell. They flee again. George tricks Nell and Queeny and spirits Prindy away. Furious, Nell and Queeny pursue George. They catch him. George kills Nell. Queeny and George kill each other. Prindy sets off alone into the wilderness.[13] The influence of the apprenticeship in 'thrill a line' plotting could hardly be clearer.

That apprenticeship left Herbert with a lifelong love of strongly dramatic scenes. Describing the writing of one such scene, he said:

> Here's a man with the gout blood of his life flowing out of his severed hand and the captain dying with a great hole in his gut. [...] I really went to town on it. You can see what a dramatic scene it is and I am a dramatic writer. I like that kind of thing.[14]

His liking for 'that kind of thing' had mixed results in the novels. In *Soldiers' Women* it produced, too often for comfort, weak melodrama such as the following:

> The battle with tongue and stick and chair raged down the stairs and through the living-room and out the front door. It was lost from the start by her who had joined it: she was now reeling, choking for breath, collapsing on the luggage, gibbering, with strange and terrible screwing up of features. A knot in the left cheek pulled lip almost up to eye and left the right side to gape and glare slackly. [...]
>
> [She] turned to snarl: 'You'll be sorry, you pair of whores. Mark my words, you'll be sorry!'
>
> She spat out of her path the red cat that would have barred it, menaced the cringing children with her wand— and was gone.[15]

A happier result of Herbert's penchant for melodrama was the success he often had in scenes of Gothic violence. In one of *Soldiers' Women*'s few really memorable scenes, for instance, a young woman slowly and agonisingly retches her life away after drinking corrosive fluid.[16] In *Poor Fellow My Country*, too, the death scenes are always powerful. The ritual rape and murder of Savitra, for instance, is a frighteningly effective depiction of brutal violence.[17]

A further legacy of Herbert's apprenticeship was his liking for plots that involved schemes and tricks. The short stories are full of 'schemes'. 'I've got a scheme!' exults the hero of one. 'Holy Moses! What a scheme', marvels a character in another.[18] So much did he enjoy tricks and schemes that, in later years, Herbert came more and more often to build whole stories around them.[19] In one of the later stories, for instance, a Greek father tricks his nephews into marrying his dowerless daughters; in another, a Japanese shopkeeper tricks two rich pearlers into parting with their money. Unexceptionable in these lightweight stories, the taste for schemes and tricks was to prove problematic for the novels. It led to scenes in which both Herbert and his characters treat childish schemes with a seriousness that to mature readers can only seem ridiculous. The following, from *Soldiers' Women*, is typical:

> After a while Rosa said, 'If only we could go to the party, and Lolly tipped Materkins off, and we worked our trick, it would give Lolly one in the eye too. [...] I'd like to get Lolly at the same time as Materkins. Wait a minute! I told her this morning I couldn't say whether we could go to the party till I'd spoken to you. I said I'd phone her. Well, suppose I do phone her and tell her we can't come because we've already got something on? If she really is spying for Materkins she'll want to know all about it...and I'll give her something red hot to report to Materkins.'[20]

The tone, as so often in these cases, is pure Enid Blyton. In *Poor Fellow My Country* we find similarly portentous treatment of a number of childish schemes: when Delacy foils Rhoda's attempt to wrest the golden horseshoes from Alfie, for instance, or when he tricks Ballywick into helping him cash a cheque. Such scenes, appropriate enough in the *Boys Own Paper*, seem out of place in an adult novel. Credulity is often strained to breaking point—and never more so than when the hitherto perfectly sensible Monsignor Maryzic sets a trap that has him crouching in one room over a dictaphone while the wicked Captain Shane reveals all to a hidden microphone in another.[21] It was just the kind of schoolboyish scheme the Herbert of the short stories loved. It is not at all the kind of thing a sensible Catholic priest would dream up.

While connections between the plotting of the stories and the plotting of the novels are relatively easy to find, the same cannot be said of stylistic connections. There seems, at first sight, nothing to explain the leap from cliché and stereotype to the irony and wit of *Capricornia*. On closer inspection, however, it is possible to see the first small signs of the talent to come. 'What is sweeter', Herbert has one of his characters say, 'than the delight of being cleverly sarcastic?'[22] It was a delight Herbert shared, and whenever he indulges it, we begin to see signs of *Capricornia* in the writing. Early in his second story, 'The Unforgivable', we find this:

> Port Morson, even after sunset, is not a very comfortable place in mid-summer. The tropical sun works overtime in North Australia. For fifteen hour shifts Old Sol diligently bakes the patient country brown, then leaves it for a space to simmer in its own hot juice.
>
> Unless you are under the influence of some solar antidote (whisky is the usual prescription) you will be liable, your attention concentrated on vain endeavours to maintain a temperature lower than that of proximate bodies, to miss what is undoubtedly the most wonderful collection of sunsets in the world.
>
> Supposing that you have rendered yourself reasonably immune to the heat, you will discover that, suddenly, with an incredible swiftness, the white, hot sun has vanished and that an unseen painter has begun to daub the western sky with every color on his spectral palette; that the lazy Timor Sea, whose vivid blue has tortured your eyes all day, has grown sadly dark, and seems to mourn in purple weeds the dying King of Day; and that the dazzling white

shores of the crescent beach now rim the silent waters
like the scalloped lips of some vast blue bowl.

Thus, if some subtle element is moving in your blood;
otherwise—even have you the soul of a Shelley—you
will remain blind to beauty, while you swat mosquitoes
and mop your steaming brow.[23]

The ironic mode suited him. While still not particularly distinguished,
the writing is certainly better here. The sentence rhythms are more
sophisticated, the inflated language used more effectively for mock-
heroic effect. 'Old Sol diligently baking the patient country' and 'under
the influence of some solar antidote' clash with gentle irony against
'whisky is the usual prescription'. The purple passages of paragraphs
three and four are brought to earth with a bump as the 'soul of
Shelley' meets the common man swatting mosquitoes and mopping a
steaming brow.

In 'The Unforgivable' the irony does not last beyond the first
page; in two other stories, 'The Atheist' and 'The Coming of Ezekiel
Mort', it is more sustained. Influenced, perhaps, by a desire to
emulate *The History of Mr Polly*, one of the few 'literary' books he
had so far read and one that made a deep impression on him[24],
Herbert moved away from romance in these stories and experimented with social satire. The results, while far from his later skill,
were promising. In 'The Atheist', for instance, we find something of
Capricornia's mocking humour in passages such as the following,
where a phlegmatic farmer surveys his devastated crops:

He was not thinking of anything in particular. To Dan
there was nothing in particular worth thinking about. Of
course his mind was active enough; once he thought of
an old pal who had gone to Sydney, then he pondered
upon the subject of iced beer, and switched on to Pringle
and the dead plough horse.[25]

In 'The Coming of Ezekiel Mort', too, there are hints of *Capricornia*:
in the balance of the sentences and, crude and heavy-handed though
it is at this point, in the irony.

Business [...] was the art, work and hobby of Alderman Giltburg. He was a jeweler because Fate and his father had made him so, and he continued to obey their decrees because there was money in it. He was Lord Mayor for several reasons. One of which was that to some extent it eased the inter-prandial gnawings of the rodent dyspepsia to snarl, *sotto voce:* 'I am the Lord Mayor of this city!'[26]

Delighted at first simply with getting published, it wasn't very long before Herbert began to want more. Pleasing the readers of the *Australian Journal* was no longer enough. He wanted to be taken seriously by people who knew something about writing. In pursuit of that aim he did two things: he embarked on a program of serious reading, and he set off north in search of new material. The journey took him to Queensland and the Northern Territory. The reading took him to the novels of Huxley, Bennett, Dreiser, Mann and, most significant of all, Dickens.[27]

Herbert encountered Dickens on the first leg of his journey north and was, he later said, 'delighted' by his style.[28] The effect of that delight is immediately apparent. The very next story he wrote opens with the hero in the grip of malaria:

> Seated beside Cadogan's bed with note-book and pencil, an engineering student (had one been in attendance) might have learned a hundred wrinkles about railroad construction. There were wild discourses on flanges, crowns and H-pieces; confidential whispers concerning fish-plates and white-ends, green ends and sleepers; hoarse mutterings about super-elevation and ballasting. But the student—provided he were not a resident of Statham—would have been baffled when the lecturer interrupted his theories with shouts of: 'That damned Carney gang,' and 'Those blasted crooks have ruined me!'
>
> Oh, what Port Statham had not already known about the John Cadogan muddle—and Port Statham is still sufficiently small, despite its claims to cityship, to interest

> itself in the affairs of its inhabitants—John himself, in the
> frankness of delirium, told them.
>
> He was a potential bankrupt. He was a high-flyer
> who had flown into an extremely tight contract at an
> extremely low tender [...]. Unfortunately, he had flown in
> without capital, had bought his plant and paid his men
> and wheeled everything on empty credit. On credit that
> squeaked at every movement like a pair of brand new
> boots![29]

The influence of Dickens is everywhere apparent: in the zest of
the first paragraph's comic exaggeration, in the final paragraph's
exploration of the comic possibilities of extended metaphor, in the
witty choice of 'frankness'. The Dickensian quality does not extend
beyond the first few pages of this story and is only occasionally and
fleetingly found in the stories that follow but it is enough to show
where Herbert first learned to strike a note that sounds so strongly in
Capricornia.

Another sign of Herbert's desire to do more than satisfy a taste
for popular romance is his attempt, in three of the early stories, to
use narrative for more serious purposes. In each, that purpose was to
express his views on gender. The first of these stories, 'The Way of a
Man', makes it crystal clear from the start what those views are. The
story opens with the hero chastising the heroine for seeking an
independent career:

> 'A whistling woman and a crowing hen, are neither good
> to God nor men?' [...] If you are a woman, be a woman—
> if you are a man then be a man. There is a job for each—
> one job. A man's is being a fighter and a worker, a
> woman's, a wife and mother.[30]

Scornfully rejecting this advice, the heroine spends the story battling
to build a career as a construction engineer, but as the going gets
tough she begins to long for 'a stronger hand, a man's hand—to
drag the burden from her weary shoulders'.[31] The story ends in her
complete capitulation.

> She smiled, just a tiny smile, through a sea of tears. Her hair was tousled, her glasses gone, her red lips moist and quivering. She was just a pretty girl.
>
> Riordan swallowed.
>
> 'Oh!' she faltered, 'Oh, Con. Will you take on the job? I—I—I can't crow any longer!'
>
> She wept her heart out on his breast.
>
> 'Don't cry little man, don't cry,' he whispered, huskily.
>
> 'I'm not a man—I'm only a girl,' she sobbed.[32]

The attempt to use popular romance to preach a message of male dominance has clearly done nothing to improve the quality of Herbert's writing. The style is still cliché-ridden. The characterisation has lurched from the stereotypical heroine of popular romance to an even more demeaning female stereotype. The dialogue is as embarrassingly inept.

The other two stories, 'When an Irresistible Force' and 'The Beauty of Barbara', were no better in quality but more interesting and potentially profitable as experiments. In both, Herbert tried mixing 'clever sarcasm' with the romance formula. 'The Beauty of Barbara', for instance, begins with the heroine 'blind and deaf to her womanhood, unconscious of the paint and powder and pretties, oblivious to the frocks and fallals and all that which usually gladdens feminine hearts'. Enter a rustic Pygmalion who teaches her the things 'indispensable to the business of the coquette', 'the art of lifting eye-brows and rolling eyes', the clever application of cosmetics and selection of dress.[33] Armed with these—the truly essential skills of womanhood, the story implies—Barbara metamorphoses from ugly duckling to swan and marries her Pygmalion. The tone throughout is mocking as Herbert turns romance into burlesque fairytale. The result is a story that is neither funny nor pleasant—but that is the fault of the gender theory, not the genre experiment. The attempt to mix romance with other genres for serious purposes was, as the novels were to prove, a step in the right direction, even though the demeaning role Herbert's gender theory allocates to women makes this story unpalatable.

Gender was, as *Soldiers' Women* and 'The Little Widow' would later prove, not the right subject for Herbert. Australia was—

and that becomes apparent every time the Australian landscape enters the early stories. In 'The Atheist', for instance:

> The drought had broken, and from the earth emanated that soft odour of damp fertility. Rivers and dams filled; the hush of the bluegum forest broke with the drought, and the great branches hummed pleasantly in the sway of the wet east wind. A hundred culverts and creeks sang merrily and the farmers of Koompartoo sang with them. Rain, Rain, Rain![34]

Already there is something of the quality that makes *Poor Fellow My Country*'s descriptions of Australia so memorable. Here, as later, the description is more idyllic than realistic. Already this is more the landscape of high romance than realism, with its soft odours, pleasantly humming branches and merrily singing creeks. Here, too, as later, the landscape is alive with movement: rain falling, water running swiftly, wind blowing. In the stories following the move north such descriptions become more frequent. In 'The Rainmaker', for instance, there is romance in the idealised beauty of plains 'where the wild emu runs to the silver dawn and the brolga dances in the painted sunset'. There is also, as in the novels, a strong sense of an Australia bursting with life: the bull grass 'eight feet high and green as only tropical grass is green', the red plain 'sunken under inches of luke-warm water and vivid with a wild rice crop', the snipe 'flittering on arrow-swift wings above the backs of thousands of sleek fat cattle'.[35] From the very beginning, the one subject that always brought out the best in Herbert was the Australian landscape.

Hard, then, though it seems at first, it is possible to find in the early short stories some evidence of the quality to come. It is there in the occasional success of the witty sarcasm, in the brief flashes of Dickensian zest, in the descriptions of landscape. These signs of developing talent, however, are few and far between and, in absolute terms, the early stories are weak—mostly very weak. Nor did Herbert's short story writing ever become much better. Between 1933, when he returned to Australia with the first draft of *Capricornia* already completed, and 1963, when he published a collection called *Larger than Life*, Herbert wrote a further twenty-seven stories, but the writing in all but two, 'Kaijek the Songman' and 'Come on Murri', remains undistinguished. It is significant that both those stories deal with Aboriginal characters.

The truth is that, while Herbert always rather fancied himself as a short story writer, it was simply not a form to which he was suited. A well-crafted story is a perfectly composed miniature in which each brushstroke is in precisely the right place. Herbert was never that sort of craftsman. He worked best with huge, sprawling canvases in which infelicities and even downright errors of colour, texture and shade are lost in, and sometimes even contribute to, the raucous, outrageous energy of the whole. It is to the first of those sprawling canvases we now turn.

PART II

CAPRICORNIA

CHAPTER 2

The Great Leap Forward

ERBERT'S first attempt at a full-length novel was called 'Black Velvet'. He wrote the book, he said, in an attempt to emulate the contemporary success of Leon Gordon's *White Cargo*, a play in which colonials in Africa are 'reduced to emaciated feverish wrecks after cohabiting with the half-naked half-caste siren Tondelayo'.[1] Why not, suggested a friend, try writing something on the same lines set in the Northern Territory?[2] And that, judging by the title ('Black Velvet' being a Territorian term for the sexual allure of Aboriginal women), is what Herbert set out to do. Whether the resultant novel treated interracial sexuality on the titillating level of *White Cargo* or dealt more seriously with race relations we will never know, since no manuscript has survived. What we do know is that Herbert set off for London in 1930 with a completed typescript in his luggage, hoping to place the book with a British publisher.

In that hope he was disappointed. The only person to show any interest in his work was Sadie Norden, a young Jewish woman he had met on the boat going over. A Londoner, returning home after a failed marriage, it was Sadie who encouraged Herbert to try again after

'Black Velvet' was rejected by the publishers. She it was, too, who gave him the seminal advice that helped him transcend the limitations of popular romance and find a voice of his own. 'If only you could write the way you talk,' she said, 'the way you tell me stories'.[3] It was excellent advice, encouraging Herbert, as it did, to give full rein to his 'delight in being cleverly sarcastic', and directing him, as it did, to do what he always did best—write about Australia. That is what he began, more and more obsessively, to do, writing, he later said, in a 'kind of trance' for sixteen hours at a time, then sleeping and waking up to find it again 'like a torrent, a river running out of my head'.[4]

The resultant first draft of *Capricornia*, however, proved no more acceptable to British publishers than 'Black Velvet', and Herbert decided to cut his losses and return to Australia. There, at last, he found someone interested in the sprawling typescript. That someone was P. R. Stephensen, a champion of Australian writing, who told Herbert he would publish the book provided it was cut back to 100,000 words and stuck 'strictly to Norman's life'. As it stood, he said, it contained 'too many explorations of side-tracks', and too much 'long-winded moralising'.[5] In 1934, therefore, Herbert embarked on a revision of the original typescript. How much help he received from Stephensen in this task later became a point of bitter dispute between the two men. To no-one but himself, however, did it matter whether *Capricornia* owed a great deal, or nothing at all, to Stephensen's editorial skill. What mattered was the quality of the book, and that, in comparison to the stories, was amazing.

There is a new sophistication, for instance, in the structure of sentences. Again and again he deftly balances one part of a sentence against another to achieve comic and ironic effects. 'As yet the children knew little that was true and nothing that was discreditable about the Shillingsworth family'[6], for instance, and:

> Oscar's age was now indeterminate, he having reached the doldrums of life, the period between thirty-five and forty-five, in which a man, not knowing whether to forge ahead and pretend to be a hoary elder or to slink back and pretend to be a youth, just drifts and lets his age be known as the—er—thirties.[7]

There is an eighteenth-century feel to sentences like this, an epigram-matic wit reminiscent of Samuel Johnson and Jane Austen. Herbert also controls the pace and structure of paragraphs better in *Capricornia* than in any of his other books. The effective-ness of his control is nowhere more clearly seen than in comic passages like the following. The train has halted. Jock Driver is bleeding to death. The first-aid box has been sent for:

> The box was set down, the stiff buckles of its mildewed straps tackled by a dozen thumby hands, the lid hurled back. To the staring crowd there was revealed a broken shunting-lamp, two greasy magazines, an axe-head, and a pair of boots.
>   'Cripes!' murmured the guard.[8]

There is a sense of comic timing here found nowhere in the short stories. The rhetorical parallelism of the build-up is tightly disciplined and beautifully paced. The deliberate anti-climax punctures the build-up at just the right point, and with just the right degree of understatement. In similar fashion, the comic chaos of the following passage is skilfully orchestrated as Herbert matches sentence rhythms to the rhythms of the event. First the sense of action slowing down as the chase ceases. Then the sharp panic as Mrs McLash foresees a new disaster. Next the sequence of frenetic action, urgent yet almost as if, dream-like, happening in slow motion. Finally, in a superb final sentence, the moment of shocked peace as humans and animals catch their breath and think about what is next to be done:

> Finding that the chase had ceased, the goats drew up and looked to see what had happened. The track was packed with them. Mrs McLash screamed as she was raised. 'My God—my goats!'
>   'Goats!' yelled the fireman to the engineer.
>   The engineer looked, then shot a hand to a valve and released a mighty jet of steam. The goats looked interested but did not move. The engineer laid hold of reversing-gear. Fireman and passengers rushed to the

hand-brakes. The locked wheels raged against the strain. Every bolt and plate of the engine rattled. Coal crashed out of the tender. Water shot out of the tank. The engine halted in an atmosphere of goats.[9]

The richly comic 'atmosphere of goats' demonstrates another aspect of Herbert's new-found skill: the deftness now of his word choice. Other typical examples are the comic ironies implicit in the choice of 'happy' in 'Mark was not in the happy state of bankruptcy enjoyed by the majority of his fellow citizens'[10] and in the choice of 'unconventional' in the following:

When the mortuary was reached, a hitch occurred in Jock's ordered movements as a corpse. The place, built to meet the requirement of normal times, was fitted with but one table, which was occupied by Cho See Kee. [...] The matron said that Cho must give precedence. He was laid on the concrete floor.

Later in the day, when the Coroner came to look at Jock, so many officials and witnesses and morbids accompanied him that, since the mortuary measured only ten by twelve and it was unconventional to stand on the body of even a dead Chinaman, Cho had to be moved again.[11]

Herbert had a lightness of touch in *Capricornia* that deserted him later. He does more in *Capricornia* with a single ironic line than he later achieves in paragraphs of diatribe. Take the final sentence of the following piece of reported gossip, for example. War has been declared and the men of *Capricornia* are desperate to enlist, but not all are acceptable:

You know Sam Stiff? Well he's got miner's complaint he got down in the West so bad he can hardly talk. Course they wouldn't look at him here. So he went down South and got away right off and got killed. Shows what you can do if you can only get down South.[12]

From the occasionally sardonic commentator of the short stories, Herbert metamorphoses, in *Capricornia*, into an ironist of stature. In the opening chapter of the book, for instance, he plays deftly with the concepts of 'honour' and 'treachery', 'civilised' and 'primitive', to mock the hypocrisies of colonial settlement:

> The first white settlement in Capricornia was that of Treachery Bay—afterwards called New Westminster—which was set up on what was perhaps the most fertile and pleasant part of the coast and on the bones of half the Karrapillua Tribe. It was the resentment of the Karrapilluas to what probably seemed to them an inexcusable intrusion that was responsible for the choice of the name of Treachery Bay. After having been driven off several times with firearms, the Tribe came up smiling, to all appearances unarmed and intending to surrender, but dragging their spears along the ground with their toes. [...] Primitive people that they were, they regarded their territorial rights as sacred.[13]

With their sweet reasonableness of tone and fierce irony, the opening pages of *Capricornia* bear comparison with Swift's ironic masterpiece *A Modest Proposal*. The irony is equally good when it exposes the purely comic side of human pretension, as when, with a cheerfully drunk mob rioting outside, 'Trooper Robbrey and Mr Gigney and several other fellows who were not good mixers maintained law and order among themselves in the police station'.[14] Or when Herbert comments on an invitation to a wedding promising free beer, 'The response was wonderful. Out of the one hundred and eighteen guests invited three hundred and seventeen arrived'.[15]

There is much, then, in the style of *Capricornia* that bears comparison with Swift, Johnson and Austen. But if it has something of the controlled wit of the eighteenth century, it has even more of the unrestrained exuberance of Dickens. Herbert and Dickens were two of a kind. Both were writers of excess. Both loved pushing an idea to its limits. There is something quintessentially Dickensian, for instance, in the following description of lawyer Bightit:

> The Shouter assumed the character of a raging bull, trampled down every Chinese witness, charged two policeman [sic] who made him see red, tossed the yellowed papers into ridicule. Then he became a crocodile and attacked and devoured Mrs Cho See Kee and her father, Ching Ling Soo. [...] Then he became a turkey-cock and strutted with many an oosht ! of spreading tail till the judge rebuked him. Then he became a cooing dove. The audience was delighted.[16]

Like Dickens, Herbert, in *Capricornia*, revelled in outrageously extended conceits. Having described, for instance, how Tim O'Cannon's thwarted patriotism led him to conduct his household 'as a sort of garrison throughout the war', Herbert proceeds to expand upon the conceit at every opportunity. Since the O'Cannon daughters are attractive and free with their favours, 'it was not unlikely that with handsome young fellows hanging round the Garrison day and night, familiarity might breed not only contempt but little recruits without producing sons-in-law'. And since the war 'story Frank told, tall though it might have been, was nothing compared with that retold by imaginative Sergeant-Major O'Cannon, [n]ight after night his children went to bed with shell-shock'.[17] How utterly Dickensian that final sentence sounds. This is no longer the witty decorum of the eighteenth century but a more boisterous delight in the resources of the English language.

That same boisterous delight is seen in *Capricornia*'s equally Dickensian love of surrealistic exaggeration: the description of a moustache, for instance, which 'looked as though the rats had been at it'[18], or of Ket having 'lately eaten so much [coconut meat] that copra bugs followed him'[19], or, most Dickensian of all, the final outrageous claim in the following tour de force:

> In fact before long the economists were boasting that they wasted nothing of a carcass, that hoofs and hairs and bones and horns were all put through some process that converted them to use, even that they used the dying bellows of their victims to blow the furnace fires.[20]

It is not only Dickens, of course, that Herbert draws upon for such flights of comic fancy: there are Australian traditions at work here, too. The earthy wit of Australian vulgarisms and the inventive exaggerations of the Australian tall story are part of the culture Herbert grew up in, and the influence of both can be seen in *Capricornia*'s comedy.

The novel is also full of what Orwell once called 'the special Dickens atmosphere'—a kind of pulsating life, the sense of a teeming world peopled by a mob of delightful grotesques, a helter-skelter of mad activity, full to excess of smells, sights, sounds. Describing how Dickens created that atmosphere, Orwell said:

> The outstanding, unmistakable mark of Dickens's writing is the *unnecessary detail*. [After quoting a characteristic passage, he continues] As a whole, this story might come out of any nineteenth-century comic paper. But the un-mistakable Dickens touch, the thing nobody else would have thought of, is the baked shoulder of mutton and potatoes under it. How does this advance the story? The answer is that it doesn't. It is something totally unneces-sary, a florid little squiggle on the edge of the page; only it is by just these squiggles that the special Dickens atmosphere is created.[21]

Herbert's descriptions are full of Dickensian 'squiggles'. The meticulous accounting, for instance, that follows a wedding feast. 'The total cost of the success to Tim, after deducting the amount he secured for the sale of two crates of butter-dishes and one of biscuit-barrels to a Chinaman in Town, was £308 13s 7d.'[22] In similar fashion, though the original founder of Red Ochre is long dead and has no role whatsoever in the plot, Herbert cannot resist telling us that he had a 'young wife whom he worked like a horse', that he 'used to weigh out the rations of his native riders in niggardly quantities on loaded scales' and that he 'was killed by a bull on the plain to the south and eaten by ants and crows and kites till buried in a sack by his wife'.[23] It is the same Dickensian detail that contributes to the slapstick comedy of Jock Driver's funeral: the mourners baling out the water-filled grave 'lest the burial should look indecently like a drowning', the undertaker's pipe slipping from his belt and falling into the water-logged grave, the mourners stopping their baling 'while he solemnly dipped for it', the holes in the coffin 'bored with care, so as not to betray the fact that rosewood might produce white shavings', the three blowflies that 'shot out of the holes in the lid and dashed off guiltily'.[24]

In a number of ways, then, *Capricornia* represents a major advance in Herbert's style. It also marks the beginning, in Herbert's work, of what Gore Vidal calls the 'natural innovation' of a writer 'absorbed in his subject'.[25] Unconcerned at this stage with what the critics might say, Herbert simply did what felt right intuitively and, in so doing, discovered original and successful ways of achieving his purposes. An example of that is the use he began to make of that most traditional of narrative elements—repetition.

Herbert's habit of repeating things is, in itself, neither virtue nor vice; what matters is the effect of the repetition. In *Soldiers' Women* the repetitions are mostly tiresome. It takes less than the first five pages, for instance, for Mrs Batt to outstay her welcome. Even the most charitable reader must weary of endlessly repeated descriptions of her staring china doll's eyes, smudged clown's mouth, unruly clown's thatch of tow-blond hair and silly little crumpled hat. We have very soon had enough of the 'sepulchral groan', the 'writhing lips' and the 'cockatoo screech' of the voice.[26] And if we are tired of these after the first five pages, how much more so when they recur relentlessly each time Mrs Batt appears, and when, making the worst of a bad job, Herbert applies the same descriptive phrases to Mrs Batt's daughter, Pudsey, with her 'clown's thatch standing out frizzy-looking' and her voice that 'screeched like a little cockatoo'.[27] It is too much. The reader wilts under the barrage.

But repetition, as Bruce Kawin in a thought-provoking book on the subject argues, does not have to be tedious. 'Everyday', he points out:

> the sun comes up, stays up, goes down. [...] We do not find the cycle boring. [...] It is not exhaustible; novelty is exhaustible. The search for novelty leads in the end to

boredom. We are bored when we have run out of 'interesting' things to do.[28]

We need to distinguish, Kawin argues, between 'repetitious' and 'repetitive'. Something is 'repetitious' when 'a word, percept, or experience is repeated with less impact at each recurrence; repeated to no particular end, out of a failure of invention or sloppiness of thought'. On the other hand, something is 'repetitive' when 'a word, percept, or experience is repeated with equal or greater force at each occurrence'.[29] Looked at with this distinction in mind, we can see that while some of *Capricornia*'s repetitions are indeed 'repetitious', most are purposefully 'repetitive'.

Examples of 'repetitious' repetitions are those places where Herbert's restless desire for 'thrill a line' plots leads him to follow a dramatic description of one event almost immediately with a cursory description of an almost identical event. The clearest example is when the powerfully tragicomic description of railwayman Ballest's death is followed by a brief statement of O'Pick's very similar death four days later. Other examples include Oscar's dramatic death followed by a cursory description of the death of Mrs Shay, and Mark's dramatic victory in a murder trial followed by brief descriptions of repetitious wins against the Labour Council and Cho Sek Ching.[30]

Most repetitions in *Capricornia*, however, are not 'repetitious'. The police make an arrest at Red Ochre in Chapter 29; they make another in Chapter 34. Each time Norman is out riding; each time he sees the buttons of the police uniforms flashing in the sun; each time he thinks, wrongly, it is Tocky they have come in search of; each time he dashes home to tell her to scoot; each time the police catch him by surprise. These repetitions are not 'repetitious'. They do not have 'less impact at each recurrence', are not 'repeated to no particular end, out of a failure of invention'. Their purpose is to establish the unchanging realities of Capricornian life. They take the individuality out of events, each repetition strengthening the sense of the conditions of life in Capricornia. Time and place change, but Capricornian life does not. Characters change, but the situation remains the same. Whites continue to pick on helpless Aboriginals.

'Ow wow—woffor?' shouts Elbert to Driver in one chapter. 'He's always pickin' on me!' roars Ket of Sam Snigger in another.[31] Orientals continue to be bashed and robbed. Mark kills Cho See Kee in one chapter; 'A Greek' tries to kill a Chinaman in the next;[32] Ket, we are told in a third, once 'battered and robbed an aged Japanese'.[33] Meanwhile a few whites continue to speak out against racial injustice. Differ lectures Oscar in Chapter 7; McRandy lectures Norm in Chapter 24.

Reinforcing the sense of the unchanging condition of Capricornian life are the instances of children repeating the actions and attitudes of parents. Like father like son; like mother like daughter. Capricornian life moves forward, only to remain in the same place. Norman and Bortells replay, a generation later, the reactions to Capricornia of Oscar and Mark:

> For look at those clerks returning to [Port Zodiac] from leave! They behaved like military majors! Norman was inclined to sneer; but Bortells was carried away by thoughts of what a pharmacist might become in such magic atmospheres, and went to truckle to Percy Potentate [...][34]

Just so did Oscar truckle and Mark sneer. Meanwhile, Norman's sister, seeking the status of 'daughter of a beef baron', tries to 'persuade her father to increase the lease and stock' just as, years earlier, her mother had urged him 'to secure more land and buy more stock'.[35]

Another type of repetition found in *Capricornia* occurs during Herbert's descriptions of the land. From book to book, as well as within the same book, Herbert, in a fashion reminiscent of Homer, gradually develops a set of recurring descriptive formulae for the Australian landscape. In the short story 'The Rainmaker' 'the wild emu runs to the silver dawn and the brolga dances in the painted sunset'. In *Capricornia* 'brolgas danced in the painted sunset and emus ran to the silver dawn'. In 'The Rainmaker' 'the red plain [is] sunken under inches of luke-warm water and vivid with a wild-rice crop' and 'Siberian snipe' are 'flittering on arrow-swift wings'. In *Capricornia* 'the scarlet plains' are 'under water, green with wild rice, swarming with Siberian snipe'.[36] When Norman, in *Capricornia*, takes his first train journey, he looks out of the window and sees 'a world of trees go spinning by in a wild arboreal corroboree. A red wall leapt at him'. Three hundred pages later, on another train, Norman watches 'the red walls leap at him and the trees go spinning by'. A few pages later, the train races on 'while red walls leapt at them clanging and trees in a wild corroboree-dance went spinning by'.[37] Years later, in *Poor Fellow My Country*, Prindy looks out of a train to see 'the trees running round and round like a big mob blackfellow in corroboree'. A few pages later he again looks out at 'the corroboree of trees and rocks dancing to the *minga-minga* music of the wheels'.[38]

The uses of repetition Herbert experimented with in *Capricornia* play an important part in later books. In *Capricornia*, for instance, the use of descriptive formulae to describe the landscape plays no very significant part in the narrative, but in *Seven Emus* and *Poor Fellow My Country*, as we shall see, it is by using such formulae that Herbert initiates his readers into the numinous world of traditional Aboriginal culture. Even more important in *Poor Fellow My Country* is the use of repetition to create a sense of timeless, unchanging reality. It is through repetition that Herbert creates a sense of the timelessness of Prindy's mythic quest and, in so doing, conveys a sense of perpetual possibility for Australia even when, in the non-mythic 'real world', all hope seems lost.

Herbert's use of repetition is one example of effective experimentation in *Capricornia*. Another is the originality of its plot structure. Ironically, it was for its supposedly ineffective plotting that Herbert was most willing to kiss the rod of blinkered traditionalism. Later in his career he was always quick to acknowledge that *Capricornia* was weak in 'the technique of novel writing'.[39] He proved himself in this a better writer than critic.

Certainly there are weaknesses in the plotting of *Capricornia*. In some places Herbert supplies details at the immediate point of need, rather than introducing them more subtly earlier. When Norman, for instance, unexpectedly finds Jack Ramble and Heather talking like old friends, there is a feeling of hasty afterthought to the explanation: 'He was not surprised to find them thus intimate. On

Thursday night he had learnt from Con the Greek, who had sought him out again, that they were lovers'.[40] In other places we find Herbert, again in crude and hasty fashion, tying up the loose ends left in the many strands he has woven. He has Norman, for instance, in a chat with Mrs McLash, learn from her:

> that he had lost his billet in Batman, that Oscar was greatly worried about his future, that Marigold was to be married to Steggles in November and was going to live in Singapore, that Gigney had only lately regained the use of his arm, that Ket was now working at the Melisande as fireman with Frank McLash on construction trains.[41]

Infelicities of this sort are, however, minor weaknesses in a plot structure that is, though Herbert himself never seems to have realised it, genuinely and successfully experimental.

Looked at as a conventional novel of bourgeois realism, the first half of *Capricornia* is perplexing. Herbert seems uncertain who to focus upon. At first, Mark Shillingsworth appears to be the central character but, after five chapters, Herbert loses interest in him, and turns for a time to his brother, Oscar. After Chapter 9, Oscar too retreats into the background, and for four chapters Tim O'Cannon holds centre stage—until death writes him out of the plot in the most final way possible. It is not until Chapter 17, when Mark's son, Norman, arrives back in Capricornia, that Herbert finally seems to make up his mind, and Norman remains the undisputed centre of attention for the rest of the book.

But there is method in this apparent madness. The purpose of *Capricornia* is not to tell the story of a single hero but to tell the story of a country. We must, in assessing the effectiveness of its plotting, stop concentrating on individuals and look instead at the characters as representatives of one or other of two groups— 'Aboriginals' and 'whites'. In studying the action, we must see all the apparently separate plots as part of one great plot—'Aboriginals and whites make a country called Australia'. Seen from this perspective, *Capricornia* falls into three clear sections, each contributing to the central plot, and each involving significant experimental strategies.

The first section (Chapters 1–5) covers the earliest contacts between whites and Aboriginals, and the period of colonising that followed. It was a section that posed a difficult artistic problem. How was Herbert to deal with so lengthy a period in such a short space? He solves the problem with an impressive piece of narrative sleight of hand. He persuades his readers to accept, simultaneously, two time schemes, by shifting imperceptibly between two types of character: on the one hand, larger than life archetypes; on the other, the characters of bourgeois realism. The Krater of Chapter 1, for instance, is a quite different character from the Krater who hobnobs with the reprobates of Port Zodiac in Chapter 2. The first is a figure of legend, physically as impressive as Zeus, and regarded with awe by the Indigenous people. He is 'Munichillu, Man of Fire', at whose 'appearance the east flamed suddenly, so that the sand was gilded and fire flashed in his beard'.[42] He stands with mythic power for the whole invading race. Outside normal time, he spans a whole period of settlement and conquest. The Krater of Chapters 2 and 3 is a different being altogether, a beach bum in ragged clothes, one of the many drunken sailors hanging round the now well-established Port Zodiac of the twenties.

Like Krater, the Shillingsworth brothers appear first as archetypes and then metamorphose into conventional characters. Unlike Krater, they are the archetypes of comedy, reminiscent in Chapter 2 of the creations of Molière and Ben Jonson. On first arrival:

> Their bearing was that of simple clerks, not Potentates. [...] When they learnt how high was the standing of Government Officers in the community [...] their bearing changed. Within a dozen hours of landing they were wearing topees. Within two dozen hours they were closeted with Chinese tailors. Within a hundred hours they came forth in all the glory of starched white linen clothes. Gone was their simplicity for ever.[43]

If Krater stands for the conquering invader, the Shillingsworths stand for a whole generation of coloniser-bureaucrats, following in the invader's wake and revelling in the opportunities for exploitation and self-advancement.

Herbert's manipulation of character creates, with deceptive ease, the dual time scheme on which the success of the first section depends. On the one hand, there is a real impression of 'normal' time, a sense that we are following the day-by-day progress of twentieth-century Mark Shillingsworth and his disreputable mate, Nick Krater. On the other, we have the sensation of being taken, in a few pages, through the whole early history of Australia, covering decades of development and change. In Chapter 4, when Krater once more takes on the stature of an archetype, his death stands for the end of an era that occurred long before the arrival of people like the Shillingsworths, yet, so well has Herbert manipulated our sense of time, no reader is disturbed by the chronological absurdity.

The first section of *Capricornia* is a story of missed opportunity. From the beginning, the trouble is as much lack of understanding as it is greed and desire for dominion. Mark and Krater trample roughshod over Aboriginal sexual taboos because they simply do not know they exist. Mark considers the Aboriginal who offers the use of his wife 'unutterably base', unable to comprehend that Aboriginals 'might love their womenfolk just as much as whitemen do, even though they were not so jealous of their conjugal rights'.[44] Here is where the foundations were laid. Whites could have learned to live *with* Aboriginals if they had only bothered to learn something *about* Aboriginals. Instead they exploited and destroyed, justifying their acts on the grounds of Aboriginal immorality and treachery, ironically the very qualities they were themselves demonstrating.

White men's feelings for, and dealings with, Aboriginal women symbolise their dealings with Australia itself. Like most Capricornian men, Mark is fascinated by Aboriginal women. Instead, however, of acknowledging his feelings and entering into a loving relationship, he resists the attraction, thinking it beneath him, and succumbing to it, when he does, secretly and guiltily. Later, he instinctively feels joy and pride in the child he fathers, 'flesh of his own flesh—exquisite thing'[45], but, fearful of public opinion, he denies the relationship, rejects the child, and leaves it to fend for itself. The story is more than just an example of white exploitation and hypocrisy; it symbolises how, in the beginning, whites could have achieved a fruitful relationship with Aboriginals, one that could have begun a fine new chapter in the old country's history. Baby Norman, product of the union between Aboriginal and white, symbolises through his golden beauty the bright future that might have been; deserted, neglected, and growing up as 'Nawnim' ('No-name') on the fringes of both Aboriginal and white society, he symbolises the failure that was and is.

And so the novel moves to the next stage of the Australian story. Chapter 6 functions as a bridging chapter. Nawnim's train trip is a journey in time as well as place, transporting readers from the world of first settlement to a world wholly and unequivocally situated in the twenties. We move from the coast to the interior, from a world of uncertain sea adventures to one of regular trains servicing established businesses.

The second section of the novel (Chapters 7–15) examines the flawed world created by the initial failure of the white invaders to respond properly to Australia. Herbert shifts now to a new mode of plot organisation, employing what, in music, would be called variations on a theme. The theme is 'Adult white man's relationship with young half-caste'.[46] The variations include Driver–Norman, Oscar–Norman, Differ–Connie, Lace–Connie, O'Cannon–Maud, Cedric–Maud, O'Cannon–Connie, O'Cannon–Tocky and Derkouz–Margaret. By replaying the crucial relationship over and over again, Herbert builds a picture of how and why whites failed to solve the problems section one has shown them creating. It is one more use he has discovered for repetition—to achieve effects of comparison and contrast. It is a use we shall find again in *Poor Fellow My Country*.[47]

The relationships involving Driver, Cedric, Derkouz and Lace demonstrate how, in different ways, white Australia oppresses and exploits Aboriginals. The response to these men's actions demonstrates white society's complicity in that exploitation. Jock Driver enslaves little Nawnim and the law allows him to do so. Lace, Cedric and Derkouz seduce and then abandon young half-caste women, and white society turns a blind eye. Welfare services are useless: the 'Native Hospital' offers Connie not the treatment she needs but simply a prison to die in. Denied the protection of society's institutions, the sole remaining hope for these abused young women is private philanthropy and, as Tim O'Cannon finds when he tries to help Connie, that can do little in the face of massive bureaucratic and public apathy.

The remaining variations on the theme involve fathers trying to save their children from the general fate. Through these variations, Herbert tests different ways Aboriginal Australians might achieve the right to fair and equal treatment hitherto denied them. The first possibility is intermarriage. Differ and O'Cannon both want their half-caste daughters to marry into white society. Differ tries but can find no white man willing to marry Connie. O'Cannon forces her white seducer, Cedric, to marry Maud, only to see her rejected by her white relations. This solution does not seem promising.

The second solution is the coward's solution of deceit or retreat. Differ seeks to disguise Connie's Aboriginality and send her away from Capricornia altogether. Oscar, borrowing the idea, sends Norman down south where he can pass as the son of a Javanese princess. But while this is an escape from the problem, it does not solve it. When Norman returns to Capricornia he soon finds, as Ket had found earlier, that he cannot hide his origins and therefore cannot escape the injustice faced by all Aboriginals.

The third and fourth solutions canvassed in this section offer more hope. The third is to win security through economic strength. O'Cannon attempts to make Black Adder a fortress of economic strength to protect his children against a prejudiced world. He fails only when death allows in the predator Derkouz to plunder his goods and debauch his wife and children. The plan is a good one but still depends on the protection of a white man. What is needed is for Aboriginals themselves to achieve economic strength, and for that they need education—the fourth solution canvassed in this section. Differ gives his own daughter a good education and urges Oscar to do the same for Norman. Oscar does so, and in the final section of the book the effectiveness of this solution is tested through Norman's attempts to succeed in a white world.

The final section of *Capricornia* begins, again, with a bridging chapter. Chapter 16 is short, reads like a history book and marks a clear break between sections. The second section ends with the problems exposed and unresolved. Whites and Aboriginals have not found a way to build a good society; nor will they while whites hold all the power. If the future is to bring a better Australia, it must be one where Aboriginals challenge that power and end the injustice of the past. The final section (Chapters 17–36) uses the career of the hero, Norman, to suggest how such a challenge might take place. Born part-white and part-Aboriginal, Norman must first come to terms with his Aboriginality and then learn to use the methods of his white inheritance effectively in combating injustice and winning his rightful position in society. Again Herbert adapts style to suit purpose, using in this section the conventions of his apprentice-ship—the conventions of popular romance—as he pictures Norman, the noble hero, taking on the oppressive might of the white world and, against all the odds, winning.

Norman's first challenge is to face the truth of his origins. He has done well down south, where he has had a good job and met with no racial prejudice, everyone, himself included, believing he is a Javanese prince. Returning to Capricornia on holiday, he does not at first understand the meaning of the slights he receives: a barman's refusal to serve him a drink, curt treatment at the hospital. Towards Aboriginals he behaves like a white man—haughtily putting Yeller Elbert in his place, 'scarcely seeing' his father's Aboriginal stock-men[48], and treating Ket, the half-caste foreman, with condescension. The irony of this condescension becomes clear when we learn that Ket, like Norman, had for a time successfully hidden his Aboriginality in order to achieve a position in Capricornia commensurate to his education. His exposure, and subsequent loss of job and social status, prove what Norman is soon to find out: that education and ability are no guarantee of fair treatment in Capricornia. No wonder Ket is bitter and that it is he who tells Norman the truth about his origins.

Chapters 22–24 show Norman struggling to come to terms with his Aboriginality. Unwilling to face the scorn of the white world, he runs off into the bush, is cut off by floods and only survives with the help of a group of Aboriginals on walkabout. When, four months later, the floods subside and he finds his way back to Red Ochre, nothing has changed. He is still ashamed of his Aboriginality.

Accused by Oscar of 'getting the walkabout habit', he eagerly protests his innocence.

It is soon after this that a meeting with Andy McRandy gives Norman's thoughts a new direction. McRandy talks to Norman about the many things Aboriginal society has achieved and urges him not to 'be ashamed of your Old People'. Rather he must 'Be their spokesman. Be their leader. Lead 'em to honour. Sit in parliament as their representative'.[49] The solution Herbert here pictures for Australia is an assimilationist one. It is the solution *Capricornia* symbolises through Norman's heroic success in the book's final section. In *Poor Fellow My Country* Prindy follows his 'own road'. Norman, in contrast, is happy to travel a white man's road, taking on whites at their own game, and forcing them to acknowledge his right to be a member of their world.

Chapters 25–29 show Norman struggling to make his mark in this world. He tries for a job his qualifications entitle him to but meets a wall of Capricornian prejudice. His surrogate white father, Oscar, dies and he becomes aimless, taking pointless trips to Singapore and Port Zodiac, trying unsuccessfully to set up as a squatter with his Aboriginal mistress Opal, and then going bush again, significantly aiming for his birthplace, Flying Fox. He meets Tocky, is diverted from his original intention and returns home. Tocky follows him, ousts Opal and for a short period there is harmony at Red Ochre, with Norman, Tocky and the Chinese cook Cho Sek Ching living happily together. For a time, half-castes and Chinese run a cattle station, free of whites and undisturbed by Capricornian prejudices. At last, it seems, intelligence, aided by education and supported by economic strength, has enabled half-castes to achieve their own solution. All too soon, however, the idyll is broken—by a white man, of course, Norman's errant father, Mark. Cho is forced out and Norman, who has earlier chosen to reject his Aboriginality, now, though regretfully, also rejects the possibility of half-caste community in favour of his white responsibilities.

That the choice is, in *Capricornia*, seen by Herbert to be the right one is demonstrated by its results. From this point on, to the end of the book, the trend is towards Norman's ultimate triumph. In

Chapter 30 it is Norman's money that saves Mark. In Chapter 32 it is
Norman's rhetoric that gains Tocky a moral victory over Hollower.
Then, for a time, the issue is again placed in doubt. In Chapters 34
and 35 Norman finds the combined forces of white laws and white
greed almost too strong, and it looks as if Red Ochre, with its
promise of economic independence, will be wrested from him. For
all his talents, Capricornia has managed, it seems, finally to defeat
him. Accused of murder, and with the evidence heavily against him,
he faces certain conviction. The only hope is to re-employ the
rapacious lawyer Bightit, but to do that he must mortgage Red
Ochre still further and risk losing his toehold in Capricornia's white
economy. The situation seems hopeless. 'The barsteds'll get me
back to the bush before they're done with me', he says, 'because
I'm a halfcaste—and they think I ought to be a nigger'. Everything
is still stacked against half-castes, however intelligent and skilled,
however much they wish to fit into white society. 'You've got your
trade to fall back on', consoles his father. 'What's the good of it here
in this colour-mad hole', Norman replies angrily. 'They'd never give
me a job.'[50]

But, having demonstrated, for one last time, the gross injustice
of the situation, Herbert finally puts it right. The conclusion is pure
popular romance. In a mere eight pages, and through a series of
amazing coincidences and strokes of luck, Norman is not only
acquitted, not only avoids the loss of Red Ochre, but is set fair for
prosperity through a combination of circumstances that bring boom
times back to the meat trade. Our last picture of Norman is straight
out of a pulp magazine. This is, without the faintest possible shadow
of a doubt, THE HAPPY ENDING!

> 'A boom!' cried Heather.
>   'Oh gosh!' cried Norman, 'A boom!'
>   'A boom!' cried Heather again.[51]

The final section of *Capricornia* marked an important stage in
Herbert's development of the generic mix found later in *Poor Fellow
My Country*, since it was here he first used romance effectively for a
serious purpose. In the stories, the final victory would have been

Norman's alone. Here, in *Capricornia*, it has a deeper significance. Norman's success symbolises Herbert's hopes for Australia, his belief, at this stage, in an assimilationist solution to the injustices faced by its Aboriginal people, one in which white Australia has learned to accept Aboriginals as equals, but in which Aboriginals have accepted and learned to work within white Australian culture. Herbert's more serious use of romance here was not, of course, new, since allegory and romance have, for centuries, been natural bedfellows.[52] But it was new to Herbert and it opened up avenues that would ultimately lead to the high romance of *Poor Fellow My Country* and its allegorical hero, Prindy.

As well as experimenting productively with romance, Herbert also began, in *Capricornia*, to discover the possibilities of the genre Frye calls anatomy. Three features of anatomy can be seen in *Capricornia*. One is what Frye calls the anatomist's willingness to indulge in 'digressing narrative'. The Dickensian 'squiggles' discussed earlier are the first examples in Herbert's work of a convention that, as we shall see later, contributes very significantly to the success of *Poor Fellow My Country*. In the final novel the brief 'squiggles' of *Capricornia* have developed into the frequent and extensive digressions so characteristic of full-blown anatomy.

A second feature of anatomy found in *Capricornia* is what Frye calls the 'stylizing of characters along "humor" lines'.[53] This can be seen both in the typecasting by name (the social climbing Shillingsworths, the established Poundamores) and in what E. M. Forster called the 'flatness' of the characters. *Capricornia* is full of 'flat' characters—characters constructed around a limited set of qualities, who do not develop and have no pretensions to psychological complexity, but who are no less lively or engaging for that.[54] Lawyer Bightit is an obvious example. Each time he appears, descriptions of him repeat the same few qualities: immense greed, a liking for the good life, a loud voice, legendary rhetorical power and an uncanny ability to win cases. Each time he appears, the same animal metaphors are used to describe him. Each time he appears, he dominates the scene with his comic energy.[55]

The third anatomy convention found in *Capricornia* is described by Frye thus:

A dialogue or colloquy, in which the dramatic interest is in a conflict of ideas rather than of character. [...] Sometimes this form expands to full length and more than two speakers are used: the setting then is usually a cena or symposium. [...] Plato [...] is a strong influence on this type, which stretches in an unbroken tradition down through those urbane and leisurely conversations which define the ideal courtier in Castiglione or the doctrine and discipline of angling in Walton. A modern development produces the country-house weekends in Peacock, Huxley and their imitators in which the opinions and ideas and cultural interests expressed are as important as the love-making.[56]

Herbert uses the convention of 'symposium discussion' three times in *Capricornia*: each time to explain ideas that are important to the novel. The first discussion, lasting for five pages, is between Differ and Oscar and deals with white Australian responsibility for the condition of Aboriginals. Oscar is used to mouth the standard exculpatory excuses ('You can't teach 'em.' 'They're dying out.' 'All the men here are loafers and bludgers, the women practically all whores.') Differ opposes this view with a picture of Aboriginal potential held back by white refusal to provide proper education.[57] The second and shortest discussion occurs when the officer in charge lectures O'Cannon for two pages on the reasons for, and nature of, the iniquitous treatment of Aboriginals in the 'Native Compound'.[58] The final symposium discussion involves McRandy and Norman, lasts for eighteen pages and begins with a discussion of foreign policy.[59] Norman puts forward the accepted wisdom of the Japanese threat, and the need to 'develop' the country; McRandy argues the case for independent nationalism. The two then move to Ramble's campfire, where McRandy gives Norman the extended lecture on Aboriginals mentioned earlier. The length and overt didacticism of this final symposium discussion are a foretaste of things to come, first in the novels of the fifties, and finally in the many lengthy discussions between Delacy and his acolytes in *Poor Fellow My Country*. The effectiveness of Herbert's use of the convention in that book is discussed in Chapter 10, as is his increasing use of digressing narrative. He became, as we shall see, more and more skilled in the deployment of both.

It is ironic that, to the end of his life, Herbert himself seemed unaware of the magnitude of his achievement in *Capricornia*, referring to it as the 'old botch' and not, apparently, understanding quite how experimental and original it was. If he had, he would never have felt the need to embark, in the fifties, on the disastrous attempt to prove originality that led to the loss of some at least of what had been gained in *Capricornia*. Nevertheless, whether he knew it or not, the fact was that, absorbed for the first time in dealing with Australia rather than simply satisfying a popular taste for romance and adventure, Herbert was able in *Capricornia*, as in *Poor Fellow My Country* later, to discover the narrative techniques he needed to convey his vision of the Australian ethos. What that vision was, at this point in his development, is the subject of the next chapter.

CHAPTER 3

In Praise of the Swagman Spirit

APRICORNIA and *Poor Fellow My Country* are similar in that both give a picture of Australia's past and present, and both express a dream for Australia's future. But there is an important difference. When Herbert wrote *Poor Fellow My Country*, the picture given of the present was pessimistic, and the dream expressed for the future was just that—a dream. In *Capricornia*, for all his criticism of past failures, the picture he gives of both the present and the future is positive and optimistic.

That the essential optimism of the book has not always been recognised owes something to an influential essay by Vincent Buckley, published in 1960. Earlier critics had been content to treat *Capricornia* simply as 'a social problem novel, a spirited plea for decent treatment of Aborigines and half-castes'.[1] And on one level they were obviously right. In this, too, *Capricornia* is a thoroughly Dickensian novel, dramatising and attacking a social evil through descriptions of the unjust suffering of a succession of half-caste characters. The description, for instance, of O'Cannon's fruitless attempts to save the dying Connie Differ invites outrage at the white community's brutal lack of concern, while descriptions of Tocky and

Christobel in the 'Halfcaste Home' expose the callous, self-righteous inhumanity with which government servants treat Aboriginals. There is, however, argued Buckley, more to *Capricornia* than 'merely social indignation'. Herbert's anger, he contended, was directed at 'a cosmic injustice done to all men'. He found in *Capricornia* 'a rejection of any conception of purpose' in a universe where 'men are fated to die by chance and misunderstanding', victims of 'metaphysical forces even more final and malignant' than any social force. Faced by such a universe, Buckley argued, Herbert's response was a kind of manic-depressive fatalism. 'Depressed by the total anomaly which he thinks the universe, [he] yet exults in the separate local examples of anomaly.'[2]

Useful though it was in challenging the limitations of earlier criticism, it was a pity that Buckley's reading became, for many years, the standard reading of *Capricornia*. A pity for two reasons: first, because it continued to divert attention from the real subject of the book, which is neither Aboriginals nor metaphysics, but Australia; second, because it diverted attention from the book's great, indeed its almost naive, optimism.

It would have been surprising if *Capricornia* had indeed exemplified a 'rejection of any purpose in the universe', since Herbert's personal philosophy was not at all pessimistic. On the contrary, he believed passionately in the power of individuals to mould their own lives and improve the lot of the race generally, as can be seen in the following expression of his lifelong views on the subject:

> All creatures exist in varying capacities to make the most of their existence. Those of us most capable of perceiving the hidden means to the ultimate to which we are compelled [...] are the people of Vision [...who] eventually will bring us to the High Destiny that must be ours as the Wonder of the Universe. [...] The only true prophecy that can be made for our species is that it will advance in the way of Truth until the Riddle of the Universe is solved—by us, who, of all creation, discovered it.[3]

No hint here of defeatism. No sense of cosmic conspiracy. Quite the contrary. Herbert's beliefs, throughout his life, were humanist and optimistic. And, contrary to Buckley's thesis, the same beliefs underpin *Capricornia*. Its world is not the world of a pessimistic fatalist but of a hopeful, though realistic, humanist. It is a world in which chance plays its normal, random part, even-handed not malign, as likely to produce unmerited good fortune as bad, a world in which humans have considerable, albeit limited, control over their destiny, and in which most trouble is caused by their own faults and follies. It is also a world in which the good may die young and the bad may prosper, since Herbert's philosophy does not deny the truths of Job, Oedipus and Ophelia.

The idea of divine influence in human affairs, whether malign or benevolent, is alien to *Capricornia*. 'God' and 'fate' are consistently mocked as excuses for human inadequacy. Humbolt Lace, for instance, after his cowardly betrayal of Connie, seeks to ease his sense of responsibility, shutting his eyes and whispering, 'Oh God forgive me—and help her—help her—I am too miserably weak'. He receives no sympathy from the author, who dryly remarks, 'That Divinity with which Messrs Lace and Prayter were on such familiar terms was apparently not so much at their beck and call as from their utterances it would seem. No blessings fell on [Connie]. Far from it'.[4] The irony is directed against evasion of human responsibility. No use blaming God for a tragedy so patently caused by human lust, cowardice and hypocrisy. No use asking for divine remedies when Tim O'Cannon later shows where the answer to human cruelty lies: in 'Courage, Kindness and Awareness, those virtues without which there can be no truly progressive human society'.[5] And if Tim is unable to save Connie, it has nothing to do with fate, everything to do with further human failure on the part of the health professionals of Port Zodiac.

In similar fashion, when Ket fails in his attempts to flee the country, Herbert's irony again ridicules fatalistic interpretations of the world. Ket feels like a 'fly caught in a vast green heaving web, trapped by Fate the Spider. He prayed to God to still the sea. The wind roared at him. The green sea spat and hissed'.[6] A Jonah in the hands of Yahweh? Far from it! The bathos of the next sentence mocks any such pretensions. 'What he thought was a hurricane was nothing but a lusty morning breeze.' Human ignorance and incompetence are at work here, not divine malignity. Herbert is of Edmund's party. For him, too, it is 'the excellent foppery of the world to make guilty of our disasters the sun, moon and the stars'. For him, too, this is merely an 'evasion of whoremaster man'.[7] 'What a world it was', he says, 'in the hands of men! Guns in the bows of ships, the widow McLash weeping her heart out in a pillow, […] Jock Driver lying on his deathbed, Yeller Elbert snivelling in a cell'.[8] Wars abroad and suffering at home are, for Herbert, caused by 'the hands of men', not the results of 'cosmic injustice'.

Turning to the plot of *Capricornia*, we find that, far from chance working in any particularly malevolent fashion as Buckley's essay suggests, it is as likely to do the opposite. Take the way chance spins its web inexorably around Norman in the affair of Frank McLash's murder. It out-Hardies Hardy! But with what result? In *Tess*, fate mocks the efforts of humanity; in *Capricornia*, humanity mocks the efforts of fate. Despite the absence of witnesses and the mass of damning circumstantial evidence, lawyer Bightit unravels the fatal web with ease and Norman is saved. In like fashion, when Bightit later turns enemy, it is chance that miraculously saves Norman just minutes before he signs away his birthright.

The novel contains, of course, its share of misadventures, large and small, and it is on these Buckley builds his case. But before too much is made of them, one should consider the nature of life in developing territories. Those who have lived in such places will respond with amused recognition to incidents such as Jack Burywell dying 'in the arms of Mrs McLash while waiting for Ganger Jacob Ledder to fish a beetle out of the magneto of the trolley on which he was to be taken up to Town'.[9] Life in such places is a training in tolerance. One learns to assume things will go wrong, and to keep calm when they do; one learns, as the humour of these descriptions shows Herbert did, to laugh, not rage. One certainly does not blame cosmic fate for all-too-human incompetence.

As for the major disasters in *Capricornia*, they too have more to do with the normal hazards of life in developing territories than with malignant fate. There are twenty-three deaths in the book (not counting those who died in McLash's train crash). Of those, ten are the direct result of human mismanagement (six murders, three drink-related deaths, one case of gross neglect), six the result of the normal vulnerability of old age and childhood, and five the result of accidents in notoriously hazardous occupations (seafaring and rail-ways).[10] Only two, those of Tocky and her baby, are caused by sheer bad luck. It is those deaths only that might seem to give some support to Buckley's thesis.

Herbert's decision to close the novel with the discovery of these deaths certainly gives the event a sense of powerful significance:

> Dry wind moaned through rust-eaten holes. He stepped up to the tank and peeped through a hole. Nothing to see but the rusty wall beyond. He climbed the ladder, looked inside, saw a skull and a litter of bones. He gasped. A human skull—no—two—a small one and a tiny one. And human hair and rags of clothes and a pair of bone-filled boots. Two skulls, a small one and a tiny one. Tocky and her baby!
>
> The crows alighted in a gnarled dead coolibah near by and cried dismally, 'Kah!—Kah!—Kaaaaah!'[11]

Why does Herbert choose to end *Capricornia* on this note? It is certainly a powerful ending and certainly makes readers think. But think about what? About the inevitable malignity of fate? Or about the unpredictability of life? The former goes against everything else in the book; the latter fits its view of life perfectly. The philosophy of *Capricornia* is not that life is a cosmic conspiracy against human aspiration but that life is unpredictable. There is a sting in the tail of even the most prosperous chain of events, and Tocky's death is simply the most tragic example of that fact. And despite its some-times tragic consequences, unpredictability is not, the book suggests, inimical to human endeavour. Quite the contrary. It is challenging and invigorating.

The chief agent of unpredictability in *Capricornia* is nature, the only superhuman force Herbert acknowledges in the book, and, though that force is often destructive, it is not pictured as hostile to humans but rather as a stimulus to their ingenuity. Faced by nature's power as he wanders alone and lost in the bush, Norman marvels 'at the phenomenon of his existence' and at 'nature's contrariety to Man that made Man's ingenuity essential'.[12] Chief symbol of that contrariety in *Capricornia* is the Cockeye Bob, a sudden, violent wind whose name, significantly, is later given to Bobwirridirridi, servant of *Poor Fellow My Country*'s 'spirit of misrule', Tchamala. A puckish spirit, Cockeye Bob keeps humans on their toes and stops them becoming too complacent. Nothing is safe from Cockeye Bob or from his fellow disrupter, the Trade Wind; they mock all man's attempts to establish permanent order. The one thing the pharmacist cannot 'control near his dispensary' is 'the Trade Wind, that hearty thing which often burst his back door in, roared through his sanctum, brought down his bottles on his head'.[13] There is no sense here of malice towards humanity. Nature simply keeps us on our toes. Storms accompany many of the important events in the novel: Norm's birth, his arrival at Red Ochre, his epiphany in the bush, Krater's death, Jock's funeral, Frank's murder, Connie's wedding, Tocky's arrival at Red Ochre. All these events involve change. Some changes seem for the worse; some for the better. Nature is neither benevolent nor malign; it simply enforces change. And change is hopeful:

> About an hour after the burial of Jock, a cockeye bob roared out of the north and tore the front verandah from the First and Last, blew two Chinese children right across Killarney Street [...] blew a few trees down, and was gone, taking the rain-clouds with it [...] As though Heaven's grief were like the grief of Man—an hour or two of weeping, then back to laughter and the workaday.[14]

The cockeye bob may blow trees down but it also blows the rain clouds away. The brightness after storm reflects the age-old truths of myths associated with spring. Change is essential. Life follows death. One thing dies so another may live.

Herbert's mood when he wrote *Capricornia* was not hard and cynical. He recounts how, stuck in foggy London, he

began to talk to Sadie about the loveliness of the land I'd
left, not simply about the violences, the harshness, the
cruelty of it—and how the people were really comical,
not so bad as mad as aren't we all. [...] And so it was that
a country of my own came into being which I called
Capricornia and it became realler than reality, and life
now became joy, because I had this world of my own
creation to live in, with its sunlight and naturalness and
comedy, against the awful background of London.[15]

Elsewhere he wrote, 'What moved me more than anything, I remember, was a vast yearning for my sunny native land, its spaciousness,
its rugged beauty, its freedom'.[16] It is not surprising, then, that the
novel is full of Herbert's love for Australia. While not blind to their
failures, Herbert saw in his Capricornians qualities he believed made
Australia, if not the best of all possible countries, at least a better
country than any found elsewhere on earth. He found a symbol for
those qualities in Paterson's 'Waltzing Matilda', which he presents as
a defining myth of Australia.

The poem is quoted in full in Chapter 24, the didactic centre
of the novel. After Mooch has sung the song, McRandy invites him to
tell Norman what some 'English musical coot' once said about it.
Herbert uses the ensuing speech to stress the defining nature of the
myth. According to the musicologist, 'Waltzing Matilda' is 'a genuine
folk-song':

That's a song peculiar to a tribe of people y'know, one't
expresses their feelin's. He says that this here Spirit of the
Land that Andy mentioned is in it. [...] [B]orn Australians
[...] look on the Jolly Swagman as a cobber that's been
martyred. [...] We look on stray things knockin' around,
such as sheep drinkin' at a billabong, [...as] property of
the tribe, same's the Binghis do things that's knockin'
round the bush. So the Jolly Swagman's the typical
Australian, doin' just what he thinks is right, like a Binghi
spearin' a kangaroo or somebody's bullock. And the
Squatter and the Troopers are the outsiders, the imported

people, the foreigners, what have a strong sense of property and a different way of looking at things.[17]

The Swagman stands for white Australians who have shaken off their colonial past, who have become truly Australian, 'doing what they think is right', not what they are told to do by others. The Squatter and Trooper represent white Australians who are still at heart colonials, who still give allegiance to European values. Throughout the novel, Herbert contrasts the Australian way of the Swagman and the colonial way of the Squatter and Trooper. In the Swagman qualities of true Capricornians, Herbert celebrates what he sees as the characteristic Australian virtues. And to emphasise the 'Australian-ness' of these virtues, he links them, wherever possible, with Aboriginal custom. The Swagman treats the jumbuck just as 'the Binghis do things that's knockin' round the bush'. He does 'what he thinks is right, like a Binghi spearin' a kangaroo or somebody's bullock'. The link is clearly stated by McRandy when he says to Norman:

> I like to think that the Great Bunyip, the Spirit of this Southern land of ours, the Lord of your Aboriginal forefathers from the beginnin' of time, and now the Lord of us who's growin' up in your forefathers' place and goin' the same old manly carefree way, wants to keep a bit of the place in its aboriginal glorious wild state and has chosen this here Capricornia for it.[18]

Not all Capricornians choose 'the manly carefree way'. Twice in the book Herbert replays the choice facing settlers: to go the way of the Squatter or the way of the Swagman. Twice Shillingsworth siblings, newly arrived in Capricornia and ignorant of its ways, choose one or other alternative. The pattern established by Oscar and Mark repeats itself, a generation later, in Norman and Marigold. Mark and Norman choose the way of the Swagman; Oscar and Marigold the way of the Squatter, with its truckling to the powerful, its concern for large ownership and acknowledged position in society. The book shows no sympathy for the Squatter choice. It is not until Oscar's squattocratic pretensions disappear that Herbert begins to treat him with sympathy. Marigold is too flimsy a character to attract the full-blooded dislike we are encouraged to feel for her mother, but her ignoble manoeuvring to escape the taint of Norman's colour invites, at best, scornful pity. By contrast, the way of the Swagman is applauded—with qualifications when it is seen in the seedy figure of Mark, but wholeheartedly in its later exemplar, Norman. Father and son both share what the novel sees as the truly Australian qualities—freedom and brotherhood—and if a certain raffishness accompanies those qualities, well, that too is part of being Australian.

The Swagman's freedom is, first of all, freedom from wage slavery. Mark rejects the steady job, concern for public opinion and social climbing of the Squatter, secure in the knowledge that, in Capricornia, freedom from the power of bosses is every man's right. 'They could not wield their whips to terrify in this true Australia Felix, Capricornia. No—because the sack meant here not misery and hunger, but freedom to go adventuring.'[19] Though there is irony in so patent an excuse for laziness, there is no irony in McRandy's later praise for Australia as

> a workin' man's paradise, which is better than it bein' a paradise for Plutes. [...] We're a great people we Australians. There's nuthen to touch us in the World. [...] There is something special about us [...] our freedom from slavery to industry and our sunshine and our elbow room.[20]

Mark's attitude may show the seamy side of Australian freedom, but it is nonetheless a freedom to be proud of, and Aboriginal custom is again used to reinforce its quintessential Australianness. 'Their tribes', says McRandy, 'are families, in which no-one is boss, in which no-one is entitled by any sort of right to bully and grab'.[21]

Swagman freedom is not only freedom from bosses; it is also freedom from restless acquisitiveness. The Swagman roams where he will, never tying himself to a job, never becoming a rich man, simply surviving—and enjoying himself. The land gives sufficient for basic needs, and true Capricornians take what is offered, refusing to tie themselves to jobs in order to acquire more than they need. And Herbert applauds this. For all their faults, the feckless reprobates Henn, Titmuss and company are infinitely more attractive than the Poundamores and Playfair Flutes, and more Australian, too, as Herbert again suggests through comparison with Aboriginal custom:

> [Aboriginals] simply preserve their game and fruits and things, by drawin' on 'em carefully, and so save 'emselves the labour of havin' to till and sow and the trouble of gettin' all mixed up financially over their stock as we do. You might call that Primitive. But lookin' at it closely and comparin' it with our system of sweat and worry and sinfulness, I dunno but what it aint quite as good. [...] What is the perfect state of society? Aint it the one in which everyone's equally happy and well fed? If it is, then Brother Binghi has it.[22]

The Swagman way is further validated as truly Australian by the fact that it is in tune with the land, unlike the puritan, acquisitive, European work ethic of the Squatter. The sensible response to Australian geographic conditions is the Aboriginal response, is Mark's response: to harvest sparingly, not exploit ruthlessly. The land resists exploitation, and that is what makes it a land in which freedom can flourish. Judged by the standards of foreign money-makers, 'it's an utterly useless land. [...] Dry Season it's a desert. Wet Season it's a lake'.[23] But it provides enough for those content with sufficiency. Booms are short-lived; the characteristic state is neither destitution nor affluence but low-key survival. There may be no market for Red Ochre stock, but there's plenty of beef for the dinner table, and it's only 'if one's heart was small' that one 'packed up and left this Capricornia that fools down South called the Land of Opportunity'. They are fools because they cannot see that the opportunity Capricornia offers is freedom, not wealth, and it offers freedom precisely because there is no incentive to slave for money in a land so stubbornly resistant to financial exploitation.

Another freedom Capricornians cherish is freedom from political tyranny. The Jolly Swagman myth is replayed again and again as troopers go out to apprehend first Mark, then Tocky, then Ket, then Norman. Always there is a sense that self-respecting Capricornians must protect freedom by opposing the troopers.

> Norman's talk of intent to betray the murderers was only blather. He had no illusions about the kind of fame he would win among his fellow citizens by doing so, nor so much love for the man-trackers that he would help them in their wretched business.[24]

True Capricornians would never choose 'to debase themselves by acting as policemen'.[25]

In Capricornia it is only the Trooper, minion of the Squatter, who seeks to limit a man's freedom, and for that he is detested by all 'self-respecting, law-despising Capricornians'.[26] The law and its servants are never seen as protectors of the weak or instruments of justice, only as opponents of liberty. In portraying the police and the public in these ways, Herbert is drawing on those realities of Australian social history that Paterson mythologised in 'Waltzing Matilda'. In contrast to the English myth of the kindly bobby helping old ladies across the road, the Australian myth grew out of the cruelties of convict overseers and pictures the police more as servants of the oppressor than as protectors of the innocent. In *Capricornia*, therefore, whatever the crime, the reader is always invited to side with the fugitive and forget the victim's claims. Con the Greek, one of the few whites to treat half-castes with humanity[27], is an attractive character. Ket, his murderer, is not. Yet once Ket is arrested, we are encouraged to forget Con's worth and Ket's crime, and think only of the right of all men (even the least attractive) to be free. The central myth dictates our response. Ket in the jungle is the Swagman at the billabong, his freedom threatened, not a greedy killer rightly brought to justice for the murder of a fellow Capricornian. In *Capricornia* the law is never seen as anything but the power enabling 'a few greedy hounds to rule and rob us'.[28]

If freedom is the first quality of Capricornia, the second is brotherhood. True Capricornians are generous-spirited. They give without counting the cost or calculating future profit. It is only outsiders like the mean-minded pommy Jock Driver who behave differently:

> An ordinary Australian of the locality would have taken Mark's word for what he said about the machine, and would have said Yes or No to the price asked, and, as a preliminary to doing business, would have stood the needy seller treat. Mark had to stand treat himself, and had to take Jock out to inspect the plant.[29]

The same goes for hospitality. The meanness of government officers brands them as Squatter outsiders. True Capricornians welcome all travellers with 'the hospitality that all in Capricornia except the Government officers [...] were always eager to extend'.[30] Again, Aboriginal custom validates Swagman ethic. Connie Differ, abandoned by her white 'protector', is 'made very welcome'[31] by Aboriginal relations, however little they can offer her in the poverty of their camp. Even outcasts like Ket and Nawnim, while not welcomed, are tolerated.[32]

Capricornian brotherhood appears also in its relationships. Vincent Buckley argued that 'in the whole book there is not one constant and satisfying relationship established'[33], but in this too he is clearly wrong. There are plenty of constant and satisfying relationships in *Capricornia*, though they are not the heterosexual relationships Buckley was perhaps looking for. The deep and lasting relationships in *Capricornia* are those between friends, and between parents and children. The relationship between Mark and Chook, for instance:

> Chook had died alone with Mark, suddenly stricken with paralysis while trying to help Mark. [...] And he died as he had chosen to live for fourteen years, a voluntary exile, a martyr to his affection for Mark. Mark had buried him with his own half-paralysed hands, weeping into his shallow sandy grave the first tears his eyes had shed for years.[34]

The love between Mark and Chook is in the Australian tradition of 'mateship' between adult males. It is characterised by total loyalty and considerable unselfishness, and expresses itself more comfortably in deed than word. It is matched in the book by the constancy of O'Pick and Ballest and the friendship between Mark and Heather. Man and woman though they are, there is more mate than lover in Heather's feelings for Mark. 'She had striven hard,' we are told, 'not with tears and common female wiles but with comradely devotion, to save [him] from his own worst enemy, himself'.[35]

The Swagman ethic is a masculine ethic. McRandy speaks of Aboriginal and Swagman sharing 'the same old manly carefree way'[36] and the choice of 'manly' is no accident. The same is true of the stress on 'brotherhood'. The term, as used in *Capricornia*, is not gender inclusive. Women are rarely included, and when they are, they become, like Heather, honorary men. The gender bias is continued in the depiction of family relationships. It is the love of fathers and brothers that is stressed. The role of mothers and sisters is either caricatured (Pansy McLash's love for Frank) or criticised (Jasmine Shillingsworth, the bad wife, and Marigold Shillingsworth, the bad sister). Male family relationships, by contrast, are consistently characterised by unselfish loyalty in time of need, and by love expressed with surprising passion during moments of crisis. When Oscar is 'accused of that worst of all offences in Civil Service— Blabbing', his brother Mark, seeing him looking 'so bemused and miserable', is 'smitten to the heart', and glories in sacrificing his own career to save his brother's.[37] In Mark's time of need, Oscar reciprocates. Though in 'no doubt about his guilt', he lies for him in court, and in so doing 'had never felt more love for Mark'.[38] The warmth between brothers is matched by that between fathers and children. If relations between husband and wife are unsatisfactory in *Capricornia*, relations between father and child are, without exception, loving. Differ, Oscar and even (except where race intrudes) Mark all cherish their children, while some of the most delightful scenes in the book are those between O'Cannon and his much-loved brood.

Freedom and brotherhood are two qualities Herbert celebrates in his Capricornians. A third is their larrikin vitality. Capricornians show little energy for the daily grind of the wage slave but have it in abundance when it comes to enjoying themselves. Nowhere is this more evident than in the relish of their fighting. Rarely is there any real malice, except again when outsiders like Jock Driver take the whole thing seriously in a meanminded, un-Capricornian way. Capricornian fights are 'matters more of mettlesome hands than malicious hearts'. The fights between O'Pick and Ballest are 'always entertaining'. Those at the O'Cannon wedding are 'grand'. And even Pastor Hollower enjoys a scrap when the Aboriginals come to steal back their women, because 'it was all great fun for everyone, including Mr Hollower, who never would admit it'.[39]

The bustling vitality of Capricornian life is further emphasised in descriptions such as the following:

> [The Paddock] was the home of scores of children of almost any colour one might wish to see, and of a multitude of mongrel dogs, and of a medley of weird sounds—laughter and chatter of strange people, tinkle and boom and wail of outlandish musical instruments.[40]

Similar crammed-to-the-brim activity runs through widely disparate descriptions of life in Capricornia. From the doctor's day ('the amputation of a gangrenous leg, the delivery of a Greek woman of triplets, the vaccination of a score of Compound natives') to the loading of cattle ('blazing lights and dust and flies and stench and din'), all is hectic in Capricornia.[41] All is a jumbled, fascinating, energetic mixture of 'mad' elements. All is alive and there is life in abundance, for 'no wind, fair or foul, ever blew in Capricornia without developing into a hurricane'.[42]

When he wrote *Capricornia*, Herbert still believed in the stereotypes of Australian 'mateship' and freedom, and his hero exemplifies those stereotypes. Buckley describes Norman as a man driven 'to a sort of permissive carelessness', and says, '[he] seems to me easily the best example in our literature of what is generally supposed to be the typical Australian'.[43] The analysis is perceptive and accurate. The only question is whether Herbert would have agreed with its critical tone. There is no hint in the text that we are to criticise what Norman becomes, and if we accept that Herbert is happy not only to accept but to extol the 'typical Australian' characteristics of the Jolly Swagman, the development of Norman should cause no surprise. He becomes a better version of his father, Mark—the Swagman spirit without its sleazy accessories. To say that Herbert had high hopes for the Swagman spirit, however, is not to say he was certain of its value. Throughout the book he maintains an ironic stance that raises doubts even as it praises:

> When the town became crowded with idlers just before Christmas, Mark, who had in him all the makings of a good Capricornian, chafed because his job went on. He was in this mood when the good Capricornian Krater came back to Town to idle.[44]

The irony of the repeated 'good Capricornian' indicates Herbert's unease, and undercuts McRandy's eulogy of the working man's paradise. Capricornian freedom and Capricornian idleness seem to go hand in hand, and the somewhat infrequent attempts of 'good Capricornians' to do something useful are mockingly exposed as foolish and ineffectual: Mark's wind-driven fans that only work when they are not needed and tide-driven dynamos that only provide light by day.

The uneasiness of Herbert's standpoint becomes even clearer in his description of the transformation of Flying Fox into the Gospelist Aboriginal Mission Station. He is torn between praising the mission for doing something useful with the land and giving purpose to Aboriginal lives, and blaming it for introducing an alien note of greedy exploitation. In one sentence his irony mocks the hypocrisy of lazy capitalists preaching the work ethic to exploited employees; in the next he ridicules the ineffectualness of normal Capricornians:

> The Gospelists, contemptible by reason of their virtue in the eyes of normal Capricornians, had done something that the normal ones had failed to do, that is, had developed methods of doing business successfully [...] Of

course they themselves did not hew and dig and sow, as
scoffers pointed out. But did Moses leading his people
through the wilderness go out and gather the manna for
them? [...] The Gospelists offered [Aboriginals] spirituality
for their labours, or, if that were not acceptable, at least
mere labour to keep their hands in trim and their minds
alive, and into the bargain taught them to read and write
and think like whitemen of the kind they were themselves. Surely better pay than a pound a month and
pigswill and the status of a dog, as prescribed by the
government?[45]

The uncertainty of the irony reflects Herbert's uncertainties. He
wanted to believe in Australian freedom and brotherhood, but he
knew they were not the whole truth about Australia. That had to
include the treatment of black Australians. Capricornian defence of
freedom stopped unforgivably short of Aboriginals; its brotherhood
was not broad enough to include them. The final scene of the
book, with its sombre reminder of the tragic and unregarded
deaths of a young Aboriginal woman and her baby, emphasises
that fact.

Nonetheless, despite Herbert's awareness of unforgivable
limitations in Capricornia's application of the ideals of freedom and
brotherhood, the novel is still full of his hope for Australia. There is
no hint of irony in McRandy's praise of 'the manly carefree way' and
the 'glorious wild state' of Capricornia.[46] Nor is there irony in the
contrast between Capricornia's freedom and happiness and the
mess the rest of the world makes of its affairs:

Thus Capricornia, freest and happiest land on earth, was
dragged into a war between kings and queens and
plutocrats and slaves and homicidal half-wits.[47]

The Herbert who wrote *Capricornia* still believed in Australia. He
saw its weaknesses, but the extent of their danger is not yet clear to
him. Between *Capricornia* and *Poor Fellow My Country* the perspective changes. It is the same Australia, but the view is different.

Optimism has changed to pessimism. In *Poor Fellow My Country* the free spirit of Australia is undermined from within as well as threatened from without. The Swagman's indomitable resistance to Trooper and Squatter has become the exception, not the rule. His successes are infrequent, short-lived and limited. The Squatter and Trooper rule *Poor Fellow My Country.* In *Capricornia,* the Swagman is king.

PART III

THE MIDDLE PERIOD

CHAPTER 4

Aboriginality as Subject, Symbol and Setting

C *APRICORNIA* was completed in 1934. Herbert began writing his next published novel, *Soldiers' Women*, in 1943. The years between were spent in unsuccessful attempts to take *Capricornia's* subject matter and themes further. His first attempt, 'The King against the Kurawaddi', was abandoned. The same thing happened to a second attempt, 'Yellow Fellow'. Unable, it seemed, to take the concerns of *Capricornia* forward in any serious way, he turned to farce and produced, in 1941, the first, shorter, version of *Seven Emus*.[1] It was something, but hardly what he had been aiming at. In 1942 the war saved him. Leaving his failed attempts behind, he went off, perhaps with some relief, to the business of fighting.

Herbert later analysed his difficulties during this period as follows:

> It seems to me that I must always have a 'deep purpose' for a novel. That in *Capricornia* was so deep that only I know it. I gave up the next effort *The King against the Kurawaddi* because it lacked a deep purpose. And the

purpose of *Yellow Fellow* was beyond my powers to deal
with at the time. The purpose will eventually (I hope) be
expressed in that idea on the halfcaste theme *Poor Fellow
My Country*.[2]

Herbert is not the most reliable critic of his own work, and what he
says here is only partially correct. It is true that the driving force
behind each of his novels is a sense of deep purpose. It is not true
that *Capricornia*'s purpose was different from the others. The
'purpose so deep that only I know it' refers to Herbert's growing
belief, in the fifties, that *Capricornia*'s 'primary purpose turned out
as bringing out the secrets of my childhood'.[3] It was an interpretation
with obvious appeal to a man who had, by then, become very
interested in psychology—especially his own psychology. But while
it is true that there are autobiographical elements in *Capricornia*, it is
not true that expression of those elements is the primary purpose of
the novel. The deep purpose of *Capricornia* was the same as the
deep purpose of 'Yellow Fellow' and *Poor Fellow My Country*—to
convey Herbert's understanding of the Australian ethos. And the
reason for his difficulties in the forties was that his view of Australia
was changing and he needed to find new ways of dealing with 'the
halfcaste theme' if he was to express that changing view successfully.
For all the difficulty and apparent failure of the period, we can, in
hindsight, see that he did indeed discover those new ways.

Before charting the changes in Herbert's treatment of 'the
halfcaste theme', however, we need to clarify the part played by
Aboriginality in his novels and to distinguish clearly between
'Aboriginality as subject' and 'Aboriginality as symbol'. The former was
well recognised from the start as early criticism explored what
Capricornia had to say about the subject of the unjust treatment of
Aboriginals. The latter, Herbert's use of Aboriginal characters and
cultures as symbols, has been less well recognised and less thoroughly
explored.

It helps, in any such exploration, to make a further distinction—between 'Aboriginality as subject' and 'Australia as subject'.
The subject that most interested Herbert throughout his writing
career was always Australia—not Aboriginality. This was true even

in *Capricornia*, where he was most the social critic, and it remained true as, in the books that followed, Herbert changed his use of Aboriginal motifs to reflect his darkening vision of both the condition of Aboriginals and the condition of Australia. In charting these changes, it is important to recognise when 'Aboriginality as symbol' refers to 'Aboriginality as subject', when it refers to 'Australia as subject' and when it refers to both simultaneously. The symbolic significance of *Poor Fellow My Country*'s Bobwirridirridi provides an example of the complexities involved, and of the need to make clear distinctions. On the one hand, as Chapter 10 demonstrates, Bobwirridirridi is important symbolically to 'Aboriginality as subject'— signifying in that context, among other things, the dauntless resistance of Aboriginals to the hegemony of white culture. On the other hand, as Chapters 11 and 13 show, he is equally important symbolically to 'Australia as subject'—in that context signifying a variety of things, including the daunting challenge Australia presents to settlers, the need for Australia to free itself of colonial attitudes and become truly Australian, and Herbert's pessimistic sense that his dreams for a better Australia are doomed to failure.

In *Capricornia*, as in *Poor Fellow My Country*, Aboriginal symbolism plays an important part in expressing Herbert's views on 'Australia as subject'. Unlike *Poor Fellow My Country*, the Aboriginal symbolism in *Capricornia* paints, for the most part, an optimistic picture of Australia. While descriptions of the unjust treatment of Aboriginals point to serious failures, the symbolism of the Aboriginal hero signifies that the Australian ethos is, nonetheless, healthy. It is, after all, the spirit of white Australia, the Swagman spirit, that Norman exemplifies. The symbolic significance attached to Aboriginal culture reinforces the optimistic view of Australia. Whereas in *Poor Fellow My Country* Aboriginal culture is used to highlight the inadequacies of the Australian ethos, in *Capricornia* it is used to validate that ethos. In *Poor Fellow My Country* white Australia is measured against Aboriginal culture and found wanting. In *Capricornia*, on the other hand, when McRandy describes Aboriginal culture, it is its similarity to, and thus validation of, the Swagman ethic of white Australia that he stresses: its opposition to the sanctions of law, its avoidance of wage slavery and its communistic sharing of goods. And, for all McRandy's praise of Aboriginal tradition, there is no suggestion that it has anything to teach white Australia. It is not Norman's Aboriginality that provides hope for the future but his 'genius' for white technology. In a revealingly racist comment, McRandy makes his (and at this stage Herbert's) assimilationist attitudes clear, when he finds it a special merit of Aboriginality that it 'breeds out' quickly. 'Three cross-breedin's and you'll get the colour right out, with never the risk of a throw-back.'[4]

The picture given of the Aboriginal hero's response to Aboriginal culture further demonstrates the difference between the symbolism of *Capricornia* and *Poor Fellow My Country*. Norman's first reaction to the knowledge that he is part-Aboriginal is to feel deeply ashamed. He goes off alone into the bush to hide and there, for the first time, encounters the spirit of his Aboriginal heritage:

> [C]rouching—at the bottom of a grey- and green-walled well of light, he sensed the Spirit of the Land to the full. Phantoms came crowding, wailing afar off, whispering as they neared, treading with tiny sounds, flitting like shadows. He felt afraid. His scalp crept. His black eyes rolled.[5]

The 'Spirit of the Land' that Norman here senses is not the 'Spirit of the Land' hymned by McRandy in the context of 'Waltzing Matilda'.[6] That is the spirit of the Swagman, the spirit of larrikin freedom after which Mark Shillingsworth's boat is named, the spirit that rules *Capricornia*. This is the Aboriginal 'Spirit of the Land', the spirit that pervades *Poor Fellow My Country* but appears only in this one chapter of *Capricornia*. In *Poor Fellow My Country* this spirit is seen as the true spirit of Australia. In *Capricornia* it is viewed negatively, as an imprisoning past from which Norman must escape if he and, by implication, Australia are to fulfil their destiny.

Faced by the Aboriginal 'Spirit of the Land', Norman is frightened, at first, back into primitive responses. A golden beetle shoots into the firelight, settles in a bush and begins a reverberating didgeridoo drone. Norman, in response, 'with eyes on Southern Cross, took up a stick and beat upon a log […] clickaclick-click'. For a moment or two the ancient Aboriginal rhythms soothe him, but then the culture of his white forefathers asserts itself. 'He dropped the stick. His skin was tingling. He looked at his hand, ashamed. Then he snatched up the stick and hurled it at the beetle.' He longs to chase away his Aboriginality as easily as he chases away the beetle. But he can't. Everything reminds him of his alien, unwanted, frightening inheritance:

> He sought companionship of stars that formerly had been as familiar as street-lamps, to find them strange, utterly strange, vastly remote, infinite, arranged now to form mysterious designs of frightening significance. The cry of the kwiluk [...] which he had heard every night since coming home but scarcely heeded, became the lamenting of the wandering Devils of the Dead. He heaped up the fire, heaped it up, poked it to make it blaze and crackle, tried by staring into it to burn from his mind his tingling fears. But the higher the fire blazed the greater grew his own black shadow, which he knew without turning round to see was reared above him, menacing. He had to restrain himself from seeking relief in the Song of the Golden Beetle. Then for the first time he realized his Aboriginal heritage. [...] He slept badly, dreaming that he was lost with some sort of silent nomadic tribe among moving shadows in a valley of mountainous walls.[7]

This is one of only two passages[8] in *Capricornia* describing those mythic elements of Aboriginal lore that pervade *Poor Fellow My Country*, and what, in the later book, is familiar and comforting to the Aboriginal hero Prindy is not so here. For Norman, the Aboriginal 'Spirit of the Land' is alien. The heavens threaten. The kwiluks frighten. Having 'realized his Aboriginal heritage' for the first time, he does all in his power to reject it. His blackness is a threat, a 'shadow' that 'reared above him, menacing'. He seeks to 'burn from his mind' the fear it rouses in him. He sees his tribal ancestry as a nightmarish prison, in which he is condemned to wander 'lost among moving shadows in a valley of mountainous walls'.

The remainder of the chapter shows Norman coming to terms with his Aboriginal ancestry, not (as Prindy later does) by accepting but by resisting it. On the following day it is when he is 'haunted by thoughts of his debasement' that he is 'more sensitive to the Spirit of the Land than ever'. Sensitivity to the Aboriginal 'Spirit of the Land', in other words, is no positive influence. Hope, in *Capricornia*, comes not from his Aboriginal heritage but from the world of the Swagman, the world of individual human genius. The escape for Norman from 'debasement' comes not by turning with pride towards the Golden Beetle, but by asserting his Western intellect:

> On the third day he became quite cheerful, as the result of discovering for the first time in his life that he was thinking deeply. This he did through solving with a minute's thought a problem in mechanics that had been puzzling him for weeks. Encouraged to ponder other problems with what he thought remarkable success, he began to feel for the first time in his life that he was clever. Soon he forgot his debasement. And he found himself marvelling at the phenomenon of his existence as a creature, of the existence of Mankind, and of nature's contrariety to Man that made Man's ingenuity essential. [...] That third night he forgot the phantoms roused by his fire in pondering over the phenomenon of combustion.[9]

Thus is the Aboriginal 'Spirit of the Land' defeated, in *Capricornia*, by white Australia's 'Spirit of Man's Genius': 'Night held no terrors for him now; and loneliness no longer troubled him. He spent the hours between sundown and ten o'clock in working out a problem in mechanics'.[10]

Three days later Norman's solitude is broken by the appearance of a 'savage [...] naked but for a belt of human hair, painted hideously, white from head to foot, and striped with red and yellow, and armed with a handful of spears' and with a 'death's-head face'.[11] It is the first appearance of the formulaic description Herbert will later use to describe Bobwirridirridi. At this point, though, Herbert is interested only in the 'hideous', alien qualities. There is nothing yet of the sense of innate dignity conveyed in descriptions of Bobwirridirridi. And, unlike Prindy when faced by a similar apparition in the opening pages of *Poor Fellow My Country*, Norman is 'terrified' by this representative of Aboriginal culture. Not for long, though, since the fearsome figure turns out to be none other than Bootpolish, a stockman from Red Ochre Station on walkabout with a group of friends, including Muttonhead, another Red Ochre stockman. Mutton-head tells Norman that, with the rivers impassable, he is stuck in the bush for at least four months. 'But I gotter get back South', says Norman, 'or I'll lose me job'. Calmly Muttonhead replies, 'More better stop. You harcarse. Plenty harcarse stop longa bush longa blackfellow. [...] Proper good country dis one. [...] More better you sit down all-same blackfella—eh Norman?'[12] For Herbert in *Poor Fellow My Country*, it was indeed 'more better' for half-castes 'to sit down all-same blackfella'. In *Capricornia*, however, neither the character nor the author sees any value in doing so. Norman remains with the blacks, but unwillingly, and Herbert proves equally reluctant to spend time with them. Norman's enforced stay with these Aboriginals gave Herbert, had he wished, ample opportunity to say something about Aboriginal culture. The fact that he devotes not a single paragraph to Norman's four-month walkabout, though he later spends a whole, and somewhat pointless, chapter on Ket's wanderings in the bush, shows how little, at this stage, Aboriginal culture interests him.

Capricornia's Aboriginal hero is very different from *Poor Fellow My Country*'s. Prindy's assured relationship with the land and its spirits is of central importance throughout the later book. By contrast, in *Capricornia* Norman experiences that relationship briefly and unwillingly. Norman in the bush is a townie out of his element, caught in life-threatening situations because he is unable to read natural signs (the behaviour of horses, the vegetation pattern by the river) that to Prindy would have spelt 'storm and flood' clearer than words on a page. The character in *Capricornia* who points the way towards Prindy is not Norman but Tocky.

Unlike Norman, Tocky is at ease in the bush:

Tocky loved frogs for their sparkling eyes and merry songs and friendly ways, but did not scruple eating them

if need be. There was need that morning. Apologetically
she slaughtered five and ate their delicate legs with dainty
bamboo-shoots, concluding her meal with native goose-
berries, a stick-load of sugar-bag honey drawn from a
hollow tree, and crystal water.[13]

There is much here that we find later in Prindy's relationship with
nature: the ease with which he finds bush tucker, the kinship he feels
with animals, the respect with which he treats them even when
survival demands their sacrifice. As Tocky apologetically slaughters
frogs, so Prindy murmurs 'Poor Bugger' as he despatches wallabies.
In other ways, too, Tocky is precursor to Prindy. Like him, she
escapes through water, is thought to have 'drowned while swimming'
and to be 'not quite sane'.[14] Like him, she plays a musical instrument
and makes up subversive songs that mock the authorities. Like him,
she disregards and evades white power rather than, like Norman,
opposing it. The difference between Tocky and Prindy is that, in
Capricornia, Herbert is yet to find symbolic significance in these
qualities.

Of the next two novels Herbert attempted, all that remains is
a plan for the second describing the intended contents of each
chapter. Short though that plan is, it is enough to show that 'Yellow
Fellow', for the most part, simply retraced ground already covered in
Capricornia. The plot includes many of *Capricornia*'s oppression
motifs: the unjust trial, the separation of Aboriginal children from
their families, the callous treatment of Aboriginals in hospitals and so
on.[15] The message conveyed by the Aboriginal hero, meanwhile, is
the message of *Capricornia* writ even larger. Parinti in 'Yellow
Fellow' is Norman Shillingsworth pushed a few steps further along
the road to success. He fulfils McRandy's dream of a charismatic
leader fighting for Aboriginal political rights. His early larrikin
aggressiveness gives way to more purposeful political action: first
some rudimentary union organisation; next the founding of a
'Euraustralian League' with himself as president; and finally a
country-wide mobilisation of half-castes that gives him entry into the
national parliament.[16] But having taken his hero to a point of real
political power, Herbert abruptly ends the book with two chapters

whose contents are described thus: 'Parinti's arrest and trial and imprisonment' and 'Parinti breaks jail, goes bush, and is killed by Tommy Lamma'. It is a strangely negative conclusion reflecting, perhaps, a pessimism caused by the failure of his own attempts during these years at political and economic action on behalf of Aboriginals.[17]

The problem with 'Yellow Fellow' was that the triumphant tale of a half-caste hero adapting to the demands of white culture was becoming a less and less functional symbol for Herbert. With his vision of the present and the future becoming darker, he needed to find new ways of using 'Aboriginality as symbol' if it was to continue to play a part in expressing his views both on 'Aboriginality as subject' and 'Australia as subject'. And, trapped though he still was in *Capricornia*'s view of the half-caste hero, Herbert did begin, in 'Yellow Fellow', to extend the Aboriginal subject matter significantly, since it is here we find the first mention of elements of tribal Aboriginality that later become central to the allegory of *Poor Fellow My Country*. In the sketch for Chapter 1, for instance, we read of the

> disappearance of [...] Jahligeeta's husband. [...] Her uncle, Tony Lauma[18] comes for her. She...runs to station [...] tells Colin Coles, manager. [...] In middle of night the blacks steal on her. [...] Coles rushes out with revolver and shoots two or three. [...] Her uncle [...] lets fly a spear and gets Coles in chest.

In Chapter 2 the black culprits are captured and tried, and Lamma 'stands up for himself and gives cheek'. In Chapter 3 Jahligeeta fears death but is told there is 'no Kurawaddi on coast'. Sketchy though the plan is, it seems clear that, like Nelyerri, Queeny and Savitra in *Poor Fellow My Country*, Jahligeeta has offended against the male cult of the Kurawaddi, and that Lamma, like Bobwirridirridi, is involved in that cult.

From the point of view of *Poor Fellow My Country*, the character of Lamma is particularly interesting. We next hear of him in Chapter 13, where 'Parinti in jail meets old Lauma [sic]. He frightens Parinti. He's mad'. Towards the end of the book, Lamma becomes more and more destructive. In Chapter 20 he spears Jahligeeta; in Chapter 25 he spears Parinti's friend Sol; and in the final chapter, as already noted, he brings the plot to an abrupt end by killing Parinti. In all this, Lamma foreshadows the nature and role of Bobwirridirridi: the one who refuses to assimilate to white ways, thought 'mad' by whites, feared by blacks, imprisoned but uncowed, ruthless enforcer of tribal custom. Where Lamma differs from Bobwirridirridi is in his relationship with the half-caste hero. Unlike his namesake Parinti, Prindy is not frightened when he meets Bobwirridirridi in gaol. In *Poor Fellow My Country* the black witchdoctor is the half-caste hero's tribal mentor and friend. In 'Yellow Fellow' that role is played not by Lamma but by another Aboriginal, Bridesman. It is Bridesman who in Chapter 7 'circumcises Parinti [...] and tells him to educate himself'. The first action points forward to Bobwirridirridi; the second, backwards towards McRandy.

In 'Yellow Fellow', then, Herbert's presentation of 'Aboriginality as subject' broadened to include elements of traditional culture that had not interested him in *Capricornia*. What symbolic part, if any, those elements would have played in 'Yellow Fellow' we cannot tell. The plan is too sketchy. In *Seven Emus*, however, there is no doubt. A shift has occurred in Herbert's use of 'Aboriginality as symbol'. On the periphery before, Aboriginal culture lies now at the symbolic heart of the book. Whereas in *Capricornia* it stood for a primitive past that must be rejected, in *Seven Emus* it points to an ideal future to which Australia must aspire. Whereas in *Capricornia* it is cited in validation of the ethos of white Australia, in *Seven Emus* it serves to criticise that ethos. And whereas in *Capricornia* the defining myth is Paterson's story of the Jolly Swagman, in *Seven Emus* it is a Dreamtime myth of Aboriginal Australia.

By the time he wrote *Seven Emus*, Herbert had lost faith in the anarchic zest of the Swagman spirit. He now sensed a spiritual malaise in the Australian ethos unguessed at before. He describes Gaunt and Goborrow as 'unsatisfied of soul because acceptance of the spirit of the land of their origin is denied them'. They do not understand, he says, that 'such things are of the soul, not of the mind, that there is no logic in them, only the psychic satisfaction that is the stuff other than bread by which men live'.[19] In *Poor Fellow My*

Country Delacy speaks in similar terms of 'the awful emptiness of the colonial-born', living 'without a country' like 'men with dead souls'.[20] This talk of 'soul' represents a major shift in Herbert's thinking. He would have been uncomfortable with the word in *Capricornia*. His view of man's place in the scheme of things has changed. Goborrow and Gaunt are castigated as 'non-believers in anything one cannot eat', men 'whose only cult was self-seeking'.[21] Herbert has lost faith in the individualism and materialism of the Swagman spirit. Something deeper, he now believes, is needed, something greater than the individual, greater even than freedom and brotherhood. He found symbolic expression for that 'something' in the beliefs, customs and myths of traditional Aboriginal culture.[22]

The defining myth of *Seven Emus* is the myth of the Emu Sisters' Dreamtime journey through Australia carrying with them 'the properties of the cult they were to initiate'. Harassed by Wanjin the Dingo, the sisters scratch out a cave as 'hiding-place' for the cult's 'sacred stones and implements' and for the 'human shades destined to be born as Emu people'. This cave is the spiritual centre of the Emu people's lives. It is 'the reliquary for sacred properties of the Emu Dreaming and bourn for spirit children of the ilk awaiting reincarnation'.[23] Its spiritual significance is so great that the Emu people's 'existence as a society depended on it'. If they 'lose 'em that, they finish'.[24] When an Aboriginal of the Emu Dreaming dies, his spirit goes back to the sacred cave to await rebirth in another body. If the sacred place is destroyed, these spirit children are lost and the tribe will die out.

In the myth of the Emu Sisters, Herbert found a symbol for what he felt was lacking in white Australians: a relationship with, and feeling for, their country that went beyond the materialism of the Swagman spirit. The beliefs and rituals of the Emu people exemplify the spiritual ties humans need, he now believes, between themselves and the world in which they live. These must, the symbolism suggests, be grounded in history and rooted in geography. The Emu people are linked to their past and their land in a recurring cycle of birth and death that is reaffirmed and celebrated through the 'things that give meaning to [their] existence, the singing and dancing, the veneration in mime of the ancient' and the art on the cave walls that 'symbolized the spirit and the history of this place'.[25] The roof Goborrow sees is 'fresh and bright from the annual painting [...] done for one more of how many thousand times', each new generation renewing its relationship with the Emu Sisters through the act of adding one more layer to the 'motionless march through the ages of the Dream-time giants' procession across the roof'.[26]

Aboriginal culture serves, in *Seven Emus* as in *Poor Fellow My Country* later, both an inspirational and a critical purpose. On the one hand, it offers a picture of the kind of relationship a people should have with their country. On the other, it becomes a symbolic measure of Australian alienation. That alienation is symbolised both by Aboriginals who have lost their culture and by whites who scorn and devalue it. In *Seven Emus* Bronco represents the former, Gaunt and Goborrow the latter.

In Bronco, we see the death of the hopes Herbert expressed through Norman and Parinti. Like Norman, Bronco aims at success the white man's way, owns his own station and leads for a time an 'arcadian existence'. Like Norman, he faces 'utter dissolution of all he had so patiently got together'[27], but then has his fortunes restored by a flood of incredible good luck. Unlike Norman, Bronco is no romance hero. He is one of the downtrodden, exploited by bank managers, swindled and tricked by Gaunt and Goborrow. Whereas before, the story of the half-caste hero testified to the strength of the Australian way, now it points to something seriously wrong in the Australian psyche that no amount of political or economic action will change. The Euraustralian League, which in 'Yellow Fellow' is real and politically effective, has become in *Seven Emus* simply a fiction, invented by wily white men to keep Bronco busy dreaming of a better future while they make off with the stolen artefacts of his Aboriginal past.

It is in his relationship to, and feelings for, that past that Bronco is most clearly different from Norman and most clearly signals Herbert's new thinking on Australia. Bronco describes himself and his fellow half-castes as 'the neither-black-nor-whites, the bloody nothings'.[28] The term 'bloody nothing' refers to Aboriginals who have lost their connection with Aboriginal culture. They are no longer part of the kinship system. They are no longer part of a world where relationship to the tribe and the land is organised, and vouched for, by relationship to one of the legendary spirits of the Dreamtime. They have lost their 'Dreaming', and in losing it have lost what gives meaning to their lives. 'Anyone got Dreamin' got strong heart for livin'', says Bronco. 'Lose 'em Dreamin', you don't care, you die.'[29] To escape from his sense of being a 'bloody nothing', Bronco, unlike Norman, instead of turning his back on Aboriginal culture seeks acceptance within it. Though 'not an Emu man himself', he believes his two children were 'born into the clan because he dreamt it'. He has also 'constituted himself a kind of patron' of the Emu cult, active in protecting its sacred cave and artwork, and eager 'to explain its rites and show off its properties to visitors'.[30] For all his efforts, however, 'the blacks did not really regard Bronco as one of them'. He is too much the white man in his regard for money and property, and 'while attraction to the ancient ways might show spiritual kinship with the Old People, no one could charge Bronco with having like mentality'.[31]

In all this we can see the genesis of three important strands of *Poor Fellow My Country*'s symbolism. The first is the symbolism of the half-caste as 'bloody nothing', which is pervasive in *Poor Fellow My Country*—found both in the picture given of half-castes in general, and in the portraits of Queeny, Nelyerri and Savitra in particular. The second is Bronco's dream of his children's acceptance as Emu clansmen, which foreshadows the later symbolism of Prindy's acceptance by Bobwirridirridi into the Snake Cult. The third is Bronco's relationship with the Emu clan, which foreshadows the symbolism of Jeremy Delacy's similarly well-meaning, similarly doomed, attempts to become accepted by Aboriginals. Like Bronco, Delacy sees himself as protector of the Snake Cult's sacred sites. Like Bronco, his allegiance to white ways of thinking ultimately prevents him from acting in accordance with Aboriginal tradition.

The connection between half-caste Bronco and white Delacy points to the fact that the position of the 'bloody nothings', or 'bloody nutchings' as *Poor Fellow My Country* calls them, becomes for Herbert a symbol of the spiritual alienation he now sees in most non-Indigenous Australians.[32] 'The introduced population', he has Professor Orbitt say in *Seven Emus*, is 'trying to find roots in a land where we are for ever alien', and since 'the fundamental happiness of mankind is in identification with country [...] colonial people are therefore never happy and so never reach a true maturity in anything'.[33] The problem, Herbert suggests, is that white Australia is cut off from its old cultural roots, and unwilling to establish new ones. He expresses this unwillingness, symbolically, in the refusal of white characters in *Seven Emus* to take the Indigenous culture of Australia seriously. 'The only history hereabout', writes Herbert, 'was the ancient black man's, enough of which these modern white men knew to create the spirit of the place for themselves', but they are too arrogant to do so. The result is that they

> live unsatisfied of soul because acceptance of the spirit of the land of their origin is denied them who are born alien to that land, and they cannot create any worthwhile spirit out of history as little as their own, nor out of the rich history of their black compatriots because that would be beneath their dignity.[34]

To emphasise the folly and the arrogance of this refusal to seek 'identification with' the new country, Herbert introduces into *Seven Emus* a character with no precursor in *Capricornia*—the character of the professional anthropologist, Malcolm Goborrow.

Herbert uses Goborrow to stress the alienation of white Australians—unable, it seems, to cut the cords that tie them to the old world and unwilling to establish new spiritual bonds with the new. And what better figure could there be to illustrate the arrogance and wilfulness of that alienation than a man who has made it his life's work to study Australia's Indigenous cultures but who remains blind to their spiritual meaning:

> Away on the plain a dingo mourned in racial memory for his ancestor Wanjin's lost loves. Up in the gorge a curlew cried of having found a spirit baby wandering too far from the Dreaming-place. That young Malcolm's interest in the primitive was largely professional was shown now by uninterestedness so obvious that almost at once he turned

to where the significance of this ancientness was to be
had as data for writing straight into a note-book, the
Joneses' place.[35]

Faced by the wonders of the Painted Caves, Fabian Cootes, the
professional anthropologist in *Poor Fellow My Country*, is similarly
unmoved, more interested in setting up his photographic gear, with
only 'a mere glance at the blazing wonder'. All he is concerned about
is the fact that the 'parietals represent as perfect an expression of the
Paleolithic ethos as you'd find anywhere in the world'.[36] In similar
fashion, Goborrow walks through a landscape alive with the mystery
of Aboriginal myth and notices nothing:

> The alien [...] went out into the shiny night that stared the
> mystery of Earth and Heaven so hard at him, that cried of
> the immeasurable soul-things so shrilly in voice of curlew
> calling of finding wandering Shade, of dingo remember-
> ing Dream-time. [...] Nevertheless he gave no more
> outward and visible sign of its effect on him than to
> slacken that city-sidewalk gait of his.[37]

The choice of 'alien' is significant. Those blind to the Aboriginal myth
meanings of the Australian night sky and deaf to the shrill calling of
Aboriginal soul-things signify through that blindness and deafness
their lack of relationship with Australia. Herbert reinforces the sense
that they are aliens in this land through the way the land's creatures
respond to them. Dogs attack Goborrow 'because they knew him for
the cheat he was'. Koodooks sweep over his head 'wing-beating with
malice' and 'grating hostile cries'.[38]

As professional anthropologists come to symbolise, for
Herbert, the failure to achieve right relationship with their land, so
Aboriginal tribal elders come to symbolise success in so doing. The
way that Herbert now begins to describe them reflects their new
symbolic importance. In *Capricornia* the description of tribal
Aboriginals goes no further than the, to white eyes, strange and
unprepossessing details: the garish paint, the nakedness. In *Seven
Emus* he insists we look beyond the surface detail and recognise a

dignity so obvious we should be ashamed for not having recognised it before:

> When they came, a couple of ancient scarecrows, with only a shirt and a pair of pants between them, they must be allowed time for leisurely fortification of themselves with tea and brownie, not in the genteel style of their betters, but off tinware, squatting with the ants in the sand outside. [...]
>
> Not that they were without dignity if one ignored the rags and studied the seamed, swart, grey-whiskered and cicatriced old faces and the heads with fat-smeared, dust-red hair rolled into daglocks and bound with fillets of ochred hair-string—faces of cast so anciently sublime, so noble, so seemingly of high intelligence.[39]

Moonduk and Mardoo may look like ancient scarecrows, but their certainty of purpose exposes modern Australia's insecurities. Secure in the age-old verities of the Dreamtime, they watch, without interest, the frenetic activity through which the white psyche attempts to shore up the breaches in its self-confidence. They have no need of the material goods and services with which white men fill lives empty of the deep certainties they are born into.

It is not, however, only in the positives of Dreamtime belief that Herbert finds the symbolism to express his changing vision of Australia. He also begins, in *Seven Emus*, to explore the symbolic potential of the limitations imposed by Dreamtime beliefs. The spiritual security of Aboriginal culture, he says, depends upon resistance to change. Tribal ritual involves not only 'veneration [...] of the ancient' but also 'mockery of the new'. It is backward-looking, 'chanting of beginning without advance towards end'.[40] Its strength is that it satisfies the need to feel at home in one's place and meaningful within the universe. But there is a cost. Anything that disturbs the ancient verities disturbs spiritual security, and therefore 'even the obvious may be rejected by the mind of palaeolithic man, should it seem likely to negate practice so anciently need-satisfying'.[41]

This conservatism in Aboriginal culture becomes for Herbert a symbol that relates both to 'Aboriginality as subject' and 'Australia as subject'. In its reference to 'Aboriginality as subject', it reflects Herbert's increasing pessimism about the future for Aboriginals who want to hold on to their culture in modern Australia. 'Their fixed ideas', Goborrow says, 'will destroy them sooner or later'.[42] And Herbert, in this at least, agrees with Goborrow. 'There is no solution to the problem,' he wrote in an essay some years later, 'at least no practical one. I made the admission [...] tacitly in *Seven Emus* which shows full bloods for what they are, a people doomed to non-progress, the poorest of the poor who will be with us always'.[43] This blunt statement is open to misrepresentation. A fuller and better expression of Herbert's views on the subject, as I demonstrate in Chapter 10, is found in the character and career of Bobwirridirridi, one aspect of whose complex allegorical significance is to represent 'dauntless but doomed tribal Aboriginality'.

In its reference to 'Australia as subject', the symbol of Aboriginal conservatism also leads ultimately towards the allegorical significance of Bobwirridirridi. Aboriginal culture, for all its inspirational qualities, is a closed system that allows for no new ideas, and has no place for newcomers: even half-castes are excluded. It thus becomes, for Herbert, a symbol not only of the tantalising possibility but also of the frustrating impossibility of establishing the kind of Australia he desired, one in which newcomers renounce old allegiances and bond with their new land. The difficulty of achieving that is expressed, symbolically, in the failure of Bronco and Delacy to win the trust of Australia's first inhabitants. Both seek acceptance; both are excluded by the logic of traditional culture. Something is needed to break the impasse. It is, again, in the allegorical significance of the character of Bobwirridirridi that Herbert finds expression for that something.

Moonduk, like Lamma in 'Yellow Fellow', is a precursor to Bobwirridirridi. Like Bobwirridirridi, Moonduk has a 'skull-like face'.[44] Like Bobwirridirridi, he is leader of a cult. But he is also different, in important respects, from Bobwirridirridi. First, he does not share Bobwirridirridi's contempt for white power. When Moonduk catches Goborrow and Gaunt in an act of desecration, he is afraid 'of the dire consequences of punishing it accordingly when the culprits were of the master-race'.[45] No such fear ever troubles Bobwirridirridi. Second, Moonduk is a mainstream leader, hidebound by tradition. The creative breakthrough Herbert achieved in Bobwirridirridi was to conceive the notion of combining traditional Aboriginal authority with outsider status. The Snake Cult in *Poor Fellow My Country* is an outsider cult, and its leader, Bobwirridirridi, is no more bound by the precedents of traditional Aboriginal culture than his master, Tchamala, is bound by Koonapippi's law. Open to new ways of doing things, Bobwirridirridi takes as acolyte another outsider, the half-caste hero Prindy, and in so doing offers symbolic hope for an Australia in which new and old can join in productive harmony.

The final breakthrough Herbert made in *Seven Emus* relates not to 'Aboriginality as symbol' but to 'Aboriginality as setting'. It was in *Seven Emus* that Herbert first attempted to create a living sense of the world of traditional Aboriginality, a world in which the numinous is natural and normal, the spirit creatures of the Dreamtime a daily reality. The technique he developed to achieve this in *Seven Emus* served him well later in *Poor Fellow My Country*. We see something of that technique in the following:

> The full moon was hanging in a golden haze above sinuous appendages of elephantine baobabs, the plain stretching away into silver nothingness in one direction, narrowing into moon-mist and shadow of the gorge in the other. By the dry river and the twinkle of a couple of camp-fires sat those of a race that from these same scarlet sands had seen the moon age and stars come and go, that had sung of its sadness and its joy with the strange downfalling plaintive lilt—tchurah, tchurah, tchurwudjeri ya!—to the click and click of music-sticks. Away on the plain a dingo mourned in racial memory for his ancestor Wanjin's lost loves. Up in the gorge a curlew cried of having found a spirit baby wandering too far from the Dreaming-place.[46]

From the start, the land had inspired some of Herbert's best writing, but it was its beauty and pulsating life, not its numinous significance, that preoccupied him in *Capricornia*. He pictures it there, as he had in the stories, as a bursting cornucopia of lush richness, with schisty rocks splitting golden waterfalls, and scarlet plains swarming with Siberian snipe. In *Seven Emus*, while description of the land is still full of Herbert's response to its beauty, it creates now, too, a powerful sense of the numinous within and behind the physical. In passages such as the one quoted, it is as if Herbert himself is using what he describes in *Seven Emus* as 'that seeing-through-things vision which makes the blackfellow [...] in looking upon his country see beyond physical features to the actuality of what the legends tell him of its creation'.[47] In similar fashion, Herbert, in his descriptions, sees not just animals but animals who reach back to their Dreamtime ancestors, not just birds but birds who still play their part in the great mysteries of human birth, life and death. It is from this new 'seeing-through-things' perspective that Herbert pictures a 'shiny night' as one that 'stared the mystery of Earth and Heaven', and 'cried of the immeasurable soul-things so shrilly in voice of curlew calling of finding wandering Shade, of dingo remembering Dream-time'.[48] Myth enters the landscape of Herbert's prose as it does the landscape of Aboriginal Australia, through the behaviour of animals and birds, and through the physical features of earth and sky.

In seeking to bring his readers into such a world, Herbert faced difficulties unknown to Homer and Virgil. Unlike them, he was not dealing with an audience that knew, and on some level at least accepted, the mythology. For him, therefore, the task was twofold: first teach the mythology, then win acceptance. And that is exactly what he did. First, always, comes the telling of a myth:

> [T]he western fire diminished with the sun's plunging into the earth's labyrinths, as local Aboriginal legend had it, in vengeful pursuit back eastward of the Moon and his wrong-side lover the Morning Star. Darkness, wrong-side in all things, which had hid all day from the Sun who is boss of the right-side, came slinking from the corners of the earth and popping out of caves and holes, with the bats, her children, in her hair.[49]

The myth once explained, Herbert proceeds to build acceptance through frequent, and increasingly matter-of-fact, references, such as: 'He staggered in there with old Kallidiwurri, the sun, glaring her last just above the rocky tumble'.[50] The result is that, by the time we come to a passage like the following, the myth has become a comfortably familiar part of the physical and spiritual landscape:

> He passed Turkey Creek, and walked on [...as] the wheeling constellations retold the Dream-time tales of the first men to the last, while the curlews came occasionally crying from their baby-spirit watching like grey nebulous shades themselves to stare with luminous great eyes at this offender trudging the weary way of transgression stooped beneath the burden of his guilt. Lastly the dingoes mourning the dying night as old Kallidiwurri, returned from never-relenting hunting those wrong-side lovers, Jalliyerri and Jitunga, through the caverns of the underworld, was heralded by the lighting of the eastern sky.[51]

It is the cumulative effect that is important. Once again, Herbert has found a productive use for repetition. The more often the myth is referred to, and the more casual and elliptical the references, the more natural a part of the landscape it becomes to readers. It happens the more quickly because Herbert limits the range of his myth elements. The effect of repetition is thus intensified, as the same few things recur. He swiftly establishes, for instance, a strong sense of the mythic realities underlying bird and animal behaviour through recurring reference to just three creatures: dingoes; kweeluks (curlews), who watch over spirit babies, making sure they are not 'wandering too far from the Dreaming-place'; and koodooks (nightjars), who are 'shade[s] belongin' to somebody what been lose 'em Dreamin''.[52] Here, as in *Poor Fellow My Country* later, repeated reference to these creatures and their Dreamtime significance plays an important part in creating a powerful sense of the reality of the numinous world of Aboriginal belief. And to have found a way to create that reality will prove, as we shall see in

Chapter 13, not the least of *Seven Emus'* contributions to the success of *Poor Fellow My Country*.

Slight, then, though it was in its own right, *Seven Emus* was a very important step on the road to *Poor Fellow My Country*. Herbert himself later said he wrote it 'to try myself out with the Ethos—in miniature'. After *Seven Emus*, he said, 'I saw what I could do with the spirit of the land, all-important in my dealings with the Australian ethos'.[53] Written with the benefit of hindsight, this makes what happened seem more planned and purposeful than it was, but there is no reason to disagree with its conclusion. *Seven Emus* did indeed teach Herbert how to use the Aboriginal spirit of the land, as both symbol and setting, to express his new vision of the Australian ethos. It was a pity that, though the seeds were there, he was not yet ready to nurture them into a stronger growth than *Seven Emus*. Instead he diverted, for a time, to less productive subjects, leaving the ground cleared by *Seven Emus*, for the moment, untilled and unplanted.

CHAPTER 5

Confession and Psycho-sexual Theorising

HAVING failed in his attempts to take *Capricornia*'s concerns further, and finding it hard on his return from war service 'to pick up the thread of writing'[1], Herbert turned again to the gender issues first canvassed in three of the early stories. The switch in subject matter coincided with, and was related to, the increasing influence in his work of autobiography, a genre Frye argues is essentially fictional:

> Most autobiographies are inspired by a creative, and therefore fictional, impulse to select only those events and experiences in the writer's life that go to build up an integrated pattern. This pattern may be something larger than himself with which he has come to identify himself, or simply the coherence of his character and attitudes. We may call this very important form of prose fiction the confession form following St. Augustine, who appears to have invented it, and Rousseau, who established a modern type of it. [...] After Rousseau—in fact in Rousseau— the confession flows into the novel, and the mixture

produces the fictional autobiography, the *Künstler-roman,*
and kindred types.[2]

From the start, confession flowed very freely into Herbert's
novels. *Capricornia* is full of characters and scenes based on the
people and events of his own life[3], and the confessional influence did
not diminish over time. In *Poor Fellow My Country* Herbert mines his
own experience even more extensively. From his stint in charge
of Kahlin Aboriginal Compound comes the picture of Alfie's tenure of
the 'Halfcaste Home'. From his war experience comes the portrait
of Fabian Cootes. His writing career appears in Alfie's literary successes. His flirtation with the Australia First party provides material for
Delacy's political activity in Sydney.[4] And these are just a few of the
many examples that could be given. The more, indeed, one learns
about Herbert's life, the more one can trace the characters and events
of *Poor Fellow My Country* back to that life.[5]

Important, however, though confession is in *Poor Fellow My
Country,* it is not quite as important as some recent criticism has
argued. His biographer, Frances de Groen, for instance, says of
Herbert that

> Over a career lasting some sixty years he moved at acceler-
> ating speed and with increasing self-consciousness towards
> autobiography. Born illegitimate and growing up in an
> atmosphere of melodramatic prevarication, he lacked a
> confident sense of self and turned to fantasy, inventing and
> reinventing himself in grandiose terms in his fiction. [...] The
> process of self-invention continued through his career, with
> Herbert adapting himself, chameleon-like, to the changing
> Australian scene. Determined to prove himself a 'genius' but
> relying almost exclusively on his own experience of
> illegitimacy and alienation for his subject matter, during the
> second half of his career he retreated into seclusion to
> recreate himself as a man and as an author by rewriting
> versions of the plot of his early life. Henceforth, this core
> narrative would take the form of the supremely gifted but
> misbegotten child's failed quest for adult self-realisation.[6]

It is a perceptive and mostly accurate assessment. In one important respect, however, I find it unhelpful. Appropriate though it is to the books of Herbert's middle period, the final sentence is not, I think, a useful description of his last novel. While *Poor Fellow My Country* does indeed involve a gifted but misbegotten child's quest, that quest is not for 'self' realisation but for realisation of the country Herbert believes Australia could and should have become. It is certainly true that Herbert's own experience informs the portrait of Prindy in a number of ways, but the significance of Prindy's quest goes far beyond purely confessional concerns.

The point at issue relates to what Herbert called the 'deep purpose' of his novels. De Groen, if I have understood her correctly, sees a confessional 'deep purpose' to *Poor Fellow My Country*. I, on the other hand, see its confessional elements, like its Aboriginal elements, as important but subsidiary to the 'deep purpose' of presenting a view of the Australian ethos. Confession was always an important element in Herbert's books but it was not always the central element. When, as in *Capricornia* and *Poor Fellow My Country*, it was subordinate to the main purpose, its effects, as we shall see, were mostly good. When it became the main focus, as it did in the middle period of his writing, the results were mostly bad.

That it was the main focus during this period is seen in the nature of the books he wrote during the fifties and early sixties. One, *Disturbing Element*, was overt 'confession' dealing with Herbert's boyhood and youth. Another, 'The Little Widow', was a confessional novel exploring events and issues of the early years of his marriage. The third, *Soldiers' Women*, while the least confessional of all Herbert's novels in content, with fewer characters and events drawn directly from life, was thoroughly confessional in its purpose: to 'discover the realities of my own existence in respect of women'.[7]

The search for what Frye calls an 'integrated pattern' that would explain and justify 'the realities of his own existence' is the driving force behind all the books of this period, and establishing the pattern was what mattered, not drawing clear distinctions between fiction and fact. Frye speaks of the confession writer's 'fictional impulse to select only those events and experiences [...] that go to build up an integrated pattern', and few writers illustrate that impulse more clearly than Herbert. In his autobiography, *Disturbing Element*, he not only 'selects' events to build the pattern; he not infrequently 'invents' them[8]—so much so that his editor felt constrained to warn him about 'turning the Autobiography into a novel'.[9] Where, therefore, there is no corroborating evidence from other sources, one can never be sure Herbert is adhering strictly to the truth in *Disturbing Element*, a fact that might cause problems for a biographer but which matters less in the present context, where the important question is not whether the events are true but what 'integrated pattern' he finds in them.

It was a pattern involving a theory of sexual psychology that provided Herbert with explanations for much that was unsatisfactory in his early relationships with his parents and with the opposite sex. It also provided a justification for the attitudes and behaviour he developed in response to those unsatisfactory relationships. It was this theory that, for a time, ousted Australia as the subject of his writing. The bad effects were both immediate and long-lasting. Immediately, it proved a subject he was incapable of handling well, hence the failure of *Soldiers' Women* and 'The Little Widow'. In the longer term, its negative effects can be seen in some of the less happy features of the characterisation of women in *Poor Fellow My Country*.

As pictured in *Disturbing Element*, Herbert's early years were not happy ones. Born illegitimate, he felt 'unwanted' from the beginning. 'Mother's favorite method of dealing with me in a row', he writes, 'was simply to disown me. She would say: "You're no son of mine."'[10] Further cause to feel rejected came from his relationship with the engine driver father whose courage and skill he admired greatly. 'Riding the iron horse', he writes, 'has always been a true man's job. [...] We knew what a brave thing it was to take a train up through the murderous tunnel newly built under Black Boy Hill'. As a young boy, he was 'always afraid when [he] rode an engine with Dad' but 'loved nothing so well' because 'whatever my opinion of my father in the end, he was my great hero in the beginning'.[11] What soured the relationship was that Herbert was a timid child. While his brother, Philip, stood on the footplate 'like a true engineman',

Herbert was 'sitting scared' back in safety. While Philip was an intrepid rider, Herbert was a timid horseman at a time when 'the horsemanship of man or boy was largely a measure of his manhood'.[12] It was no surprise, therefore, that he reacted badly to his father's attempts to 'make a man of him'. He speaks of 'having my head knocked off [...] in slaps delivered in boxing contests' and 'being flung up [...] on to tall horses that immediately bolted'. He became convinced, he says, that his father was an 'enemy', his mishandling 'malicious'.[13]

Reflections of the unhappy relationship with his father can be found in all Herbert's novels. Norman in *Capricornia*, Pudsey in *Soldiers' Women*, Prindy and Clancy in *Poor Fellow My Country*—all have fathers who reject them. It is surprising, therefore, that though he comments in *Seven Emus* that 'nothing hurts anyone, perhaps, like having a father who is ashamed of one'[14], he spends little time in the novels on any such feeling. Norman does not feel it. As a child, he has no knowledge of his father, and as an adult knows himself to be admired by that father. Pudsey, for most of the book, feels loved by her father; rejection comes only at the end. Prindy has no knowledge of, nor interest in, his father, and is loved by almost every other adult he comes in contact with. Only with Clancy does Herbert touch, briefly, on the feelings of rejection he explores so passionately in *Disturbing Element*.

Of greater influence on the novels was Herbert's sense of having failed to measure up to his father's standards of courage. A boy who wept easily in a society where 'real men don't cry', he berated himself as a hopeless 'sissy' whenever he did so.[15] 'Scared of any show of belligerence by [...] playmates', he feared the 'cow blows' exposure as a coward would bring. Convinced of his cowardice, he began to welcome physical punishment as a means of proving his manhood. He was, he says, 'a sissy in pretty well everything' except the capacity to endure a beating and never learned to box because he 'sought rather to be hurt, as proof of manhood, than to hurt anybody'.[16] The need to prove his manhood by passing self-imposed tests of physical courage was one that remained with him for the rest of his life.[17] In the light of all this, it is not surprising that physical courage becomes the mark of worthy masculinity in his novels. Real men, like Hannaford, Ferris and Delacy, are intrepid riders of horses, drivers of trains, pilots of planes. Real men never back away from fist fights. Old though he is, Delacy's punch is famed and feared and never fails. Unworthy men, on the other hand, shit themselves in planes, like Sergeant Sims, or baulk at restive horses, like Esk's pommy jockey, or scream for help in a fight, like Fabian Cootes.

Early in *Disturbing Element*, Herbert blames his cowardice on his father's 'mishandling'.[18] Later in the book, he blames his sexual difficulties on his father's failure to 'show me how to conserve that power from my genitals'.[19] Deprived as he felt he had been of effective guidance from his own father, Herbert, as he grew older, came to enjoy relationships with admiring younger men towards whom he could play the mentor role. His response to the young editor assigned to *Poor Fellow My Country* was typical. 'I really love him', he said, 'like a beautiful intelligent son—and am sure he returns the feeling'.[20] As in life, so in his novels, Herbert liked to create mentor relationships whose idealised perfection was the opposite of his father's remembered inadequacies. As if to expunge the disappointment of his own relationship with his father, Herbert tends to sentimentalise these fictional relationships. The tone of the following is typical. Oscar is worried that Norman may be getting 'the walkabout habit':

> 'Aw Dad!' gasped Norman, seizing Oscar's arm and look-ing at him miserably. 'Aw Dad—dinkum I never!'
> Oscar saw tears in his rolling black eyes. 'All right, Sonny, all right,' he said, and drew him close and kissed his cheek.[21]

In *Capricornia* Oscar and McRandy are kind mentors to Norman. In *Poor Fellow My Country* Bobwirridirridi, Brew, Delacy, King George, Nugget Knowles, Barbu and Maryzic all provide Prindy with wise, loving mentoring. The mentor role is also seen in Delacy's relation-ship to Bishoff, Fergus Ferris and Dr Solomon. (There is, of course, considerable irony in Delacy's dual role—as unsatisfactory father to Clancy and Martin, wise mentor to these others.)

As described in *Disturbing Element*, Herbert's relationship with his mother, Amy, was no better than his relationship with his father. Herbert pictures Amy as a strong, ambitious woman, chafing under the restraints of her situation, managing her husband with contemptuous ease[22] and ruling her children with a rod of iron. She disciplined them with a sharp tongue and frightened them with exaggerated threats of bodily harm if they did not behave.[23] Herbert's response was inglorious. 'She had only to crook her finger', he writes, 'to have me rushing into her arms to put on a show of mother-and-son love'. The 'frank contempt' he saw in the eyes of the rest of the family[24] as he did so no doubt fuelled the bitterness seen in the following passage from his confessional novel, 'The Little Widow':

> Just as Amy, straight from abusing her sons for toads and turds, would march proudly forth hanging on their arms to show them and herself to the world as the perfection of loving motherhood and filial devotion, so would that virago who bore me and who never ceased to scold because I had not come out of her in the exact and perfect image of her conception of herself.[25]

His mother is twice damned here—as the widow, significantly named Amy, and as the narrator's 'virago' of a mother.

If relations with his mother were unsatisfactory, relations with girls were no better. They added further to his sense of inadequacy. Playing opposite his 'first sweetheart' in a play, he is laughed at in rehearsal for being 'such a sissy' that he was 'afraid to kiss' her, and then humiliated in the actual performance when, tricked into a public kiss, he burst into tears and bolted as 'the town hall rocked with mirth'.[26] Later experiences proved equally humiliating. Infatuation with one girl, given the pseudonym[27] Lucille in *Disturbing Element*, ended when she played a cruel trick on him with the connivance of his best friend. Infatuation for another, called Kathy in *Disturbing Element*, exposed him to the mirth of the whole town when his lovesick antics were mockingly reported in the local paper.[28] Apart from the humiliation they caused, these early experiences made him doubt his own virility, and the fear of being thought 'laggard in love' recurs frequently in *Disturbing Element*.[29]

No-one likes feeling humiliated. We all look for ways to restore our pride. One of the ways Herbert did so was to cast himself in the role of sexual conqueror. The fact that the stories of sexual conquest in *Disturbing Element* are probably fictitious[30] tells us even more about Herbert than if they had been true. That he may have invented the nasty details he recounts with such pride reveals how unpleasantly his attitudes towards women had been affected by the need to boost his sense of self, and how blind he was to that unpleasantness. He could hardly have revealed those attitudes more clearly than in the description of what he claims was his first successful seduction. It took place, he tells us, on the very day Lucille betrayed him. The chronology is surely invented, his placing of both events on the same day a clear indication that masculine pride, bruised by failure with one girl, could only be restored by triumph over another.

The story, as Herbert tells it, has him spending the whole day brooding on his 'first agony of disillusionment in love'. That night, as he returns sadly home, he meets Maggie, a girl he has been told is 'a good thing. Billy Walsh and Wokka Williams been up 'er'. He invites Maggie for a walk on the beach where, 'no longer at a loss for anything, I forced her to go back into the sandhills, and there wrestled her down'. He describes how she 'fought for a while' and 'whimpered' but then succumbed passionately. Afterwards, sated, elated and thoroughly proud of himself, he can't wait 'to get away from her clinging and snivelling' and goes home 'swaggering, marching, whistling and humming a song I'd heard sailors ashore from a warship singing: *I laid my hand upon her breast, and the wind from her arse blew west-sou'-west'*. He proceeds to preen himself on the 'utter intrepidity' with which he subsequently visited her:

> [S]imply going to her whenever I felt like it and popping in through her bedroom window. It was even better tupping her while her saintly Pa was snoring in just sleep across the passage way. Besides, under the circumstances I was spared poor Maggie's incessant imploring and

snivelling. After such an excursion I would be so stimu-
lated, or relaxed [...] as to be positively brilliant at my
studies for days.[31]

There is no hint of self-criticism. Far from seeing anything wrong in
taking advantage of a vulnerable girl, he is proud of it.
The pride is pride in what he sees as proof of masculinity.
Real men are sexually successful and Herbert was desperate to prove
his own virility. He was as fearful of failing in sex as he was of failing
in courage. He needed to lay to rest the fear of being thought a
'laggard in love'. The 'success' with Maggie did not achieve that. His
'manhood', he felt, 'was not yet vindicated', because in his milieu 'the
proper manly thing' was 'to go the molls' and his own first attempt at
'forthright handling of a moll in a moll shop' had ended in
humiliation when he failed even to achieve an erection. Worse, the
story got around and he had to endure the taunt that if a woman
offered 'it' to him, he would 'put 'is 'at over it and run'. Salvation
came, significantly, in the shape of an attractive 'halfcaste aboriginal'
prostitute in whose arms 'desire swept over [him] like a surging
wave' and he was able to prove his 'manliness' in a fashion his peers
would recognise.[32]

Now began, he tells us, 'the phase of my career in which I
was the complete roué, whose dedicated purpose was to have carnal
knowledge of every desirable female who came into my ken'. He
made, he claims, 'a list of females I was resolved to debauch' and
'ticked them off as they fell to me'.[33] The motivation was still at least
as much the need to prove virility as satisfaction of desire. He speaks
of 'fighting as hard to best [Kathy] because I felt it would settle
eternally any suspicion that I was a laggard in love'.[34] That suspicion
never seems to have been conclusively settled. Frances de Groen
describes how, later in life, he 'added [Beatrice Davis] to his list of
conquests':

> After much alcohol and endless talk he at last wore her
> down. Pursuing her gleefully into her bed he embraced
> her with the triumphant cry of 'gotcha' but to her puzzle-
> ment the occasion was never repeated.[35]

The 'gotcha' says it all. The rampant male adds scalps to his belt in order to prove, once again, his virility and, having conquered, loses interest.

Occasionally in *Disturbing Element* the picture of 'Herbert the ruthless seducer' metamorphoses into 'Herbert the parfit, gentil knight'. He tells the story of a one-night stand with a married woman who taught him 'that the male's part is not to satisfy his own superficial lust' but 'to rouse the deep desire of which the female is capable'.[36] He meets an old conquest and says that though she 'had been one of my successful kills of the seduction list, I had no such interest in her when I met her again. I was too well aware now of my responsibility to what I had learnt were truly the weaker sex'.[37] The role of 'parfit knight' and 'ruthless seducer' are, of course, similar in one respect. Both allowed Herbert to construct the male as dominant and powerful, the woman as weak and subordinate, and that was the way Herbert liked to picture women. 'To me,' he once said, 'women are frail things...sensitive frightened things'.[38]

As for women who were not frail or frightened, whose assertiveness challenged his sense of virility, them he accused of penis envy. Having, in real life, made a fool of himself over Kathy, he turns the tables in *Disturbing Element* by describing her as 'an unhappy mixture of prude and wanton' who wants 'to be debauched [...] for the power she would have had over men'. Kathy was, he says, 'jealous of males', destroying them 'like a female spider', encouraged in so doing by his own mother, the 'harpy' who had 'emasculated' his father.[39] The accusation that these strong, independent women used the power of sex to emasculate men was a predictable rationalisation of Herbert's early sense of discomfort and humiliation. It was to become one of the most passionately argued points in his theory of sexuality.

Having cut women down to size as would-be castrators, Herbert further asserted his masculine superiority by learning, he says, to master the desire that put him at their mercy. In *Disturbing Element* he describes how, discovering a way to precipitate climax without actually masturbating, he nonetheless felt 'emasculate, shattered, ashamed' each time he succumbed to temptation. He later learned, he says, to control and sublimate sexual desire.[40] In 'The

Little Widow' his alter ego Frank achieves 'a degree of continence' that 'released' him from the 'all-absorbing preoccupation of the sexually mature human male with sexual indulgence' and allowed him to redirect the 'force of sexual desire' into 'noble achievement'.[41] Frank's continence is a fictional version of the self-imposed 'celibacy' through which, Herbert claims, he achieved 'the state of saintly ecstasy' in which he wrote *Soldiers' Women*. 'I used', he said, 'to stay writing in my camp, in complete isolation, for twenty-one days at a time. Then I would go down to Sadie at Redlynch for rations and a day or two of talking with my kind—never for anything else though: for celibacy I had acquired'.[42] The idea of sublimating sexual desire into creative achievement derived from his reading of Freud. It, too, became an important part of his theory.

His early experiences as a pharmacist offered Herbert further opportunities to construct women as dominated. Apprenticed to a chemist whose practice 'was largely in the venereal field', he watched, part-scornful, part-envious, as women were taken into the back room for consultation. 'The chemist', claimed his master, 'is the girl's best friend' because it is to him they turn for help in dealing with the functioning of their bodies.[43] It was, for Herbert, an alluring position of power. As a pharmacist, he saw women at the mercy of their own bodies—and at his mercy. In one of *Disturbing Element*'s nastiest stories, he describes with relish the 'reeking greasy tack' he dispensed to one girl for an ugly skin condition. He jokes behind her back about her 'blushing' red bottom and, with a delightful sense of superiority, diagnoses the cause as 'hot emanation' of unsatisfied sexual desire.[44] This view of woman, as dominated by what he calls in *Soldiers' Women* 'the grisly facts of female functioning'[45], is another element in his theory of sexuality.

Of the many ways in which Herbert dealt with uncertainties about his masculinity, none was more significant than his choice of Sadie Norden as his lifelong partner. Sadie had left her first husband partly 'because she felt her "ambitions" would not be fulfilled by staying with [him]'. With Herbert they were, and, his biographer says, 'she identified completely with his ambitions and basked in his fame'.[46] She had every right so to bask. From the start she was a partner in the enterprise. Herbert did the writing, Sadie the managing and encouraging. She it was who gave him the confidence to begin *Capricornia*, and who looked after him as he wrote it.[47] She it was, throughout his life, who managed things so that he could concentrate on writing.[48] She it was, above all, who provided him with the uncritical, admiring audience he needed. Her interests were practical, not intellectual. She was not a great reader, preferring the radio to books.[49] She was, therefore, perfect for a man whose need was to be admired and reinforced, not criticised. While perfectly capable of standing up to him on other matters, in the area of his ideas and his writing Sadie was happy to accept him at his own valuation.[50]

In the matter of sex, too, Sadie seems to have been willing to subordinate her needs to his. 'A recurrent nuisance, his philandering', says de Groen, 'was not a serious threat to their partnership and she generally responded to it with sardonic humour'.[51] Herbert himself, in a letter to a friend, claimed that Sadie

> has virtually told me to 'Go in unto mine handmaiden' to straighten difficult matters out. Not that the lady is wanting in anything feminine. The contrary. I've had to admit, as on a couple of occasions to bawdy friends, that 'She's the best performer in bed I ever struck' […] She is an 'Orgasm woman' a rare type. […] There is always a sense of Renewal in such dealings with her…which of necessity must be rare.[52]

The letter reveals, once again, Herbert's twisted attitudes to women. It is an appalling way to think, let alone speak, of a loving and loyal wife: as a sexual trophy to be waved triumphantly in the face of envious friends.

Supportive as Sadie was, Herbert came to assume it as his right that their lives should revolve around his needs. 'What a pair of idiots we were to let me get caught like this', he says of a temporary job taken while writing *Poor Fellow My Country*. 'And yet I feel it's been all to the good, that an enormous benefit will accrue from it, which must be shown in the task itself, since that is the final expression of my development.'[53] Note the personal pronouns. 'We' take responsibility for 'me' and 'my development'. For Herbert it is axiomatic that Sadie will subordinate her needs to his.

The full extent of his selfishness appears in an episode late in their life together. Sadie had been seriously ill in hospital for some weeks and was at last well enough to return home. Herbert knew she was longing to get home, but felt her return would interfere with his writing. Even to explain this to her would, he felt, destroy the peace of mind he needed when he was writing, so he sent a telegram to a mutual friend, asking him to break the news to Sadie that she was not welcome home. He then sent her a letter, sublimely confident that she would share in his joy that he had been 'relieved' of his 'panic'.

> It was a strange thing yesterday how I got that sense of panic on me on hearing of your being likely to come home next week. [...] I saw it was the ancient panic that seizes me when I am utterly engrossed in work and something intrudes to pull me away. [...] I guessed you would want to come home and feel rejected if prevented. I was in a bit of a stew till I was having my shower. Then I thought of the telegram [...] I was instantly relieved of the panic when I saw the cause of it. I prepared the work nicely by taping and then was up at 2.10 a.m. to work till 10.45 ever so nicely. It's something we have got to face and accept, that odd state I get into when writing properly.[54]

This is self-centredness on a grand scale. The assumption that, even in these circumstances, his smallest need must take precedence over Sadie's far greater needs has a quality of complacent selfishness that is startling.

Self-absorbed as he was, it was predictable that Herbert would generalise and idealise Sadie's intelligent accommodation to his needs into a universal theory of femininity, one in which the perfect woman is as undemanding and long-suffering as Griselda in Chaucer's *Clerk's Tale*. But Griseldas are not the best women on whom to model a general theory of womanhood, and Herbert was not the best man to construct such a theory. Though claiming to know much about 'love', there is little evidence of any such understanding in his own relationships. Though claiming to understand women, he seems to have spent little time thinking about the needs or feelings of the women in his own life. It was his own needs and feelings that absorbed him. He needed women very much, as demonstrated by his undignified attempts, following Sadie's death, to persuade a succession of women to come and live with him[55], but, resenting his dependence, he took every opportunity to cut women down to size. He probably thought of himself as 'having a soft spot for the ladies' but came closer to the truth when he wrote once to Sadie, 'Wimmen! 'Ow I 'ate 'em!'[56] It's meant as a joke but it's uncomfortably close to the truth.

Interesting though they might be to a biographer, Herbert's problems with relationship and identity would not have warranted the time spent on them here had they not given rise to theories that significantly influenced the way he characterised men and women in his novels. What those theories were and how they influenced Herbert's characterisation can be seen most clearly in *Soldiers' Women*, a book whose stated aim was to allegorise and popularise Herbert's views on the nature of men and women.[57] They were views derived in part from his reading of Freud and H. G. Wells.[58]

The influence of Wells can be seen in the biological determinism of Herbert's explanations of human behaviour. 'The basis of human association', he states early in *Soldiers' Women*, 'is satisfaction of need, and one's need is part of one's destiny, and one's destiny is the expressed meaning of one's existence'.[59] One further thing about 'one's destiny' that soon becomes very clear is that it is predetermined by one's gender. The advancement of the species, says Leon, depends upon females 'nurturing the progeny of their eggs [...] against the harshness of the environment, ever giving of themselves to the next generation in nurturing, while the males gave in striving to eclipse their sires and brethren so that the next generation must ever excel'.[60]

The 'nurturing' role pictured in *Soldiers' Women* is a limiting one that puts women totally at the mercy of men. A distinction is made between woman's 'need' for love and man's 'acceptance' of love. 'Love', Herbert says, 'is no true need of man's. It is woman's need. It is man's weakness to meet it: and it is his destiny, part of his fulfilment if the woman's need is honest, his damnation if it is otherwise'.[61] A woman's life, in other words, has no meaning unless she finds a man to love, whereas a man can choose. He can fulfil himself by responding to a woman's love and taking her with him as he pursues his destiny, or he can forge ahead on his own. No such choice for a woman. She needs a man to make babies for her to nurture. And she needs a man to protect her. Ideally she will find a man who can 'meet her primary needs and win her admiration, since love, apart from the hysteria of mating, is need plus admiration'.[62] But if she cannot find someone worthy to love, she is bound by her gender to subordinate herself to some less worthy man, because only a man can satisfy her needs. When Selina says to Leon, 'I need you so badly', his strangely cold reply undercuts the sense of personal choice her statement implies. 'You need someone to protect you…a man. That's all.'[63]

Since woman's primary needs can only be satisfied by men, it follows that attracting men is one of her most important skills. A psychologist in *Soldiers' Women* is described as so tall, 'young men must have looked with alarm rather than desire'. It was, writes Herbert, 'that altitude of hers which perhaps had made her a doctor rather than a housewife'.[64] Higher education, a career, independence—all these are unimportant compared to a pretty face and nice figure. A woman's main task is to get her man. Hence the obsessive concern in *Soldiers' Women* with dress and cosmetics. Hence the stress on the magnificence of Pudsey's cooking. Hence the stress on the twin attributes of beauty and culinary skill in *Poor Fellow My Country*'s Rifkah.

The limitation of the woman's role pictured by Herbert is further seen in his stress on the supreme importance of the menstrual cycle. As Pudsey's teacher drones on about geometry, the narrator imagines the lesson she might more usefully be teaching:

> Our subject is menstruation, by which is measured the rhythm of a woman's life. Live by that rhythm and you will be happy. […] Woman's rhythm of life, her monthly renewal with her patroness the Moon, is the most important thing in her existence.[65]

Forget advanced mathematics; the monthly period is what matters. The moon 'renews [women] for positivity every twenty eight days'. A woman who does not make babies is 'doomed' to 'negativity'.[66] Thus Rosa, having contracted venereal disease, is inconsolable until assured that her reproductive system is undamaged and she will be able to live 'the way [she was] made to, with a handsome husband and lovely children'.[67]

The powerlessness of women in the face of their biologically determined destiny is further emphasised by the distinction Herbert makes between male and female desire. In sexual desire, too, woman submits, man controls. However powerful male desire may be, a mature male can control and direct it away from women, can sublimate it into other achievements. 'True eroticism in the female', by contrast, is 'as far beyond control of will as the tide pulled by the moon'.[68] Ida's claim that 'a woman can desire any time. It depends on her mood'[69] is rejected for Madeleine's view that it is only when her eggs are ready to be fertilised that a woman feels desire. A woman, says Herbert, is 'bound periodically to enter oestrus, the "ripe-time", in which her whole being [is] preoccupied with mating with man'.[70]

The trouble with desire, even the constrained version Herbert allows women, is that it still tempts them from their ordained, circumscribed role. Even a good woman like Selina becomes 'inclined to indiscretion under the influence of the hormonic tide rising within her'.[71] It comes as no surprise, therefore, to find Herbert building into his theory a firm proscription against such indiscretion—nor that, unequally treated in this as in most else, it is only to women that this proscription applies. Along with moon-ruled sexual desire, Nature, Herbert argues, has built strict codes of sexual fidelity into women. 'Female virtue', he says 'is no accident. It is inherent in the womb for protection of the species'.[72] In typically unequal fashion, male virtue of a similar sort is not necessary for protection of the species. Nature does not tell Leon, though he has a wife and 'two kiddies', that it is wrong to take another woman; it does tell married Selina she must not take another man.

In Selina, Herbert presents his ideal; in Ida its opposite. In Ida we see the demonisation of those qualities in women Herbert felt threatened by: independence, strength and the power their sexual attractiveness gives them. Female virtue, says Herbert, 'is to be found only in wombs fully female, not in hens that crow or women that whistle. Whores are not made, they're born'.[73] Ida, the born whore, has none of that female virtue the race needs to protect the species. She is unashamedly promiscuous—not, womanlike, betrayed by the irresistible prompting of her hormones but, in masculine fashion, deciding when, where and with whom to indulge herself. She also, and emphatically, rejects the demands of maternity. From the beginning she neglects her children, and does so from deliberate policy, explaining that 'indulgence of them would mean surrender to them and surrender to all hope of liberty'.[74] So lost to ordinary womanhood is she that, when her house burns down with her children trapped inside, she watches with 'cruel joy'[75], welcoming their deaths as relief from responsibility. Unwomanly in her response to sexual desire and rejection of motherhood, she is unwomanly too in her desire to dominate men. She stands 'shining with triumph' when she has Leon in her toils, and when, with male strength of will, he resists the force of his desire, she is 'like a child from whom something it had contrived to get possession of has been snatched away'.[76]

There is one aspect of Herbert's theory on which he is strangely silent in *Soldiers' Women*. It is referred to often enough in letters. We find it, for instance, in the following:

> A woman's power is her sex [...] And a woman's sex is expressed in either of two ways, begetting and nurturing the children of her body or of [sic] identifying herself with a unique man and hence serving the genius that makes him so.[77]

The word 'power' is, of course, disingenuous since women are actually powerless to do anything but accept one of two choices, both of which depend upon attracting men. What is interesting, though, is that linking your destiny with a man is not here seen simply as the necessary precursor to having children but as a valid alternative to having children. The second choice offered, that of 'identifying with a unique man' and 'serving his genius', is described in more detail in a letter Herbert wrote to Beatrice Davis, the editor of *Soldiers' Women*:

> Dear One, we are man and woman, and we fell in love according to the formula of need and admiration [...] the deep purpose of our love creation of this work of art. [...] My feeling was that after a struggle you would accept my masculine power, that this acceptance would signal your full development [...] the discovery of your feminine purpose and that thereafter you would give all your power and talent to the [...] nurturing of the truth that I and others like me whom you'd seek, have the genius to find and the courage to deliver to mankind. [...] Now comes the great moment of your life when you must decide whether this force that has drawn you irrevocably into its orbit is a bright comet on which you will ride to high destiny or a dark-star in whose negative void your soul will die.[78]

The arrogance is staggering. A position of responsibility in a publishing firm is not enough. The knowledge that she is one of Australia's finest editors is not enough. A woman without children, her 'feminine purpose' can only be achieved by 'nurturing' Herbert's male 'genius'. Such nurturing is seen in Estelle's relationship with Frank in 'The Little Widow', and Nanago's with Delacy in *Poor Fellow My Country*, but is found nowhere in *Soldiers' Women*.

Also absent from *Soldiers' Women* is any serious exploration of what Herbert says is man's primary role in evolution: 'striving to eclipse their sires and brethren so that the next generation must ever excel'.[79] It is to Frank in 'The Little Widow' and Delacy in *Poor Fellow My Country* we must look for examples of this aspect of Herbert's theory. In *Soldiers' Women* it was not man's 'striving' that interested Herbert but his relationship with women, particularly the two aspects of that relationship that most concerned him: male power over women, and male response to sexual desire.

The novel's position on both these matters has already, to some extent, been covered. On the question of sexual desire, what Herbert is concerned to stress is that men should be in control of, not controlled by, their desires. On the question of power, he starts from the premise that it is right for men to have power over women, wrong for women to seek power over men. *Soldiers' Women* invites no question on that. Its aim is rather to demonstrate how male power should be used, and what qualities a man needs if he is to use it properly. Those qualities are 'courage, strength, [...] gentleness' and 'intelligence'.[80] A man who lacks any of these will fail either in wielding power over women properly, or in controlling his desire properly.

Through the ironically named Fortitude, Herbert demonstrates that failures in courage prevent a man taking the dominant role that is properly his. Lacking the courage a man needs, Fortitude allows his mother to rule him. When she disapproves of the girl he loves, he weakly marries the one she chooses for him. When he wants to do some real soldiering, she stops him. So devoid of male strength is he that it is only when his more determined girlfriend intervenes that he finally escapes his mother and sets off to war.[81] And war, that 'periodic primitive lad-testing with murder', implies Herbert, is what men like Fortitude need if they are to develop the courage of true men.[82] The self-imposed physical tests of courage so important to him in his own life are here incorporated into his general theory of masculinity.

Important, however, though courage and strength are, they are dangerous if not accompanied by gentleness. Without gentleness, strength may be used to oppress, not protect. Eugene, a man who gains his sexual pleasure from brutalising women[83], is only the most extreme example of a misuse of male strength all too common in *Soldiers' Women*. Again and again soldiers take women swiftly, brutally and against their wishes.

> Bill looked in leering: then he barged in guffawing when she squealed and tried to cover up her nakedness. And he tore the cover from her, gasped at the sight of her, stared: then seized her despite her desperate pleas, silenced her with frantic kisses, flung her on the bed amongst her pretty things, and, fumbling and snorting and bucking like a berserk beast, dealt with her in the ancient way.[84]

Two men only in *Soldiers' Women*, Leon and Jed, demonstrate the qualities of true masculinity—Leon in full measure, Jed partially. Jed has the right combination of strength and gentleness. He is 'the protecting type to whom any woman would go in need', a 'full male' who 'would not be dangerous to women'. In one respect, though, he falls short of Herbert's ideal. 'Big of body', he is 'small of brain'. Strong in the protective role, his 'simplicity' leaves him vulnerable to the wiles of unworthy women.[85] Faced by the 'shining miracle of [Ida's] nakedness', Jed 'surrender[ed] his giant's strength to her' and in so doing proved himself 'a man so limited in striving that he could give his soul to a dainty-feasting harpy'.[86] In contrast, though Ida's beauty awakens the 'warmth of Leon's desire', he is a 'master of restraint', recognises Ida's 'spiritually futile game' and 'turns away sharply' until firmly in control again. Leon knows that 'without awareness one can spend one's courage and kindness foolishly'.[87]

Herbert's psychological theories had predictable effects on the picture given of women in his other novels. The negativity of that picture becomes apparent when one examines the sum total of white female characters in *Capricornia* and *Poor Fellow My Country*. There are bitter, dissatisfied wives, who dominate their husbands: Jasmine and Mrs Bightit in *Capricornia*; Alfie, Rhoda, Mrs McCusky, Mrs Turkney and Mrs Trotters in *Poor Fellow My Country*. There are women unhappily and unnaturally fixated on fathers, sons or brothers: Mrs McLash in *Capricornia*; Lydia, Alfie and the Cahoon sisters in *Poor Fellow My Country*. There is the pitied old maid, Kitty Windeyer, and the mocked lesbian, Fay. The only white women presented at all sympathetically are Heather in *Capricornia* and Rifkah and Bridie in *Poor Fellow My Country*. Significantly, two of these work in pubs. Working behind the bar, Heather and Bridie have become honorary men, 'mates' rather than 'women'.

Things are no better when one examines the details of the picture. Though Herbert tries to hide the ugliness of his attitudes with talk of protection and unselfish love, when he actually describes women, the real nature of those attitudes cannot be hidden. His need, for instance, to put women down appears in the delight he takes in picturing them in undignified, crudely physical situations. He stresses the brutal physicality of Alfie's attack on Rifkah. 'Red claws extended', she 'hooked the claws into the distorted face beneath her, dripping her streaming bloody spittle onto it'.[88] He delights in unnecessary descriptions of women urinating. Lady Lydia is a particular favourite, perhaps because there was special relish in cutting a British aristocrat down to size:

> She pulled her pants down, squatted, gave the parched earth a drink such as it never had before. She called Jeremy back while she was still buttoning up, standing boldly over the damp erosion, and smirked at his evident embarrassment.[89]

In the space of ten pages Lydia is described urinating four times. Each time the description is crudely physical. Each time he stresses the woman's shameless coarseness, the man's embarrassment.[90]

One of the least happy results of Herbert's attitude towards women was the voyeuristic tone that frequently appeared in his descriptions. Viewing women as sex objects, he was incapable of recognising the prurience of descriptions he probably regarded as tributes to female beauty. His descriptions dwell, in men's magazine fashion, upon bums and tits. Alfie's 'pretty bum wobbled' and her 'little tits filled her red-piped breast pockets'. Fergus admires Rifkah's 'spreading thighs' and 'shapely bottom wobbling in the tight pants'.[91] Again and again readers are placed in the position of voyeur. Sometimes we watch alone, as when Alfie 'pulled her pants down and did a bit more larding, round and round the beautiful gluteal curves'. Sometimes we watch with a male for whom a woman strips, as Lydia does for Delacy, and Alfie for Frank, at the Rainbow Pool. Sometimes he gives us the peeping Tom's view: of Nelyerri showering, Rifkah skinny-dipping and Rifkah sleeping.[92] Descriptions concentrate on breasts and crotch and the tone is pornographic:

> What he saw caused his breath to catch—the slight-spread ivory thighs, bare almost to the crotch, the outline of what lay beneath the tight-drawn silk there plain to see, above that goblet of the navel in the strip of white belly revealed by updrawn shift, a small breast half-revealed.[93]

When he describes Aboriginal women, Herbert's sexist attitudes have the further effect of betraying him into expression of the very racism he sought to attack. Descriptions intended to demonstrate appreciation of Aboriginal beauty actually reveal something rather different:

> One who was observant and aesthetic would have gloated over the perfect symmetry expressed in the curves of the wide mobile nostrils and arched septum of her fleshy nose, would have delighted in her peculiar pouting mouth with thick puckered lips of colour reddish black like withered rose, in the lustrous irises and fleckless white-of-egg-white whites of her large black slightly-tilted eyes.[94]

The word 'gloated' gives the game away. This is to look with the eye of a prospective purchaser: the plantation owner selecting the young black slave, the customer selecting the young black prostitute. Though critical of white men for not acknowledging their sexual relations with black women, he is unconcerned about the exploitation involved. Instead of condemning white men for taking advantage of Aboriginal women, he paints it as natural and acceptable. 'I reckon any normal healthy man'll fall for 'em if he'll expose himself to the risk', says the significantly named McRandy, whose prurient description of young black concubines is offered not for criticism but as an example of lack of prejudice. In contrast to Chaucer's clear-sighted scorn of the old lecher in *The Merchant's Tale*, Herbert's sympathy is with McRandy as he dwells on the nubile charms of the young black girls he buys for his bed. '"You've got a peach," [says Norman] "Plum!" hissed Andy. "Sugary black plum. A damson—Ha!" He attacked his food with zest.' McRandy is simply interested in having unfettered use of young black bodies. And the author finds no cause for criticism in that. It is McRandy's neighbour he mocks, for treating them as more than bodies, for getting emotionally involved and pursuing them when they return to the tribe. In contrast, McRandy's cynicism is offered as an admirable piece of commonsense: 'They're just gettin' nice and fat and cheeky, when their bucks come round and sneak 'em back. But it never worries me. I soon get another'.[95]

It's a small step from McRandy's exploitation to the more brutal exploitation of rape. Indeed there is little difference, in *Poor Fellow My Country*, between the way Nelyerri's white 'lover' treats her and the way she is dealt with by her white rapists. Her lover 'hissing [...] forced her down to the sawdust'. Her rapist, 'hissing in her face, forc[ed] her down to the streaming floor'. Her lover takes her 'loins and breast to his lips [...] slobbering'. Her rapist 'wallop[s] about on top of her [...] slobbering'.[96]

Herbert's sexual theories appear also in the characterisation of women who know their place (Nanago and Rifkah) and women who don't (Alfie, Queeny, Nelyerri and Savitra). Both Nanago and Rifkah are confessionally linked with Sadie. Rifkah is Sadie when Herbert first met her, the beautiful, foreign Jewess. Nanago is Sadie, the devoted wife. Herbert once praised Jewish women and black women for a 'singing strength' that makes them 'not mere men with tits as most breeds of women are'.[97] It is clear, though, that their 'strength' is not one that sets itself in opposition to men, and if it sings, it does so very softly and soothingly. Nanago is, Delacy says, 'the perfect wife'. All she wants is to be his 'servant'. His needs are paramount. When she sees he loves Rifkah, she urges him not to hold back. 'Aren't you jealous?' he asks. 'Only white woman get jealous' and 'want to be boss of man', she replies.[98] Nanago may not want to be boss, but even she threatens Delacy's independence. She promised, he says, 'she wouldn't intrude on me' but 'subtly she has...snaring me with the comfort she's provided. She'd do it again. All women will. Emasculating the male is the female's business'.[99] Women just can't win with Herbert. They must be perfect in servitude, but are then blamed for trapping men through the very perfection of that servitude.

In contrast to Nanago, Alfie Candlemass seeks to emasculate males in culpable ways. Alfie is Ida revisited, the 'enchanted one' who with 'amorous look' holds men 'spellbound'. All fairy beauty by day, she moves witch-like at night against Delacy's masculine integrity, 'slinking down [...] to scuttle across the yard, with her short shadow bobbing along beside her like an attendant gnome'.[100] Alfie, like Ida, like Kathy, like Amy Herbert, is 'woman as castrator'. Nanago calls her 'Min-minya', the 'debil-woman' of Aboriginal legend who, when she finds a 'weak' man, lures him into her vagina in order to 'suck him dry'.[101] The story is paralleled in *Disturbing Element* where Herbert's mother holds her hand 'with the tips of thumb and fore finger pressed together' and tells Kathy, 'Keep him there, my dear!' 'I used to think', says Herbert, 'the gesture meant simply to keep a grip on a man, till one time it struck me, like a cold douche, that it was erotically symbolic'.[102]

The other women in *Poor Fellow My Country* who seek to rule rather than obey are Nelyerri, Savitra and Queeny. They would be better, Herbert implies, for some of the 'Aboriginal wife's traditional putting in her place'. He approves when Savitra, a mixture of 'white shrew […] docile Indian and the slave-rebel lubra', is punched on the nose by Prindy to show her who is boss[103], just as, in *Capricornia*, he approved when Norman decided 'cuffing' Tocky was 'the most effective way of dealing with her'.[104] Again, for all the talk of 'gentleness' and 'protection', he cannot disguise the essential brutality of his attitudes to women. It is no surprise to find that strong, independent women often meet unpleasant deaths in Herbert's novels. Tocky starves to death. Alfie is blown to pieces. Fay in *Soldiers' Women* and Queeny, Nelyerri and Savitra in *Poor Fellow My Country* are brutally murdered. The relish with which Herbert describes those murders is significant.

Herbert's theory of sexual psychology had, then, a number of bad effects on his writing. It was not, though, the root cause of *Soldiers' Women*'s failure. It is not the quality of its theories that determines the success of a novel. The historical theory articulated in *War and Peace* is simplistic, the novel complex and satisfying; conversely, the ideas in Huxley's *Island* are stimulating, its success as a novel limited. The problem with *Soldiers' Women* is not its ideas. D. H. Lawrence's views on sex and gender are no less partial, no less distorted by rationalisation from his own weaknesses and inadequacies. Why, then, did one man produce *Women in Love*, the other *Soldiers' Women*? The answer is found in their different talents as writers, not as thinkers. Herbert had qualities Lawrence did not possess, but they were not qualities that fitted him for the kind of novel he attempted in *Soldiers' Women*. To write that kind of book, you need to be skilful at creating the kind of character E. M. Forster called 'rounded'. The reason *Women in Love* succeeded while *Soldiers' Women* failed was that Ursula, Gudrun, Birkin and Gerald fascinate, while Pudsey, Ida, Jed and Leon irritate. Unfortunately for Herbert, as we shall see in the next chapter, he simply was not suited to creating the kind of characters he needed for a book like *Soldiers' Women*.

CHAPTER 6

Confession and the Construction of Character

FOR all Herbert's interest in psychological theory, he never found it easy to create a sense of psychological depth in his characters. One reason for this was that he did not really know enough about anyone except himself. During the first half of his life, his experience was varied. 'I can boast', he said, of 'being sailor, soldier, stockman, railwayman, airman, anthropologist, deep sea diver'.[1] But wide experience is no guarantee of deep understanding. If you are self-absorbed, judge others on the extent to which they feed your amour-propre, and prefer talking rather than listening, you may not learn very much about the people you meet. You are even less likely to do so if, in the second half of your life, you opt for isolation from, rather than engagement with, your fellows. And from 1949 onwards, that is exactly what Herbert did. Living in solitary fashion in a small Queensland town, he speaks of 'escaping from my fellows' by 'going to bed early, stuffing my ears and having rhythmical sound to help drown the discord of the world'.[2] 'No wonder people hate me', he writes on another occasion. 'They must read my remoteness from them in my eyes. How deeply have I hated the whole world always, because of its pettiness, its stupidity, its ugliness, its meanness.'[3]

He was, on occasion, forced by circumstance to emerge from his isolation and live in more sociable fashion. In 1968, for instance, he spent four months working as a relieving pharmacist at Innisfail Hospital, and in 1974 he was in Sydney for two months overseeing the publication of *Poor Fellow My Country*. His letters to Sadie on both occasions reveal that, while he enjoyed these forays into the outside world, they did little to deepen his understanding. Rather, acting like a binge on a confirmed teetotaller, they seemed to go to his head. We find him alternately exhilarated and repelled by the social demands made upon him: now longing for the peace of home; now revelling in the novelty of new relationships; and all the while making broad generalisations about the people he meets, generalisations that mostly appear ill-judged and sometimes downright strange.

Self-absorbed as he was, Herbert was prone to fantasising about the people he met, creating emotional adventures for them in which he assumed a larger importance in their lives than common-sense suggests he actually had. He then analysed their feelings and motives so as to support this Herbert-centred view of reality. Character analysis so based is neither convincing nor profound, as can be seen from his descriptions of three members of staff at Innisfail whom I shall call Anne, Carol and Barbara.[4] Herbert's interpretation of their behaviour depended on his belief that, at the age of 67, he was still so attractive that all three women were consumed with desire for him. Nothing in the events he describes lends support to his analysis of their feelings. The signs he interpreted so portentously sound no more than friendliness mixed with a little tongue-in-cheek flirtation once they realised the old gentleman liked that kind of thing. What an edifice of sexual psychology he built on these foundations! Barbara becomes a monster of frustrated lust:

> Both [Anne and Carol] have been equally mad to get possession of a part of me [...but Barbara] is different. She has wanted me, all of me, body and soul [...] I have felt keen fear of what might happen if she laid hands on me. She'd really hurt a man—I'd think even injure him deliber-ately in the frustration that must come from combination of her greedy need and a man's natural loathing of such a

creature. [...] She hasn't dared to do anything [...] but it glitters in her pig's eyes.[5]

As for Anne, when Herbert's expectations fail to materialise, far from admitting he has misinterpreted her friendliness, he explains her behaviour thus:

> Anne has no heart, nor even womb. Her ovaries are testicles up near her back bone, and the bag beneath it only a trap for the weakness of the male she hates because she was denied the male things he has. [...] She had no plans, only a trap that kept luring and luring, and which, knowing mouse that I am and brave one, I've pretended to approach nearer and nearer [...] No doubt about it she likes me. But I'm certain that she wouldn't go to bed with any man. That's probably why she drinks as she does. Some inadequacy. She's a boy-girl. [...] I think deep down she is very frail, has had a couple of disappointments with men and is determined not to have any more—or rather, is sure she'll never have anything but disappointment with men, because she'd have to dominate. The type of man she'd want she knows she couldn't boss. I've got very close to her. I'd say I've got as close to seducing her as any man has in many a year. I've done it deliberately to try and understand her type—truly I think I've done it very cleverly.[6]

It's *Soldiers' Women* psychology: the behaviour of real women distorted to fit the psychological scheme Herbert has constructed. Rather than using experience to test and qualify his theories, he cuts and pastes real life to fit the theory.

Herbert's ability to assess other people's characters was further hindered by the fact that his judgment was too strongly influenced by their response to him. He criticises one of the Innisfail doctors for being 'a petty, jealous creature', two others for being 'nitwits'. It is clear, though, from the reasons he gives for these judgments, that they derive not from genuine character defects but from the failure of these doctors, in Herbert's view, to show him sufficient respect as a fellow professional.[7] In contrast, a fourth doctor is described as 'really a nice intelligent boy' who 'knows a lot about me [...] and respects me. [...] I've never known one of his breed to be so respectful'.[8] It's clear where this doctor's real superiority lies—not in the 'intelligence' area but in the 'respecting Herbert' area.

Another handicap for Herbert the novelist was his lack of interest in listening to other people's stories. 'People bore me', he told Sadie.

> What dreadful bore [sic] practically all people are! All my life I've suffered with swelling of the feet thro' having to listen to people's dull, dull talk. You can hear anything the average person has to say on any subject in about 3 mins.[9]

The conversations he enjoyed were those in which he talked and others listened. On one occasion he records:

> I spent two hours with [Gough Whitlam] and talked to him and he listened most of the time—one of the journalists said to me [...] 'Don't you ever listen to what people say?' I said, 'I am listening all the time and the only time people tell the truth is when they want to sneak a word in.'—The thing was that I was getting his guts all the time more than he was getting mine.[10]

Herbert might have done better with characterisation if he had realised you don't 'get the guts' of other people by closing your ears to them.

Ill-fitted though he actually was for balanced judgment of character, Herbert was convinced he had special expertise in this area. He described himself as 'essentially the student of human nature'[11], and frequently cited 'perspicacity' as one of his great strengths.[12] In a speech given at the end of a stint as a visiting fellow at Queensland University, he told his audience:

> To be a novelist you need only one quality—a tremen-
> dous perspicacity. [...] One looks at the world and one
> estimates it. [One becomes] an expert in the observation
> of one's fellows. [...] One has to assume the ability of
> isolation—that is the second quality a novelist needs. [I
> shall now] go away back into the solitude to try and
> discover the truth about this business of relationship.[13]

It was dangerous, this belief that he could, through infrequent
observation followed by extended isolation, achieve deep understanding of his fellows. He would have done better to test his
theories on human nature by taking a daily interest in the thoughts
and feelings expressed by those he lived among. 'People to me', he
once said, 'are vast and dangerous mysteries. I exaggerate their
potentialities in action—although I'm dead sure of my reading of
these in rest'.[14] The first two statements were true; the last a
dangerous misconception.

Herbert's attitude to people in real life had predictable effects
on the way he presented them in his novels. It comes as no surprise
to find the picture is unsympathetic and unflattering. He favours
verbs with demeaning connotations. People in his books 'babble and
bray' rather than speak, 'goggle and gape' rather than look, 'cringe or
strut' rather than walk. Their eating is greedy and gross. Reverend
Tasker 'smacks' and 'swigs' his way through the ginger beer. The
race mob 'guzzles' and 'gorges' their curry.[15] Their lovemaking is as
greedy as their eating. Fergus 'laps up' Rifkah's kisses. Clancy
'devours' her lips and 'slobbers' her mouth.[16] Even smiling and
weeping are treated unsympathetically. Herbert's characters don't
cry; they 'snivel' or they 'blubber'. They don't smile; they 'snigger and
snicker' or 'leer' or, most commonly of all, they 'smirk'. Lydia smirks
as she urinates. Alfie smirks as she guzzles.[17] Cholly, Rosa and Ida
spend a whole page doing little else.[18] It's a mean little word—
'smirk'. That Herbert selects it so often for one of the more attractive
human behaviours says much about the view of humanity he
presents in his novels.

Another predictable result of Herbert's attitude to people in
real life was the difficulty he had, in his novels, whenever he tried to

write dialogue dealing with complex emotions. Had he been a better listener, he might have found it easier to recognise and reproduce the subtle ways in which humans reveal their thoughts and feelings. His difficulty with dialogue of this sort becomes most apparent in *Soldiers' Women* because of the nature of what he was attempting in that book. The following, between mother and daughter, is typical:

> 'Have you been with a man?'
>
> 'Y—yes.'
>
> It was a moment before Materkins dared ask the next question: 'You...you have lain with a man?'
>
> A quivering moan.
>
> [...] 'Answer me! You have lain with a man?'
>
> 'Y—yes.'
>
> 'Good God!'
>
> Now it was all Materkins could do to breathe. [...] When at last she could articulate it was almost to croak: 'Have... have you done this...this sort of thing before?'
>
> 'N—no.'
>
> 'Did...did you take precautions?'
>
> Felicia smothered her shame in slender hands.
>
> The croaking became strident: 'Fool...miserable, damned, hopeless, helpless, half-witted thing that you are...to think you're a child of mine...tchah!'
>
> [...] Her voice rose in a tiger's scream.
>
> 'Strumpet...but you'll ruin no plans of mine with bastardy. [...] If you're pregnant I'll have it taken away... you filthy fornicator...slut!'[19]

It is not good writing. The language is stilted. The characters wear their emotions firmly on their sleeves. There is none of the equivocation, the silence and half-truth, that bear so much of the meaning in real conversation. Nor is he any better with the dialogue of male characters:

> 'Please, sir, send me back to my squadron. [...] You understand, sir...you've been through it. Materkins

doesn't understand. Please, sir, *please...*' It ended in sobbing. [...]

'I understand, my boy. But I can't gainsay your mother's wish.' [...]

'If you would give me the order first, sir, I could take it to her and tell her I would be away only for a little while. [...] If I had the order she'd have to let me go.'

'But what about me? I have to stay here and face her!' [20]

Only a writer as 'un-listening' as Herbert would have an Australian soldier refer to his mother as 'Materkins' and his commanding officer swing from the awkward pomposity of 'I can't gainsay your mother's wish' to the guilty childishness of 'What about me? I have to stay here and face her'. The tone is wrong, the psychology incredible. Nor is this the worst he is capable of. Unable to catch the subtler differences between the way individuals speak, he is betrayed, too often for comfort, into caricatured speech reminiscent of the bubbles in a comic strip. A tetchy old army officer cries, 'Dad-blistering damnation, sir!' [21] And middle-class outrage is, again and again, conveyed by 'How dah you'.

Another result of Herbert's attitude to people in real life was that, in creating fictional characters, he concentrated on what he knew something about, the external, and avoided, as far as possible, what he knew very little about, the internal. We see this in the point of view he adopts, in his excessive dependence on body language to reveal emotion, and in his painstaking attempts to record accurately how characters speak and dress.

The authorial point of view Herbert favoured was a rigorously external one. The stance taken in his novels is that of the intelligent observer who draws conclusions on the basis of observable data. 'Let us', he says of one character:

hazard a bit of guessing, without pretending to discover anything like the facts about him—which would be soothsaying—but simply to make deductions on the much that was unknown about him from the little that was known, with fair certainty of getting enough evidence for our purpose, which is to establish some sort of understanding of the man [...][22]

While not claiming the privileges of an omniscient author, Herbert does, in his books as in life, claim special skill as an interpreter of observable behaviour. When, in *Soldiers' Women*, for instance, Pudsey takes Athol to a secluded house, the author first tests a number of possible hypotheses to account for the available data:

> The reason was certainly not desire on her part, because in submission to the inevitable she was as reluctant and non-cooperative as last night. Nor could it have been for the perverse pleasure of reducing her swain to that state of imbecility inevitably the lot of the male who copulates for his own selfish easement, common enough revenge though this is that women take on men they hate: for to do this she would have waited till they got home so as to complete the humiliation by leaving him alone with his feeling of negation.

Next comes the chain of argument leading inexorably to the correct conclusion:

> To call Athol a cad for what happened when, after a lot of clumsy contriving, he got her into the bridal bed, would be unfair. She knew the formula by which good girls keep that way, but used no part of it. Hence it must be presumed that she had as much to do with the manoeuvring as he, that virginity was irksome to her now, that in response to the urge of her destiny she had with deliberation chosen to be rid of it by using this oaf.[23]

You can almost hear the murmured 'Elementary my dear Watson!'

The point of view reflects Herbert's complacent certainty in real life that he could plumb the depths of character simply by observing the surface signs. It is not an easy point of view to sustain without sounding laboured and unconvincing—particularly when a character is on their own. On one occasion, for instance, Delacy sits looking out of a plane window at the country below and Herbert wants to tell us what he is thinking, but, having deprived himself of the powers of an omniscient author, he can only do so in the following clumsy and unconvincing fashion:

> By the way he half-frowned, perhaps Jeremy was wondering whether modern means of getting about his environment would so demean it to Man that he would not scruple to destroy it. [...] Yet is destruction of one's true mother's womb even thinkable? And is not one's country one's mother, too, since one takes one's first substance from it? Are not its features as much to be beloved? So might Jeremy have been thinking, being the man he was [...][24]

Yes, he might. But he might just as well be thinking of a thousand and one other things. There is simply not enough external evidence in situations like this for the internal workings of the mind to be 'guessed at' in such detail and with such confidence.

Herbert's concentration on the exterior signs of character is further seen in his heavy reliance on a set of stereotypical body language signifiers that he uses to indicate emotion. These signifiers become more and more obtrusive with each book. 'Fighting for breath', for instance, signifies 'in the grip of strong emotion', and characters are much given to 'heaving' and 'panting'.[25] Strong feeling also gives rise to much quivering, jerking and shaking—of mouth, cheek and face most often, but also of head, shoulders and body. Often these movements are accompanied by a reddening of the face.[26] A further sign of strong feeling is a voice that is 'strangled', that 'husks', that 'croaks'.[27] Vulnerability is indicated by 'crumpling' or 'puckering' of the face[28], surprise by 'popping', 'rolling' or 'goggling' of the eyes[29], submission by blinking.[30]

Another body language marker to which Herbert attaches significance is eye colour. Present already in rudimentary form in *Capricornia*, a semiotics of eye colour has, by the time he wrote *Poor Fellow My Country*, become firmly established. Green eyes signify the larrikin. In *Poor Fellow My Country* Cahoon, Hannaford and Ferris all have green eyes, as does Lolly, Fortitude's feisty girlfriend in *Soldiers' Women*. Grey eyes, on the other hand, signify maturity and thoughtfulness. McRandy's misty grey eyes are found again in *Soldiers' Women*'s Erica and *Poor Fellow My Country*'s Jeremy Delacy and Monsignor Maryzic. Prindy, too, wise beyond his years, has grey eyes. Brown eyes signify the 'good woman'. Rifkah in *Poor Fellow My Country* and Selina, Rosa and Madeleine in *Soldiers' Women* are brown-eyed, as was Sadie. Fortitude's brown eyes, meanwhile, add to the suggestion that he lacks masculinity.[31] Black eyes signify women who use their sexuality aggressively. Alfie, Savitra and Bridie in *Poor Fellow My Country* all have black eyes. So fixed in Herbert's mind does this semiotics of eye colour become that, more than once, it betrays him into unintended inconsistency. When, for instance, in *Soldiers' Women* Lolly looks at Fortitude with 'the expression of a mother seeing her little boy come battered from fighting', Herbert describes her with 'troubled searching in hazel eyes', forgetting the larrikin green eyes he has given her elsewhere in the novel and replacing them momentarily with the brown eyes of motherhood.[32]

A final indication of Herbert's stress on the exterior in characterisation is the importance he placed on recording accurately the sound of speech and the details of dress. Unsubtle in catching the nuances of dialogue, he is rigorously accurate in recording the phonological features of a character's dialect: Barbu's 'It is t'e vay of t'e country', for instance, and Rifkah's 'I only vont mek ze poor people 'appy'.[33] In similar fashion, in *Soldiers' Women* he describes in meticulous detail the dresses his characters wear. The result is description uncomfortably close to a cadet journalist's fashion piece.

> The outfit today was in cerise hopsack, with large organdie collar colourfully embroidered in cornelli style, white gloves, red shoes, little red hat trimmed with red-eyed daisies [...][34]

It comes as no surprise to learn he used to 'cut out pieces from the newspaper of different women with their different clothes and get them that way'.[35]

Given his limitations, it is not surprising that Herbert had most success with character types that did not depend on deep understanding of one's fellows. One of those was the type found in anatomy, the type E. M. Forster calls 'flat'.[36] Herbert did not need to delve deeply into his Capricornians to create their lively energy. What he did need was to base such characters on people he had actually known. The more he relies on invention, the less his flat characters convince. Roddy, Mrs Batt and Mrs La Plante, the invented flat characters of *Soldiers' Women*, are unconvincing caricatures. In contrast, the flat characters of *Poor Fellow My Country*, based as they were on people Herbert had actually known[37], are vigorously alive. Judge Bickering, for example:

> When Bobwirridirridi was duly escorted into the dock and Judge Bickering looked at him amiably, he grinned broadly, saying, 'Goottay, Boss!'
>
> Judge Bickering was well known at the Jail, not simply as Chiefest of Turnkeys, Master of Screws, but as an amiable visitor, who often went out to see how those who had lost the game with him were getting on, to consider releases, even to take small gifts. He called it Tempering Justice with Mercy, and often declared in his Court that while he enjoyed his power as a judge he preferred the exercise of it rather in ordering release of a prisoner than in committing one. Now he winked rapidly at old Bob, but addressed him in a tone of true judicial gravity: 'Prisoner at the Bar, know you that you are in flagrant contempt in so addressing me? Nonetheless, Goottay to you, too!'
>
> Bobwirridirridi flung his grey head back and opened the crack of a mouth wide in joining the wholesale laughter.[38]

The *Capricornia*n skills are back. The humour is back. The characters lack depth, but they are full of life.

Confession is not always, though, so positive an influence on the flat characters of *Poor Fellow My Country*. Herbert does least well when he uses fiction to pay back old scores. Confession allowed him, for instance, to denigrate two old enemies, P. R. Stephensen[39], the editor of *Capricornia*, and Bill Stanner, the anthropologist who 'conceived and developed the North Australia Observer Unit' in which Herbert served from 1942 until 1944.[40] Herbert resented being placed under Stanner's command and came to dislike him intensely. He often threatened 'to put the bastard in a book'[41] and put him in he did, in the character of the epicene Fabian Cootes. Stephensen meanwhile appears in the character of 'The Bloke', the Free Australia movement's would-be little Hitler.

The problem as far as the novel is concerned is that both characters are so viciously pilloried by the author that even as flat characters they simply become incredible. Whenever Cootes, for instance, appears, he is placed in situations designed to make him look foolish. He is persuaded to wear full academic regalia in court and then mercilessly mocked by the judge for so doing. He claims skill in horsemanship and then, ignominiously, falls off the most docile horse Lily Lagoons can offer. He is tricked into eating pigeon offal to prove his bush skills, rushes away to vomit violently, and is then made to look even more foolish when he denies having done so. He is described as vain, self-seeking, cowardly and effeminate. Faced by an irate priest, his voice rises 'shrilly', his eyes 'wobble', he 'squeaks' commands and then, dumped in the sea, 'bob[s] up again gasping and flapping wildly and looking scared to death'.[42] The more Herbert warms to the task of character assassination, the less credible becomes the character. One might accept, for instance, an ambitious man angling for a position on a general's staff but not when he uses language straight out of 'The Sneak of the Lower Third':

> Cootes's voice became a little boy's pleading: 'I could hand over that command, Malters...General...and I would so love to be with you. I...I've had enough action...for the time.[43]

We know from other sources that the portrait of Stanner is historically unjust.[44] It is also artistically inept. It is impossible to imagine anyone handing the leadership of anything to a character whose folly and cowardice are relentlessly exposed every time he appears. Yet we are asked to believe that the army hierarchy is so blind to his all-too-obvious faults that, despite his lack of any military experience, it entrusts him with command of the whole of northern Australia.

Ineffective though the portraits of Cootes and The Bloke are, Herbert's successes with the 'humours' of anatomy far outnumber his failures. In this type of characterisation, his limitations in human understanding and preference for looking at the surface of characters were no hindrance. Nor were they a hindrance to creating the characters of high romance. Romance characters, says Frye, 'are heroic and therefore inscrutable'.[45] So it is with Prindy and Bobwirridirridi. They are powerful characters precisely because Herbert does not go below the surface. With them, his limited interest in other people becomes unimportant. Since neither expresses his thoughts and feelings except to the other, and since we are never privy to their conversation, they remain a mystery throughout the book—which is precisely why they are powerful figures. Frye's 'heroic and therefore inscrutable' might equally well be expressed as 'inscrutable and therefore heroic'. Words circumscribe; the imagination has no bounds. Had Herbert attempted to convey the motives and thoughts of either character, he must inevitably have fallen short of the mark. Romance characters must remain impenetrable if they are to convince. Prindy and Bobwirridirridi live powerfully in the imagination precisely because they remain enigmatic.

The characters of romance, like the characters of anatomy, were unaffected by Herbert's limited interest in his fellows. It was quite otherwise with the characters of the 'novel', characters of the type Forster calls 'rounded'. It was this type he needed to create for a book like *Soldiers' Women* to be successful, and concentrating on the external is not the way to achieve that. The first five pages of *Soldiers' Women*, for instance, catalogue the external features of Rosa, Materkins, Ida and Mrs Batt in exhaustive detail, but the characters remain lifeless and insubstantial. Mrs Batt, for instance:

> A gaunt woman, gaudily attired in lavender and red, with
> a silly little hat crushed into a shock of tow-blond hair

that looked like a clown's thatch above the smudged painted face and bulbous brow [...] great staring eyes, like the china eyes of a doll, magnified with tears; and her mouth, with lipstick widely smeared to make it look like the painted mouth of a clown, writhed with speech that came forth as a sepulchral groan [...] a lean blue-veined hand [...] a cockatoo-like screech.[46]

It is the crime reporter's view of humanity, an exhaustive (and for the reader exhausting) catalogue of external features that gives little sense of the person behind the detail.

Herbert's problem in *Soldiers' Women* was that he simply did not understand people well enough to make its 'rounded' characters convincing. If we chart the relationship between Ida and Rosa, for instance, we find the power shifting in strangely inconsistent ways. It is not that we expect humans to behave with robotic consistency, but there is a human logic to the behaviour of real people that is absent here. The first time we see them, they behave 'like newly met lovers, prattling eagerly, searching each other's face with swift shy glances'. The shift to first-name terms becomes matter for 'delight'. At this stage, Rosa is the dominant partner, making the running with 'Couldn't we meet some time soon?' Ida responds with delight. 'Oh yes, I'd love to—whenever you like.'[47] And so it continues for a time, with Ida treating phone calls to Rosa with all the fear and joy of a teenager in love. Then suddenly, for no good reason, there is a complete turnaround. On their first outing together, Rosa becomes the dowdy country cousin, Ida the aloof princess:

> [Rosa] expressed her humility, saying, 'I suppose to be a smart dresser you have to be born that way.'
> Ida was remote in answering: 'Well...really, it's a matter between you and your dressmaker.'
> Rosa did not dare to voice the favour, could only ask it with pleading eyes.
> Still remote, Ida answered: 'If you like, I'll introduce you to Ramona Kelly.'[48]

Some time later, the two visit Mrs Batt, a working-class mother who chooses, for reasons unexplained, to act like royalty. Ida is now the one who is ill at ease. We are asked to believe that 'playing ladies scared Ida, but not Rosa'. It seems highly unlikely. It seems even more unlikely that when Pudsey ridicules her mother's behaviour, 'Ida responded to the covert smirking with tiny smiles when it was safe: but not Rosa, whose glassy staring in obvious disapproval soon put an end to it'.[49] The aloof Ida of the trip to town has become a schoolgirl rebuked by the friend she patronised in the world of fashion. It strains belief. The problem is that Herbert simply does not have a rounded conception of any of his characters. Therefore, they behave erratically according to his conception of the thematic or dramatic needs of particular scenes.

It was, again, the genre of confession that provided a partial solution to Herbert's problems with 'rounded' characters. One reason he found it hard to create the characters of *Soldiers' Women* was that none of them was 'taken from life'.[50] Had there been a confessional element in these characters, they might have been less ineffective. But only slightly so, since there was only one person Herbert knew well enough to form the basis for an effective rounded character and that person did not provide the material needed for a group of society women. The person was, of course, himself.

Since he needed to draw characters from life to have any chance of success, and since the only person he knew well enough to provide material for a psychologically complex character was himself, Herbert's increasingly frequent intrusion into his own novels, while it has often been criticised, had much to recommend it. He needed, though, to learn how best to use his knowledge of himself. In the early books, it is mostly the mistakes we notice—mistakes such as the appearance of Herbert's voice and opinions in the mouths of inappropriate characters. It strains credulity, for instance, to find a tough, ignorant, feckless young prostitute speaking remarkably like a certain knowledgeable, middle-aged pharmacist-turned-writer:

'That's the only safe way [abortion] can be done,' said Fay.
'My friend used to do the job herself, but had so much

trouble with the difficult jobs she nearly got landed. So
she took to teaching her patients how to do the job themselves. That's a hundred per cent safe, because the patient
knows just how far to go without hurting herself enough
to cause shock. Shock is the great danger in abortion.'[51]

It strains credulity, too, when the fit between Herbert's
experience and the character to whom he gives that experience is
poor, as happens in an unconvincing scene between Pudsey and her
psychologist. At their very first meeting, Dr Dickey urges Pudsey to
write 'the story of your struggle with your mother for the love of
your father'. 'If you were to tell it in its every detail', she says

> working not only with your talent, but with your courage,
> inspired by the sense that you were making a great
> contribution to knowledge by baring your own soul [...] it
> could be one of the great literary and scientific efforts of
> the period.[52]

Dr Dickey's assessment of her young client derives from Herbert's
view of himself and what he was doing in writing books like
Soldiers' Women. It has no credible basis whatsoever in the situation
pictured. The only evidence offered to account for the doctor's
belief, on the basis of so short an acquaintance, in this unprepossessing adolescent's capacity to write 'one of the great literary and
scientific efforts of the period' is a short story Pudsey tells the doctor
she has written, but which the doctor has not even seen.

By the time he wrote *Poor Fellow My Country,* Herbert had
become much better at using himself as the basis for characterisation.
He includes aspects of himself in a number of this book's characters
and, in each case, the fit between Herbert's experience and the
character is comfortable. In the enigmatic figure of Prindy, Herbert
finds an infinitely more credible repository than Pudsey for 'the part
of my character [...] that can't be fully understood', the 'genius' part.[53]
In Clancy, Herbert convincingly incorporates the less satisfactory
aspects of his experience as a young man.[54] Alfie, meanwhile, is a
complex mixture of confessional elements. Based on two women

involved in the Australia First movement (Adela Pankhurst and Miles Franklin)[55], she is presented as just the kind of managing, intellectual, man-dominating woman Herbert hated. She is also, however, based on the two aspects of Herbert's own experience he was most proud of: his role as champion of Aboriginals and as writer.[56] Herbert's success in dealing with these contradictory confessional elements demonstrates that he is doing two things much better now. He no longer ascribes his own experiences inappropriately to characters, and no longer has them speak with his voice unless that voice is appropriate to them. Thus he limits the 'Herbert element' in Alfie to aspects of his experience that fit comfortably with a character based on Adela Pankhurst, the social reformer, and Miles Franklin, the writer. And he makes sure that neither his speaking voice nor his ideas are allowed to creep into Alfie's dialogue except when she expresses the joys of novel writing, speaks out in defence of Aboriginals, or champions Australian independence.

Of all the characters in *Poor Fellow My Country*, none is more closely based on Herbert than Jeremy Delacy. He was, Herbert said, created 'out of bits and pieces of myself' as 'a character on my own nature (without the genius, which I've given to the little boy)'.[57] There are, of course, dangers in creating such characters. It is hard to remain a clear-sighted judge when dealing with your own fictional self. For Herbert, the task was made more difficult by the fact that he was no better judge of himself than he was of others, prone to overestimating his strengths and blind to his own weaknesses. It is not surprising, therefore, that his judgment of a fictional character based so closely on himself proved equally fallible. As one early critic commented, 'Jeremy is intended, one guesses, as one of nature's bush gentlemen' but is actually 'an inverted racist, sexist, ruthlessly selfish, and hopelessly thoughtless, self-deluding old hypocrite'.[58] In an incensed rebuttal, Herbert claimed he had not intended Delacy to be seen as a 'bush gentleman' and that he had 'deliberately' included the racism, sexism, selfishness and hypocrisy.[59] There is, though, scant evidence to support these claims. In the book itself Delacy is criticised for only one fault, the one Herbert does not share, his 'negativity'.[60] Nowhere is there evidence that Herbert is any better able to recognise Delacy's sexism, racism, selfishness or self-delusion than he is able to recognise his own.[61] Apart from the negativity, Delacy is Herbert, and Herbert admires him.[62] Delacy is, he once said, 'my kind of hero [...] He won't tolerate dishonesty, cowardice, sloth. That's why they hate him'.[63] Even his negativity is pictured as the result of his essential nobility. Nanago calls him a 'brave, kind, clever man' and says, 'Da's what git him down...what you call negative...all meanness, unkindness, cruelty in country, in world'.[64]

Herbert's blindness towards Delacy's faults should, one might think, have created major problems. That it did not was thanks to the non-intrusive authorial point of view he favoured. By drawing upon his knowledge of himself, he was able to present an accurate picture of the flawed, self-deluding character Delacy was, while the lack of omniscient authorial comment protected him from conflicts that might otherwise have occurred between his own and his readers' judgment. How effective the result was can be seen in the final scenes between Delacy and Nanago. By drawing upon memories of his own relationship with Sadie, Herbert creates in these scenes a picture of ruthless selfishness and self-deluding sexism that is as clear to the reader as it is hidden from the author. The genre of confession, in combination with a non-intrusive authorial point of view, has enabled Herbert, for the first time, to create a 'rounded' character of real psychological complexity.

The parting between Delacy and Nanago results from the army's ordering all civilians to leave northern Australia. Delacy is determined to remain in defiance of the order but insists Nanago must go, even though she is passionate in her desire to stay. Before anyone goes, however, there is the 'Blackfellows' Christmas' to be organised. The traditional patroness, Lady Rhoda, has left and Delacy leaps at the opportunity to take over. 'If this is to be the last of squattocratic *noblesse oblige* in these parts', he says, 'I want Nan to have the honour of it. Her Ladyship is sure to hear and be sour about it'.[65] A typical piece of self-deluding selfishness. Unwilling to give Nanago what she really wants, permission to stay in her own home, he dresses up a petty desire to score points over his ex-wife as something done for Nanago's sake.

The final night at Lily Lagoons arrives and Nanago wants to spend it with Delacy in the annexe. 'Don't you want to sleep the last night in your own house?' he asks:

She shook her head. 'I have no own house.'

He took the hand from his hair, pulled to round his neck, fondled it. 'This house is yours as long as it stands [...] it's yours to come back to as mistress.'

She sipped. 'I am not mistress...I am servant.'

He looked at her shocked. 'Eh...what's this?'

She removed her hand, to resume stroking his hair, looking at him with the great calm of broad, sweet, dark countenance that was usual when she spoke seriously. 'Always you have been my master...I your servant.' The patois was dropped.

He burst out: 'But this [is] silly! I made you my wife. You have been full mistress here ever since I brought you to the place.'

'For all other people I am mistress. For you I am servant.'

'You mean that's all I wanted you to be?'

'No...all I want to be for you. I tell you before like this. You don't listen.'[66]

Herbert achieves here something he rarely achieved: dialogue in which the subtleties of human emotions and relationships are allowed to reveal themselves through what is not said as much as through what is said, in nuances rather than grand gestures. Delacy's self-deluding complacency is confronted by the honesty of 'Always you have been my master...I your servant'. Typically, Delacy cannot match that honesty. Though his behaviour in refusing to allow Nanago to stay shows that the master–servant relationship is highly congenial to him, he deludes himself into thinking otherwise. His 'You mean that's all I wanted you to be?' is clearly a prelude to fierce denial, but any self-justification is undercut by Nanago's calm acceptance of responsibility: 'No...all I want to be for you'. Her 'I tell you before like this. You don't listen' sums up beautifully Delacy's attitude to her.

As the scene continues, Nanago's honesty continues to expose Delacy's selfishness:

'Always I am servant of Jeremy Delacy. Time I can't be his servant, I don't want to live.'

He pulled her somewhat roughly into his lap. 'Now listen...we've had all this out. You promised to go away and look after the others.'

She kissed him, with passion, then relaxed, saying, 'I do dat, because you tell me...and I am your servant.'[67]

'We've had all this out', says Delacy, but it is clear 'we' have done no such thing. 'He' has laid down the law and 'she' has been willing to accept it. Again her honesty contrasts with his self-serving self-delusion. The scene's conclusion is equally revealing:

He talked of what he wanted her to do to maintain the pride of race that had been taught here as religion to crossbreds ever since it had been made a refuge for them [...] how he wanted her to fill in her empty time with showing herself in her pride to those who would be sympathetic towards her and learn from her the problems of being Euro-australoid [...] how he relied on her to teach the difference between yellow-fellow and black-fellow and stop the destruction, moral or otherwise, of those the country really belonged to, before it was too late [...] If she were his beloved servant, here was her service. She fell asleep listening to his droning.[68]

Again we see Delacy's self-absorption, his insensitivity to his wife's needs. She, meanwhile, as no doubt often before, loving the man and not his theories, retreats into sleep.

The final parting, some days later, is further testament to the value of the confessional element in Herbert's writing. This was just the kind of emotional scene he normally found it impossible to deal with successfully. This time he manages a scene whose understated simplicity has real conviction and power:

They walked as before. But now mostly she went with hanging head.

At length he asked, 'Are you crying?'

She shook her head, but blinked hard. He stopped, to

raise her face, to kiss the welling eyes. He whispered,
'Please be brave, my dear.'
  She choked: 'I got to cry lil bits…I lose my country.'
  'You'll be able to come back to your country some day.'
  Her head fell again. 'You are my country.'[69]

The Herbertian stereotype of the willing slave-wife may jar upon
some readers, but there is no denying it is an infinitely subtler and
more human presentation of that stereotype than he achieved in
Soldiers' Women.

It is unlikely that when Herbert wrote the scenes between
Delacy and Nanago, he was aware of the picture he was actually
giving, but so long as he maintains a non-intrusive authorial point of
view, his own blindness to Delacy's weaknesses does not matter.
There are, however, situations in which the non-intrusive point of
view is not enough to protect Herbert from the dangers involved in
creating a character so closely confessional. One of those situations is
when the author's own faulty judgment appears in the response of
one of the other characters. One of the less attractive aspects of the
author's own character, for instance, can be seen in an incident
involving Herbert and one of the nurses at Innisfail. Having invited
her to a party, Herbert became irritated about something and refused
to drive her home. She was, not unnaturally, annoyed. His description of the sequel exhibits all the weaknesses of his handling of such
scenes in his novels: the melodramatic tone, the serious treatment of
trivial events, the obsessive interest in demeaning manoeuvres:

> I felt […] that I just had to save my face. […] At breakfast
> it occurred to me to write a humble note. I typed this […]
> and gave it to [Ross] who was pleased to see me acting
> like 'The Master' as he said. […] He was to give it to her at
> breakfast. But you can never tell what a woman (or that
> kind of woman) will do. Soon after he went off, Anne
> popped into the [dispensary…] and after a short good
> morning, to which I replied kind of breathlessly said, 'I
> simply can't understand you.' I muttered something, and
> said I'd written a note of apology. She said there was no

need for one because the thing was beyond excuse. In
the note I said that my only excuse was the threadbare
one that I was drunk. In a moment she was gone but I
guessed I was beginning to win. [...] I was very excited
because the victory would mean much to me—I mean
the saving of the situation. [He arranges a meeting] and
with cleverness that I never thought I had, lied my way
out of it. [...] I brought her down in the funny old lift
which I stopped half way so as to kiss her—and arrived
at the bottom to be caught by [Ross who] greeted me with
some droll fitting comment at the same time eyeing us
shrewdly and seeing that the Master was again in control.
[...] I'm glad [...] as never before in dealing with a woman
of her kind of my mastery.[70]

In *Poor Fellow My Country* there are a number of scenes
in which Delacy is involved in similarly petty and demeaning
manoeuvres. The success or failure of such scenes depends upon
whether Herbert's flawed pride in that behaviour is allowed to
appear through the response of other characters. One of the failures
is the scene in which Alfie comes running to Delacy, asking for his
help in 'defying' his ex-wife Rhoda, who is trying to prevent Alfie
'helping the Patron in drawing' the golden horseshoe raffle. Alfie has
been told to give up the list of entrants and has refused, she tells
Delacy, because to do so will 'give [Rhoda] a victory...not only over
me, but over you'. She asks Delacy to 'give me courage to do what
you'd do yourself', saying, 'It's what you've done's inspired me to do
the same'. It's a ridiculously large mountain to build out of an
infinitesimally small molehill, but, as Herbert himself would have
done, Delacy responds with intense seriousness. 'We can't just barge
into it', he says. 'The thing's got to be planned so that there can't be
any failure.' He outlines the following plan:

> I suggest that Alfie keeps out of the way till the last
> moment...but not you, Frank. Gilling is sure to ask you
> where she is. You say she's around somewhere and will
> be along any minute...with what he wants. Any suspicion

they might work up over her non-appearance'll be smothered by my appearance. [...] I'll stroll in...with Alfie. But you'll have to take Alfie off my hands at once. [...] If Gilling should come to you in the meantime, put him off by saying, sort of whispering and all amiability, that she'll give it to him as soon as the draw begins. [...] Then Alfie marches up to the Patron. [...] They might be too scared to ask you for the things after they've seen you with me...but if they do [...] well [...] you refuse, addressing yourself to the President. [...] If he asks for the thing, say that first you'd like to know the *exact* reason why you're being done out of something you'd looked forward to with great pleasure. However it goes you should sink 'em...because everybody'll know what's supposed to happen, and if they haven't the courage to tackle it, the laugh is still on them. Got it?'

So overwhelmed by it was Alfie that the big black eyes swam, and she came and reached for the ruddy hands, choking, 'Oh, you're marvellous, Jeremy...you're wonderful!'[71]

For Delacy to take this nonsense so seriously is no problem. It only becomes a problem because the author, too, is seen to take it seriously. In this case, the non-intrusive point of view provides no protection. The author's own misreading of the situation, damagingly at odds with the reader's, is here revealed through Alfie's admiring response.

Another situation in which the author's close confessional relationship with Delacy caused problems was when Herbert was unable to resist the pleasures of wish fulfilment and pictured Delacy achieving successes that were simply not grounded in the logic of character and situation. In Delacy's sexual prowess, for instance, Herbert vicariously indulged the dreams of an old man whose ability to seduce young women had long since departed. Not so his alter ego. Despite Delacy's age, young women queue to share his bed. First Lydia, then Bridie, then Alfie and finally Rifkah fall under a spell that is far from obvious to a reader.[72] Delacy is old enough to be their grandfather and does nothing but lecture them, but still they besiege him. With credulity already stretched to the limit, readers are then asked to believe that the husbands and fathers of these maidens, far from objecting, are downright eager for Delacy to take advantage of the sexual favours so prodigally offered. Alfie's cuckolded husband positively begs him to continue.[73] Alfie's father, far from taking out the horsewhip, 'heartily approves'.[74] Most incredible of all, even that tough old protector of his own territory Finnucane, far from objecting to the bastard Delacy has fathered on his beloved daughter, is 'proud av it, because always have I wanted to mix the blood of Finnucane and Delacy'.[75]

The incredibility of Delacy's sexual successes is matched by the incredibility of his military and political successes. The responses to him by Esk in the military sphere and Alfie and Fergus in the political arena are far beyond what Delacy's past experience or present actions could realistically have given rise to. Basing his decision solely on an impression gained in a few conversations and the fact that Delacy had served in World War I, General Esk appoints him '2-IC Northern'. He would also, he says, 'gladly give you command of the Division I hope to God I'll have in Malaya [...] because no man could handle it better, or deal with the British Brass [...] more effectively'.[76] It is hard to fathom how Esk can think Delacy the best man for this job: a man who mistrusts the British and whose conciliatory skills, as demonstrated by relations with his own countrymen, are abysmal. The belief expressed in Delacy's political skills is equally hard to understand. A man with no political experience and a history of being extremely unpolitic in his own social circle would seem the last person to turn to for leadership. What possible grounds can Fergus Ferris have for saying the leadership of the Free Australia movement is 'your job...only you can do it'? And why would national figures down south, including the Prime Minister, be interested in his ideas?[77] What is actually happening here, of course, is that Herbert, to the detriment of Delacy's credibility, is enjoying in fiction the military success and political influence he would have liked to, but never did, achieve in real life.[78]

Nevertheless, though it sometimes caused problems, the effect of confession on Herbert's characterisation was largely positive. His many successful 'flat' characters were all based upon people he had known; where his characters move towards 'roundness', they are always more effective if based either on himself or on those he knew best; and the only truly complex character he ever created was based firmly upon himself. It was all a matter of learning to maximise strengths and minimise weaknesses. Temperamentally unsuited to creating the kind of characters expected in the genre Frye calls 'novel', Herbert learned instead to achieve his purposes with character types he was better suited to, the types found in romance, anatomy and confession.

CHAPTER 7

Didacticism and the Role of Romance

THE didacticism seen in a few of the early short stories had, by the time Herbert wrote *Soldiers' Women*, become a very significant element in his writing. One reason for this was his belief that he had discovered great truths about life, and that his contribution to the advancement of the species must be to pass those truths on to his fellows. Of *Soldiers' Women*, for instance, he wrote:

> It is women I aim to teach, for in their hands lies the future of the species, in their capacity for sacrifice of the petty power they wield over men through men's weakness [...] The allegory won't change the behaviour of mankind but it will prepare the way for preaching the doctrine of sexual sublimation as the means of Man's attainment to the fullness of his powers, to his Salvation, his enthronement as a god. I do truly believe that the publishing of this ideal will have as great an effect upon mankind as had 'The Origin of the Species'.[1]

Later he was to speak in similar grandiose fashion of *Poor Fellow My Country*, describing it as 'a monument [built] out of the truths I have collected' and saying 'I can smile when I die looking up at that monument, knowing that I have contributed to the advancement of my species'.[2] The book would, he said, teach his 'fellow countrymen the reality of their existence' and make them 'a better community of men than they have been hitherto'.[3]

A second, and more mundane, reason for Herbert's increasing didacticism was simply that having devoted a lot of time to broadening a previously rather limited education, Herbert couldn't resist showing off his new-found knowledge. Long-suffering Sadie bore the brunt of it. His letters to her are peppered with patronising little snippets of information like the following:

> For quite a while now I've been sending these *billets-doux* as I call them (French, but in the dictionary—means actually love-letter). [...] The Aboriginal name for mother is Breasts—my Breasts means my mother—and so it may be in all languages. It certainly is in universal language derived from the so-called Indo-Germanic (the Aryan)— MAMMAE being the Latin for TEATS—hence Mammy and Mummy and Mumma and Mum.'[4]

'Monday 00.15,' he begins another letter, and continues, 'meaning 15 minutes after midnight, or just 15 mins of new day—the way they would give the time and date in aviation is 0015 29, meaning 15 mins of the 2nd day of the 9th month. [...] Formerly it was written 0015/2/9'.[5] If Sadie did not understand the twenty-four hour clock by the end of 1968, she never would! Letters dated 28 August, 1 September and 4 September relentlessly repeat the same lesson.

Nor was it just Sadie who had to put up with Herbert's pontificating. He was happy to lecture any captive audience, from the chance-met priest who received an unsolicited lecture on 'Jews, Catholics and sex', to the academic who received one 'on the Psychopathology of everyday life'[6], to that most captive audience of all, the readers of his novels. From the 1950s onwards, they too are bombarded with snippet after snippet of information—delivered, all too often, in the patronising tone of the know-all. 'Of course, Hogmanay properly is what the Scots call New Year's Eve.' 'Patriotism, of course, comes from *Pater*, Father, one's Fatherland.' 'Of course the word ["gin"] really meant simply *woman* in classic Greek, *gyn*, of very ancient usage, without malicious intent, like *nigger*, simply being from the Latin, *niger, black*.'[7]

The increasingly didactic tone was a potentially dangerous development. Readers of novels do not like being lectured at. They like it even less when the content of the lecture is a lot less clever than the lecturer thinks. And that posed a problem for Herbert, since he very often overestimated the quality of his ideas, as the following extract from a letter to Sadie illustrates:

> My yesterday's joke was a beaut. [...] Now there is a thing in modern medicine called the mille-equivalent (m/eq) a method of measuring dosage according to atomic weight of substance. There is also a creature known as a mille-pede, which perhaps you know, one with a vast number of fine legs, you sometimes see in the garden—name means in Latin 'thousand legs'. Well my joke was: 'Doctor thinks a mille-equivalent is a kind of centipede.'[8]

The pride and laboured explanation are revealing. Only a rather simple thinker could find this as clever as Herbert obviously did.

Similarly revealing was the way he kept returning in letters, articles and interviews to the same few ideas, the same few examples. On the English language, for instance, he keeps referring to a single item gleaned from his reading of Fowler's *Modern English Usage* as if it, and it alone, were the measure of grammatical scholarship. In a typical example, he tells Sadie that his publishers at Collins have

> great fun trying to trap me with a Fused Participle— which believe it or not, they'd never heard of before, but now are quite mad about. There is a screed on it in the latest Fowler, still giving the same support for it and stating, as Fowler did and I have always maintained, that

the language could be *destroyed* by not recognising its value.[9]

It is hard to decide which is the more naive: the idea that these professionals are 'quite mad about' a single grammatical pedantry, or the belief that 'the language could be destroyed by not recognising its value'.[10]

Herbert's unquestioning acceptance of Fowler was typical of his mode of thought. He had an absolutist view of 'truth'. Modern grammarians might point out that rules of grammar are the servants of usage, and fused participles are only ungrammatical so long as the majority of standard dialect users reject them, but to Herbert such thinking would have been alien. He preferred his authorities absolute. Had he been a religious man, he would have been a funda- mentalist. Unlike jesting Pilate, he firmly believed one could find and fix 'the truth' about things—and was all too ready to believe he had himself done so. 'The Danes', he confidently tells Sadie, 'are all [...] mean faced and pin-headed'. With similar confidence he assures her that 'A Lutheran parson is about the worst thing on earth' and 'Australian women are either creeps or bullies'.[11] He rarely provides convincing argument in support of such statements. Even on Aust- ralia, the subject on which his books can be genuinely illuminating, it is as prophet, not political scientist, as visionary, not thinker, that he achieves his insights. He is least convincing when he attempts to argue a case. He is passionate, for instance, on the value of 'Commonwealth', but asked to define what he means by this, he retreats into vague idealism:

> The Commonwealth is a sharing, it is not just a sort of an alliance. It is a brotherhood, it's something very different. Well it's more than a brotherhood, call it a fraternity if you like.[12]

Try to push Herbert's thinking on 'Commonwealth' beyond 'brother- hood' towards practicalities of social and political organisation and you find contradiction and confusion. 'You have to establish a Socialist State to have a true Commonwealth'[13], he says at one point but elsewhere condemns socialism scathingly. 'The Union boys [...] solution [...] is Socialisation', he says, and scornfully continues, 'as if Australia wasn't socialised up to the neck already'.[14] Herbert's real strengths were not intellectual. He was a passionate believer, not a rigorous thinker, and if he wanted to use his novels to teach, he needed, as he had done with characterisation, to find ways of playing to his strengths rather than exposing his weaknesses. He did so by learning, through trial and error, how best to use the genres of romance and anatomy to achieve his didactic purposes.

In discussing Herbert's developing use of anatomy, it is useful to distinguish between the 'homiletic' and 'satiric' conventions of the genre. The homiletic conventions include displays of erudition and symposium discussions. The satiric conventions include ridicule of folly and pretension and stylising of character along humour lines.[15] As *Capricornia* had already proved, anatomy's satiric conventions were well suited to Herbert's type of thinking. Satire comfortably accommodates authoritarian and simplistic ideas. Satirists think in black and white, not grey; their job is to home in on a target, not explore the territory. There is, however, one proviso: a certain lightness of touch is needed. In *Capricornia* Herbert had that light touch, which is why we are amused rather than irritated by its generalisations. It is easy to accept pontificating when it is leavened by epigrammatic wit:

> To say that the citizens of Port Zodiac were delighted with the bloodshed would be true but perhaps unfair, since like folk of any Anglo-Saxon community they preferred to appear doleful in the presence of human death, to say of it How Sad! when they meant How Interesting![16]

In *Soldiers' Women* such generalisations have become merely irritating. Without *Capricornia*'s sardonic wit, statements such as 'playing indifference is rightful for a woman, but only spiteful for a man' and 'despite his polygamous tendencies, the average man's heart belongs to only one woman: mother, sister, first sweetheart, or wife'[17] sound like what they indeed are—the sweeping generalisations of a not very profound thinker.

Well suited though the satiric conventions of anatomy were to expressing the negative, critical side of Herbert's didacticism, he was never again, after *Capricornia*, very successful in using them for that purpose. Between *Capricornia* and *Soldiers' Women*, he seems to have lost much of his earlier wit and humour, and, without these, satire turns to diatribe. In *Soldiers' Women* the cheeky larrikin has turned into a self-righteous preacher relentlessly pounding the pulpit. In the books of the fifties we hear only faint echoes of the laughter that rolled through *Capricornia*. There are occasional flashes of the old Dickensian zest—in a doctor's voice, for instance, that has 'an edge to it, as if she had it touched up occasionally with her scalpels'[18]—but, more often, what once was delightful Dickensian grotesquerie has become forced and tedious. Throughout *Soldiers' Women*, for instance, Herbert labours the 'human as animal' metaphor. Roddy the taxi driver is a rat 'surveying the field with rodent's caution' and speaking 'in a subdued squeak'. Prostitutes in the hands of policemen are 'bright moths in the grip of great black and silver spiders'. Women constables are the 'females of the species [...] plump black widows with eyes eager for a moth-killing'. When Erica visits Ida, she comes 'barging along the path [...] looking rather like a hippopotamus' as Ida 'bounded away' like 'a gazelle' and Rosa followed 'like a monkey'. When Rosa visits a lingerie shop, the owner appears

> like a great bright-feathered bird of prey, to pounce on Rosa as on a silly fat rabbit and bear her away. But if it were like a rabbit that Rosa went, she came back like a weasel or some such sleek and lissom creature [...] the effect of her new girdle.[19]

This is no longer the Dickensian relish for pushing an idea to lunatic extremes for the sheer fun of it. This is a painstaking attempt to fit everything into the equation 'Humans = Animals'. And 'fitting everything in' is not at all the same as being unable to stop everything bursting out.

With his sense of humour disappearing, Herbert turned more and more towards anatomy's homiletic conventions. Symposium discussion became, in the books of the fifties, the main vehicle for his positive message. And therein lay a problem, since homily, even in the mouths of great preachers, rarely inspires—and the preaching in *Soldiers' Women* is anything but great. There was cruel truth in a contemporary review that spoke of its 'long slabs of barber-shop philosophy'.[20] His editor did her best to help. 'I don't think anyone will read all this', she said of Leon's lecturing. 'Could you cut while giving the impression of a long and fascinating dissertation.'[21] Her advice went unheeded. Far from curbing his use of homily, Herbert moved in his next book, 'The Little Widow', even further towards pure sermonising. The scene between the hero and Mrs Beaky is typical. It begins with the hero in the role of Socratic questioner:

> 'Do your children rave and shout at your grandchildren?'
> 'Of course, when necessary.'
> 'What decides when it is necessary?'
> 'You mean who decides...the parent of course.'
> 'By what right and rule does the parent decide?'
> 'It's a law of nature. It's a kind of instinct you have as a parent.'
> 'And it could never make mistakes?'
> 'Sometimes.'

After a great deal more of this, the hero shifts to monologue:

> Listen to an intelligent man's idea of what a child's mind is like, gained first from experience of a none-too-satisfactory childhood and then from a lifetime of observation with a mind trained to deal in scientific facts not fantasies and finally a good deal of reading of the observations on the subject of some of the most brilliant minds of our time. To begin with, will you concede that there is nothing we know that is the equal of human intelligence [...]

And off he goes, pontificating on and on, until at last: 'In the great eyes now I thought I saw dawning realization of the truth...and my heart leapt to the joy of winning a disciple'.[22] Realisation of the truth might dawn in the great eyes of the puppet figures Herbert manoeuvres so lifelessly through this utterly misconceived book, but it will not dawn in the eyes of its readers. The homiletic conventions of anatomy have, as we shall see later, their valid uses in Herbert's fiction, but they are not the inspirational uses to which he put them in the fifties. Homily will never inspire readers with the passion Herbert wants them to feel for the truths he taught. For that he needed something different. For that he needed romance.

Romance was a genre for which Herbert was temperamentally well suited. 'The marvellous', writes Gillian Beer, 'is not crucial in the definition of medieval romance because emotions and everyday activities are perceived by true romance writers as equally marvellous'.[23] So it was with Herbert. 'There is', he once wrote, 'a marvellousness about life. [...] Life is really larger than it appears to be'.[24] He saw the wondrous in his own life wherever he looked. The word 'wonder' and its derivatives fill his letters and punctuate interviews. His relationships at Innisfail are 'the wondrous things that are happening to me'. In chilly Sydney a friend lends him a coat and he marvels at his generosity, saying, 'I won't wear it. It is too wonderful a thing'.[25] On being ousted by Sir John Kerr, Whitlam says, 'Now come on the Republic', and Herbert comments ecstatically, 'But isn't it wondrous that he should say that at that moment'.[26] Where others saw only the mundane, Herbert saw the marvellous, and it was this that enabled him, when the conditions were right, to transmute the base metal of simplistic didacticism into the golden visions of the prophet and dreamer.

Herbert once wrote that he 'belonged in two worlds [...] that of my imagination, and the real one, but have had the talent to change the real and work-a-day somewhat, for periods, to meet the make-believe'.[27] A classic example of this capacity for living within a self-created world of make-believe was his flirtation with Judaism during the editing of *Poor Fellow My Country*. Treated with kindness by two Jewish employees of his publisher and taken by them to the synagogue, Herbert's wild enthusiasm awoke, and, over a period of weeks, he became more and more divorced from reality until we find him writing thus to Sadie:

> The logical conclusion is my acceptance by Jews as as
> great a force of friendship as they have ever had. If no
> one else could declare the truth about Australia Felix as I,
> no one can declare that about the House of Israel as I.[28]

Four days later he has persuaded himself it is his destiny to teach the
whole Jewish race

> the truth that I believe I alone can convince them of,
> which is of their greatness above all other humans. [...] I
> feel that I am bound to pronounce this truth someday—
> and that it will be taken seriously. [...] I've made a great
> discovery [...] that should be the making of Israel (if it is
> to survive) if it is proved true. It boils down to this—the
> question: 'Why did you (Herbert) have to link your life
> with Sadie?' The first answer is: 'Because she is a Jewess.'
> Why that? I've answered: 'No [...] woman of any other
> breed [could] have brought me to fulfilment.' But why?
> Simply because of her Jewishness. And that broadly
> applies to the world—and that is why all the gentile
> world is anti-Jew—they can't accept [...] the fact that of
> all forms of human society yet tried, the single one that
> fills the bill of primary brotherhood [is Judaism].[29]

If Herbert's belief that these muddle-headed ideas will lead to his
acceptance as the saviour of Israel reveals a monumental lack of
commonsense, it also reveals a profound capacity to transmute
mundane reality into rich fantasy. For those with feet more firmly on
the ground, his delusions of Messianic grandeur seem as ridiculous
as Quixote tilting at windmills. But it was precisely because he had
the ability to believe in things against all reason that he was able to
create, in his best novel, such a powerful romance. The same naivety
that produced this Messianic nonsense also produced Prindy,
Bobwirridirridi and Tchamala.

Herbert was not only well suited to creating that sense of the
marvellous without which romance fails; he was also well equipped
to exploit the allegorical possibilities inherent in the genre. Where

others saw scenes, it was natural for him to see meanings. At Innisfail, for instance, an Aboriginal girl sought his help in escaping 'from the "mongrels" as she calls them who live in squalor in the towns'. He described seeing her off at the station thus:

> There was the poor thing all alone with her shabby suitcase [...] Yet looks so nicely dressed. [...] She was just going to board the train—all alone. There were few on it—one of those wretched old bombs of things—a couple of awfully foreign-looking cane-cutting types, and some blacks. It was all so poor and mean—in this land of sunshine and plenty and liberty, equality and fraternity.[30]

There is no doubting the human sympathy that moved Herbert to help the girl, but it is as symbol that the situation most resonates for him. Here, as so often in his novels, he reads the Aboriginal situation as a comment on the state of Australia. Here, as so often in the novels, the picture becomes the meaning. In *Capricornia* children shut up in the squalor of the 'Halfcaste Home', listening to the drunken revelling of matron and her visitors, 'mean' all the injustice and hypocrisy of white bureaucracy, 'mean' all the callous mistreatment of Aboriginals in Australia.[31] In *Poor Fellow My Country* houses with 'strange squashed faces' because only the essential back areas had ever been built 'mean' foreign banks foreclosing on mortgages, 'mean' the hard labour and disappointed hopes of ordinary Australians.[32] The ease and economy with which Herbert, at his best, is able to convey abstract meaning through pictures are reminiscent of his great seventeenth-century namesake. When Delacy and Maryzic, for instance, leave the Leopold Island Mission:

> The grey hairs of the two passengers sitting amidships blew in the rising sou'easter as they waved their hats, the squatter's wide-awake, the cleric's black, to the waving crowd ashore. [...] Still they stood staring back, till with the curving of the channel, the dream-thing behind vanished like a dream.[33]

Explanation is unnecessary. The picture conveys the meaning. The old power groupings of church and squattocracy have no place in a new Australia in which migrants and Aboriginals attempt to achieve a brave new world, free from the old conflicts and failures.

All this, of course, raises an obvious question. If Herbert was so well suited to allegorical romance, why was neither the romance nor the allegory very successful in *Soldiers' Women*? There were three reasons. The first was that, although he had had plenty of experience with popular romance, *Soldiers' Women* was his first attempt at high romance and it posed new problems: above all, the problem of how to incorporate the magic of romance into the mundane world of the novel. At one point in her comments on the manuscript, his editor gently complained, 'It's always moonlight. It never rains. There are never any clouds over the moon'. In the margin Herbert scrawled in exasperated riposte, 'So what!'[34] The standards of realism, he is saying, no longer apply. He is trying to create a world where enchantment rules and natural law is suspended, a world where mundane reality is transmuted into fairytale perfection, where a spoilt society lady driving a gawky schoolgirl home through the sprawling suburbs becomes a fairy godmother transporting Cinderella through a world of magic:

> They had turned into South Head Road and were heading for the greater heights above the bay, whereon suburban roof-tops reared like ebony castles in a fairy tale against the shimmering gold of the peeping moon. And soon they reached that castellated crest, to glimpse the vast expanse of inky bay twinkling with the lights of shipping like sprinkled gems, then plunged, it seemed, into the very magic circle of the moon herself hanging ready to receive them.
>
> They went through the shopping-centre of Bayview Heights, skimming a golden highway flanked with shops with gilded windows.[35]

It was a difficult balancing act to maintain—between the mundane normality of 'the shopping centre of Bayview Heights' and the romance perfection of the 'magic circle of the moon' and the 'golden highway'. In *Soldiers' Women* such descriptions more often exasperate than entrance, but already the intention, if not the execution, is right. It is through heightened description that Herbert beckons us into the rarefied world of romance. It is a world where, as in traditional romance[36], the colour gold predominates: the golden moon, the golden highway, the gilded windows; Ida's children 'coming forth to greet the golden day' and opening 'the front door to let in a flood of gold, to see the sun leaping in golden flame'.[37] There is magic in this world. It is, at one and the same time, the world of wartime Sydney and the world of a Grimms fairytale. Pudsey is a Cinderella transformed for a time by the magic wand of the beauty parlour. There are chattering elves in the telephone static; the lighthouse makes oracular pronouncements. Ida, the fairy godmother, is also Ida the wicked witch, her familiar the cat whose carnal interest in her nakedness marks him as more than feline.[38] Like Snow White's stepmother, Ida's beauty masks a cruel heart: as her children burn to death, her face is 'scarce human: a mask of demoniac glee'.[39]

It was daring, this attempt to mix the nineteenth-century realism of Zola with the conventions of romance. It is no small matter to mix two such opposed genres. The conventions of extreme realism can so easily send romance toppling into the ridiculous. Ida's 'mask of demoniac glee', easy to accept within the conventions of a fairytale, strains credulity in the world of the novel. Our enjoyment of romance, writes Beer, 'depends upon our willing surrender. [...] The absurdities of romance are felt when we refuse to inhabit the world offered us and disengage ourselves, bringing to bear our own opinions'.[40] A book that keeps shifting between romance and realism is, by its nature, constantly 'disengaging' readers, constantly allowing them to 'bring their own opinions to bear'. Hence the peculiar difficulty of achieving, within such a text, that willing suspension of disbelief upon which success depends. The problem in *Soldiers' Women* was that Herbert had not yet found a way to solve this difficulty.

Another reason for the ineffectiveness of Herbert's use of romance in *Soldiers' Women* was his decision to link it with the negative rather than the positive. In *Capricornia* he had used anatomy for the negative, romance for the positive. Through the satiric conventions of anatomy, he poked fun at Capricornian folly, reinforcing the criticism through occasional use of the homiletic convention of symposium discussion. Meanwhile, through the progress and ultimate triumph of the romance hero, he expressed his faith in Australia's future. In *Poor Fellow My Country* the relationship between genres and didactic purpose is the same, though the balance within each genre has shifted. On the negative side, the balance has shifted towards the homiletics of anatomy; on the positive side, it has shifted from popular to high romance. In *Soldiers' Women* Herbert uses romance differently, mixing it with satire, and enlisting it on the side of the negative, not the positive. That not only deprives his positives of the enriching power of romance; it also works uncomfortably against his natural bent. His capacity for wonder was best suited to creating a world that really is golden, really is magical. In *Soldiers' Women* he is uneasily imprisoned in the role of cynical unbeliever. The golden world he creates is all pretence, a child's illusion. 'There are no enchanted cats, except in fairy tales. There is no enchantment anywhere, for grown-ups anyway.' The world of *Soldiers' Women* is 'only a mockery of fairyland'. Pudsey tries so hard to enter the world of her own fairy story, to become Cinderella to Ida's fairy godmother, but instead, 'slinking like the hunted criminal waif the processes of her destiny had made of her, she headed southward, carrying her golden shoes [...] a midnight-mooching Cinderella who had not caught the Prince's eye'.[41]

In *Soldiers' Women* 'Herbert the dreamer' has become 'Herbert the killjoy', pretending to create a golden world, only to rip the tinselled facade aside, revealing it as tawdry illusion, a painted curtain behind which stands a grubby reality peopled by tired, disgruntled actors. The seeming romance is nothing but a cruel joke: not a promise that dreams come true but a reminder that humans always and inevitably fall short of dreams. A typical episode begins with a vision of heroines sallying forth 'into the lovely world [...] breasting the tide of reality, their magic going before them to clear the way'. As 'blue-eyed shepherdess[es]', they are 'wooed' by 'Captains Perseus and Phaeton'. But then Herbert shatters the illusion:

> Paradise in pieces [...] vanished winged sandals, celestial
> aureoles, magic cloaks. Two coarse-voiced young men

were saying, 'That's us, sweethearts...gotta beat it. Nice
knowing you. So long!' The nymphs drooped heads
together in their weeping [and then went] out into the
world of work-a-day, of disappointment, lack-illusion,
love-lack.[42]

The bathos is deliberate and recurrent. When Ida and Bill seek 'a
corner in which to yearn together undisturbed by the rest of the rude
world [...] it seemed by their expression that they'd escaped from
others, were beyond reach on the dewy arch of a rainbow'. But then
'the crude rude world rushed in to bump buttocks again with them.
There again were Dolph and Pudsey [...] hepping madly'.[43] In
Soldiers' Women the crude, rude world always does come rushing in,
bumping its buttocks against the dewy rainbow. Romance has
become a satiric tool, mock-heroic instead of heroic. And what suits
a cynical intellectual like Pope does not suit an enthusiast like
Herbert.

In *Poor Fellow My Country* the world of romance is created as
a dream to believe in. It is set within the 'realistic' world of everyday
Australia, but the drab reality of that world is unable to destroy the
nobler reality of Prindy and Rifkah and Bobwirridirridi. In *Soldiers'
Women* things are different. Under the facade of romance, pessimism reigns. Grandma Fry seeks 'to make the world of grown-ups
abandon alcoholic illusions for the stark misery of the reality of their
mostly negative existence'.[44] Felicia and her boyfriend drive

down through the mean world of shuttered houses wherein
bonded wifes [sic] dreamed of love's perfection beside their
lords snoring in the pig's clover of satisfactory conjugal
rights, down to the sea-shore whence the silver flood of this
night's tidal fullness had ebbed to leave stinking slime for
the minutely monstrous matings of the crabs.[45]

Like Webster, Herbert in *Soldiers' Women* 'sees the skull beneath the
skin'.[46] 'How different', moralises killjoy Herbert, 'was [Ida and Bill's]
return journey, in the harsh light of day with the reality of what
they'd dreamt of riding with them like a grinning skeleton!' 'Hell is

not beyond the grave', glooms the lighthouse, 'but here in life where humans vie in their stupid arrogance'.[47]

The problem with turning the dreams of romance into Jacobean nightmares was that pessimism was foreign to Herbert's nature. He did not write well when he allowed it sway. His nature was hopeful: his dreams were real dreams, not nightmares; his inspiration optimistic. *Poor Fellow My Country*, he once said, was

> essentially the reconjuring of the Dream, for all its irony, mockery, bitterness in expression of utter failure [I have a] hope of a miracle that I may be able to work by the depth of my feeling. [...] If only I can do what I strive for...to make my fellows realize that there is truly a place called Terra Australis del Espiritu Santo, and that it can by the perfection of its people become the example of the perfection that can be mankind.[48]

Though there was a part of Herbert reminiscent of Swift's 'saeva indignatio', it needed to be balanced by the part that believed passionately in the wonder of existence. Where that was absent, his fiction faltered.

A further unhappy result of his decision to stress the pessimistic was that, thwarted in one direction, his passion for the wondrous bursts out in other and, for his novel, dangerous directions. He is too often seduced, despite his opposite intention, into seeing the trivial and the tawdry through the transforming prism of romance. Dressing for a party, for instance, is described thus:

> Last phase of the exciting business began at sunset, when the bay was a lilac lake low over which hung the golden moon at fullest promise. This was the dressing-up, a slow process for all the trembling eagerness with which it was undertaken, rather an evolution, from the simplicity of scantiest slips of silken underwear into the complex gorgeousness that, when presented to others of the household, caused eyes to pop as if at the appearance of a brace of fairy queens.[49]

Herbert's innate romanticism betrays him. He cannot help joining in. When he talks of 'the exciting business', we can hear that he really does find it exciting. And the reader does not. All too often in *Soldiers' Women*, though the aim is mock-heroic and the intention to expose meretricious lives, Herbert enters too wholeheartedly into the description, and the writing suffers. Herbert was an enthusiast, a dreamer, a lover of the wondrous, and when the subject is right his descriptions can soar and uplift. Descriptions such as the one just quoted don't soar—they gush. It was one of the least happy results of *Soldiers' Women*, the gushing tone that was one of its by-products and that reappears, too often for comfort, in *Poor Fellow My Country*.

Herbert's thwarted romanticism bursts out, in *Soldiers' Women*, in one other direction—with happier results this time. The lush writing that is simply embarrassing when used to describe the world of fashion has a genuinely powerful effect when applied to the reverse side of romanticism. Easily the most successful scenes in *Soldiers' Women*, the ones that remain quite powerfully in the memory, are scenes of Gothic horror. Rosa 'sprawled with blood oozing from broken nose and mouth, snoring for breath' after a vicious beating. Felicia's drowned corpse, 'the glassy golden right eye wink[ing] alone […] the left eye […] gone to the fishes'. And, most memorable of all, the scene in which Fay, tricked into eating corrosive poison, retches her life away, 'gasping, gurgling, clutching at throat and stomach', 'reeling away to the bathroom' to emerge 'with ropes of bloody vomit hanging from her gaping mouth'.[50]

The final reason for the failure of *Soldiers' Women*'s romance is that Herbert was over-conscious of the allegorical meaning he sought to convey. In the best allegories the relationship of plot to thesis is organic. The writer sets a plot in motion in order to explore a thesis, but once in motion the thesis develops in tandem with the plot, neither dominating or dictating to the other. This is what happens in *Poor Fellow My Country*. The relationships between Prindy, Rifkah and Delacy are set in motion in order to set the allegory in motion, but both plot and allegory swiftly move beyond the control of Herbert's conscious mind. The characters develop in the ways his intuition tells him they must, and, as they develop, allegorical meanings also grow, in a rich, living complexity beyond anything Herbert's conscious mind could ever have created.

In *Soldiers' Women* the created world and its allegorical meaning are not in a relationship of productive equality. Plot and character are here subordinate to thesis. The result is an allegorical meaning that is unambiguous and characters who, rather than growing beyond their author's original conception, continue, in their wooden fashion, to follow his dictates and exemplify his thesis. Unenriched by a developing plot and characters, the thesis is constrained by the intellectual limitations of Herbert's conscious mind. Obedient to the demands of the thesis, the characters are puppets dancing to a very limited tune, the strings manipulating them all too evident. An obvious example is the scene in which Ida attempts to seduce Leon. At first it seems she will succeed, 'the warmth of desire darkening his skin and lighting his eye'. But then, writes Herbert, Leon 'frowned, turned away sharply. [...] Then as suddenly he turned back, with a new expression, eagerness, in which for a moment he studied her face intently. "I'm an artist of sorts. Would you let me do your portrait?"'[51] The sudden switch from lustful male to dedicated artist is psychologically unconvincing. It occurs because Herbert is less interested here in getting the characterisation right than in illustrating part of his thesis, that it is wrong for women to use sex to gain mastery over man and right for men to sublimate sexual desire into worthy creative endeavour.

Though Herbert's attempt at allegorical romance in *Soldiers' Women* has to be judged a failure, there was at least one pointer towards what he would later achieve. It came, significantly, in descriptions of the character most clearly exemplifying the positive. Throughout the novel Selina, allegorically the good, nurturing mother, is described in emblematic passages full of soft browns, moonlight, children and animals:

> [Selina] went with haste, like a brown and white lady-bird out late and fearful for her children at home. [...] Her dog, trotting beside her, cocked his wise old head as if trying to divine what she was thinking: and her patroness the moon seemed to come closer to offer counsel. Her cats

went leaping on before, to be sitting on the gateposts of
home to greet her.[52]

In descriptions like this, Herbert comes closer than anywhere else in
Soldiers' Women to creating a real sense of the world of romance. It is
through Selina, too, that, if only in the final pages of the novel, his
allegorical writing becomes more successful. Selina is returning home.
She had planned to turn her back, for a time, on the responsibilities of
maternity. She gets as far as the ferry boat, which would have taken her
to Leon and a clandestine love affair, but finds, at the last moment, that
her sense of morality will not let her do it. She tells the taxi driver to
take her home. And so to the concluding paragraphs:

> As they entered Marine Parade, beyond Fry's foundry, to
> run southward beside the sea they could see the S.S.
> *Zephyr* skimming on her wanton way over the dancing
> blue. Selina looked beyond the ship, to its destination,
> New Sorrento, a blur of red and white and silver in noon-
> day mirage: or was it tears that made the blur. Her cherry
> lips moved in soft utterance:
>
> 'Good-bye...dear American soldier!'
>
> Then she turned the way they were going, towards
> reality, blinked away her tears, got out her compact.
>
> Soon they were through the tunnel at the foot of
> Tumbledown Stairs and bowling along Bayview Terrace,
> now out of sight of the sea. They came back into sight of
> it as they passed the samphire-bright escarpment below
> which lay Shellybeach: a charred shell about heaped rusty
> rubbish that had been its luxury, a ruined castle of which
> a squatting ginger cat was king.
>
> Then they were at Silvery Waters, where on the gate-
> posts sat her own cats as if expecting her, and her dog
> came up roaring to pop his great head over the gate and
> laugh for the joy of seeing her. She entered her gate,
> looked down upon the familiar scene, not seeming to see
> what lay beyond, the shimmering sea-scape with far-away
> places beckoning, looked down clear-eyed upon her

queendom. She went down the zig-zag steps with her frolicking menagerie, in by the fluted door that could put on illusion of magic, into the quiet reality of her existence.

But it was not quiet at the moment. From the kitchen sounded a tintinnabulation that could only be Sausage banging her battered dinner-plate with her spoon to show that she had had enough of what was being fed to her.

Sure enough, Sausage was at table, sitting in her high-chair, still wearing the saucy chignon over an ear, now with chin and bib well decorated with dribble and the remains of lunch. She saw her mother at the door, whooped, sent spoon and plate flying, held out her arms, crying, 'Mummy...Mummy!'

Selina swooped on her, lifted her from the chair, hugged and kissed her, dirty face and all, whispering, 'My beautiful...my baby!'[53]

While falling far short of the romance in *Poor Fellow My Country*, this is richer than Herbert's writing elsewhere in *Soldiers' Women*. Analysis of its effects is harder: there is more going on beneath the surface. His love of the wondrous lifts him; his sensitivity to symbol allows him to suggest in three pictures more than he states in three hundred words elsewhere. The equivocal nature of a love relationship with Leon is explored through the oppositions set up as 'Zephyr', 'skimming' and 'dancing blue' clash gently with 'wanton' and come to rest against 'blur' and 'mirage'. The implications of her decision are softly implied as she 'bowls along' but 'now out of sight of the sea'. Part of her reason for rejecting Leon is seen in the 'ruined castle' that resulted from Ida's sins. And finally the more positive reasons for choosing as she did are exemplified in two vignettes: the first, her entrance, welcomed by animals, and looking down on 'the familiar scene'; the second, Sausage, symbol of 'the quiet reality of her existence', noisily banging on a battered dinner-plate, whooping and dribbling and sending spoon and plate flying. It is an earnest of Herbert's greater success at this point that he comfortably incorporates the excessively mundane within the glow of romance. It is still a long way from the Australian idyll of Prindy and Rifkah but it is a start.

CHAPTER 8

Curiouser and Curiouser:
The Style Thickens

O F all the things Herbert did in the fifties, none was stranger than the way he tampered with his prose style. He did so, he said, in response to critics of *Capricornia* who suggested he should 'overcome [his] pedestrianism by emulating the passionate originality of Thomas Wolfe', and 'curb [his] prolixity by study of that master of succinctness, our own Cecil Mann'.[1] It was not good advice. *Capricornia*'s style was not pedestrian, and its wordiness was an important part of its effect. Unfortunately, Herbert had neither the confidence to reject the advice altogether nor the ability to respond to it sensibly. Focusing solely on the charge that really rankled—'pedestrianism'—he decided to do something 'original' simply for the sake of it. The fact that what he decided to do actually increased 'prolixity' to a point where it really did become a problem escaped his notice, so fixated was he on the simplistic notion that 'novelty equalled originality' and 'originality equalled literary quality'. 'I couldn't copy anyone', he later said. 'To do so would be to betray unoriginality, the first attribute [sic] to literary distinction. So I invented a syntax of my own. I reckoned that that, if nothing else, would win me recognition for literary genius.'[2]

It was actually more a method of punctuation than a syntax that he invented, but it certainly had effects (all of them bad) on his syntax. The idea was to limit himself to one sentence per paragraph and, within that sentence, to indicate breaks with a new punctuation mark of his own invention—the 'double dot'. Semicolons were abolished altogether. Commas and colons were allowed but used sparingly. The all-too-predictable result was a series of very long sentences and a prose style that was ponderous and unwieldy, as the following paragraph, from the first edition of *Seven Emus*, demonstrates:

> It was from what Goborrow confided to the local low-brows in those bouts of boozy condescension that it became generally understood that there is more to anthology [sic] than mere study of man . . it seeming that field surveys such as Goborrow's study of the Tjingali tribe might not be made so much with the simple impersonal motive of acquiring knowledge as with the very personal one of collecting, first of all material for writing a thesis that would get the collector his Master's degree or doctorate, and then a swag of primitive implements and works of art for presentation to the anthropological museums of such universities as favoured him, universities abroad, of course, since one must get out of this colonial dump, where appreciation was limited to sport, to have one's special qualities appreciated . . therefore, possessed of a novel bit of ethnological material, the doctorate, and the swag, one wrote away to universities in other English-speaking countries, describing one's discoveries, letting it be known that one was about to travel abroad and would not be averse to giving a series of lectures, not forgetting to mention the swag . . this matter of contributing to the treasures of anthropological museums of universities being of first importance, particularly when dealing with those of the U.S.A. which set much more store on what is called visual education—'Hence the comic strip!' as Goborrow was wont to say with a high-brow's smirk.[3]

It is hard, at first, to believe that Herbert changed his style for change's sake, simply to achieve 'originality', but all the evidence points that way. He did, after the event, attempt to justify the changes on aesthetic grounds, saying things like, 'A paragraph consist[ed] of an entity of the whole composition that was self-contained and hence could have but one initial capital and one concluding stop' and 'I believed that by my system emotion could be better expressed than with the conventional which would demand conventional reading'.[4] But the tone of the following explanation, given in 1970, suggests that the real reason for change had nothing to do with aesthetics, everything to do with pleasing the critics:

> *Seven Emus* was an experiment with Style. All around me were the Stylists, being patted on the head, while I was being ignored as Pedestrian (actual Critic's word). It was also an experiment with sentence construction. What is a Sentence? What is Punctuation? Why use a Semicolon (which is an ugly thing) when you can use a Colon, which has symmetry? Why use a full stop in a Paragraph at all? Why not write in Lines, as in poetry—all that sort of thing.[5]

The dismissive tone of 'all that sort of thing' makes it clear how unimportant to him were these rationalisations. It was being 'ignored' that rankled, and the whole point of the 'experiment' was to prove himself a 'Stylist'.

The first test of his new style came with the publication of *Seven Emus*. So adverse was the reaction, Herbert allowed Beatrice Davis to restore *Soldiers' Women* and subsequent editions of *Seven Emus* to more normal punctuation, though still insisting on 'no semicolons'. The humour and good sense of her response highlight the naivety of his thinking:

> I shall not insert *one* semicolon, in view of your objection to this, I am sure, well-meaning little symbol, but I shall try to get rid of the *two* dots wherever possible, using colons or dashes where they will fit, and the normal *three*

dots for pauses and hesitations. Why not? There is no need to be deliberately different, since all good punctuation is completely unnoticeable by the reader anyhow.[6]

The two dots were mere affectation, easily rectified. Sentence structure was less easily restored. With the change to paragraph-long sentences, the Augustan balance of *Capricornia* was replaced by the heavy pomposity of passages like the following from 'The Little Widow':

Why did that man, who of all others was moved to broach to me the subject of my puberty, not pursue it, not explain to me that shortly my entire being would be changed by the progeneration of a new dynamic, a volcanic potential that with its violence was going to bewilder me, stupefy me, distort me, even perhaps destroy me, that certainly was going to torture me as nothing before in my life had or ever would again, unless I recognised it for what it was, understood that it was the burgeoning of masculinity, of the primary force in the second great urge to existence, propagation of species, the same that caused the savage, street-rutting of dogs, that would cause a man himself to rut like a dog unless he exerted that self-control which differentiates him from the animals, which he is bound to exert since so bidden by the precepts of his noble kind, on pain of being classed an animal and put away, but which he should first *want* to exert by reason of his human dignity, which indeed he must learn to exert for the joy in the courage it takes, all the courage a man has, so that half-men only half-exert and cancel out the man-purpose which each seeks in his fullness in brave endeavour, unless I understood that in Nature it is only complete males who are the propagators, the sires of the next generation to which for the purpose of never-ending advance of species every generation is dedicated, but the immature gain in the general striving, their easement expended energy, their fulfilment increased stature, that herein lies the means of a boy's acquittal of himself in the ordeal of puberty with the dignity and premium that should be his, since the force is essentially physical, it may be spent in physical exertion and turned to account as visible achievement.[7]

The first thing one notices about this, apart from the sheer length of the sentence, is its excessive use of subordinate clauses. The penchant for clausal complexity was not a wholly new thing. Already in *Capricornia* we find Herbert using clumsy double and triple negatives such as: 'Not that Lace did not respect her nor feel concerned about the burden that so angrily she often told him he had thrust upon her'.[8] In *Capricornia*, too, there are confusing, albeit syntactically pure, uses of the relative pronoun such as: 'Miss Carrie Oats, holidaying niece of the Government Secretary, promise of conjugality with whom had made thoughts of going combo baser still'.[9] From the start, Herbert had favoured an old-fashioned ornateness in clausal construction. What prevented this preference becoming a problem in *Capricornia* was the control he imposed through judicious use of balanced structures and short sentences:

> That it was swollen much above Dry-Season volume was apparent, as also that the volume had increased through comparatively light showers that had fallen in the last two days. This much he realized. What he did not realize was the river's capability of swelling rapidly and mightily. He could not have realized the rapidity without seeing it for himself; but he might have understood its potentiality for rising mightily if he had studied the scored and snag-littered bed of the grassy spaces flanking it.[10]

The first sentence seems headed for disaster, but is rescued by the quite complex yet unobtrusive way Herbert balances and links the remaining sentences. Only occasionally, in *Capricornia*, does he lose control, and then it is we get a taste of what the future will bring:

> Oscar was soon moved to consider quitting the rather
> poor bachelor-quarters in which they had been placed
> and taking a bungalow such as married officers occupied,
> with a view not nearly so much to making himself more
> comfortable as to advancing himself socially and in the
> Service by getting into a position in which he could
> entertain his superiors as they now condescended to
> entertain him.[11]

The balance of the middle clauses here is not enough to save a
sentence whose beginning and end ramble. In *Capricornia* these
occasional lapses are the exception; in the style of the fifties they
have become the norm.

The second thing one notices about the new style is its use of
the hackneyed tricks of political rhetoric. There is excessive use of
parallel structures ('bewilder me, stupefy me, distort me [...] destroy
me'). There is much apposition ('the primary force [...] propagation
of species'; 'the propagators, the sires of the next generation'). And
there is a preference for pompous over simple vocabulary ('progeneration', 'burgeoning', 'easement'). One can make a case for this
type of prose when it is used, as it is in *Seven Emus*, for mock-heroic
effect. But even in that book Herbert seems dangerously enamoured
of pomposity for pomposity's sake: as when he writes, for instance,
that the sound of a car disturbs 'the gently sonant quietude of this
backwater of frustration' and when he describes Goborrow as
'captain from the beginning despite apparent equipollence'.[12] In
Soldiers' Women the ponderous style is even more obtrusive. Again
it is sometimes used for mock-heroic comment. But whereas
Capricornia's irony prompts favourable comparison with Swift and
Austen, the mock-heroic in *Soldiers' Women* leaves one longing for
the defter touch of Pope[13]:

> Thence unto fashion's temple, into the holy calm, the
> silence, the shadeless brilliance, the redolence of new-
> spun cloth and naphthalene: one to enter with the mien
> of pious communicant, the other with proselyte's wide-
> eyed awe: both soft-footed on crimson pile, being

multiplied in mirrors and mingled therein with other devotees and black-clad priestesses.

At last the high-priestess came to them, prim, spare, black brooding eyes, nose like a cherry, corrugated lip. She looked not at their faces but their dress, dismissed the proselyte's with a terrible glance, eyed the communicant's moss jersette as if looking at some sacrilegious usage.[14]

If only the heaviness was limited to such overtly mock-heroic passages! It isn't. It pervades the book. Herbert has become incapable of straightforward description of even the simplest things. Drinking a milkshake becomes 'satisfying gastronomic greed [...] with the essentially infantile [practice] of gorging milk-concoctions'. The taste of a hamburger becomes the 'insidious alliaceousness [that] can seduce all but saints and the worst dyspeptics'.[15] In *Capricornia* Herbert's word choice is deft and witty. In *Soldiers' Women* he simply opts for the most ponderous available. It comes as no surprise to learn that in 1940 he borrowed a friend's dictionary with the intention of adding twenty words a day to his vocabulary.[16]

The negative effects of Herbert's ill-conceived experiment in style remained for the rest of his writing career. He acquired habits too deep to be wholly eradicated and the results are seen, in *Poor Fellow My Country*, in sentences that seem sometimes to move backwards rather than forwards, as clause follows clause, qualification follows qualification, before, finally, he remembers to get to the point.

> When Mr Eddy McCusky told Prindy and his mother that he would be seeing them tomorrow, as he did when greeting them on New Year's Day, he was not being merely boozily patronising to people who, because he was officially responsible for them, might, by such as he, be thought to feel in need of his patronage, as soon revealed. [...] As things turned out, Mr Turkney had them, as he put it himself when driven at last to complain about his superior's inordinate failure to comply with what he had committed himself to, not merely in

hand but *on his hands* for three full days of waiting, on
each of which McCusky had declared by telephone that
he would be along as soon as he got things sorted out.
Probably it wouldn't have mattered so much to Turkney,
surely used to having people on his hands, since the
population of the Compound ran into hundreds, had it
not been raining hard during those three days, and the
man, being told to have the pair on hand and not being
completely heartless and having no other handy shelter
for them, had been compelled to have them close
enough to be irritated by their presence—by their
windging [sic], as he called it, because they naturally
grew irritable hanging about.[17]

Here, as in the fifties, Herbert overuses subordinate phrases and
clauses to the point that sentences become tiresome to the ear and
confusing to the mind. How confusing they can become is illustrated
by the following, in which all but the most alert of readers may find
themselves wondering why the termite nests are called 'Ant Beds'
everywhere except along the creek-bank:

The sandstone of the locality, projection of a distant Plateau
to be just glimpsed through the ragged open forest to
northward, and the dark red sandy soil and forest, soon
gave way to grey plain with meaner growth and a
profusion of small spiked termites' nests, or Ant Beds, as
called in these parts, except along the creek-bank, where
water gums and coolibahs and the like grew stoutly despite
the dryness that would obtain for most of the year.[18]

Herbert's decision to tamper so drastically and foolishly with
the style that had served him so well in *Capricornia* is, at first sight,
perplexing. Why, when his first novel had been very well received,
was he so badly affected by a few negative comments? Why, when
he had always claimed to scorn academic critics, was he prepared to
make such radical changes simply in order to win their favour? And
why, when he did make changes, did he make such silly changes?

The answers to the first two questions lie in the circumstances of his early life.

As we have already seen, from the beginning Herbert had felt rejected and undervalued. Had he been born with a more confident streak, the effects of his parents' perceived rejection might have been different. As it was, his sense of self-worth and confidence both suffered. He felt 'doomed to be a fool at everything [he] did'. At school he 'quickly became one of its prize dunces, and remained so for the length of [his] mostly wretched term there'. He was unfortunate in his teachers, one of whom, called Grassopple in *Disturbing Element*, beat him unmercifully and publicly humiliated him by putting up a list headed 'Mental Defectives' containing only three names, Herbert's being one.[19]

They explain much, these early experiences. They left Herbert with a burning desire to 'prove them wrong', and, more than that, to get 'them' to admit they were wrong. 'What made me, who hated school from the first day, stick at it so long and unnecessarily', he later said, 'was some sort of complex engendered by dear old Mr Grassopple's declaration of me as mentally defective'.[20] Describing his feelings on being accepted by Melbourne University, he writes, 'I had come all the way a schoolkid had to, under the lash of the cane and of my own self-doubting […] I had arrived!'[21] This was not the first time he felt he 'had arrived'; nor would it be the last. The phrase occurs again and again in *Disturbing Element*. He 'had arrived' when he got his first job; he 'had arrived' when he was accepted into a Christian Brothers' College; and he 'had arrived' when a middle-class friend invited him home for the first time.[22] Each arrival he hoped would be 'the' arrival, the one that would establish him unequivocally in the eyes of the world. The trouble was that no success is ever as unqualified as Herbert needed. There is always someone who criticises. Thus it was that each success turned sour on him, leaving his uncertainties to fester. 'Although I went on to university', he wrote:

> it seemed only to be an amazing series of flukes, as if the few things my half-wit intelligence could grasp of a particular subject were always set at the examinations I sat for. At least that was the impression I was given by my

teachers and other superior people with whom I rubbed shoulders.[23]

It is in this context that we can begin to understand Herbert's response to *Capricornia*'s reception. When, to his 'joyful astonishment', the book won the Literary Society's Gold Medal, he was determined to 'make the most of my first achievement, my great victory, my laurel-getting'. At last, it seemed, he really had 'arrived'. Surely there could be no question of it this time. This would finally show all the Grassopples. But again he wanted too much and again the result was, in his eyes, another failure:

> The teachers and the editors and the critics and my own literary mentors turned up in force and told the crowd that I had not passed on my merits at all, that it was a fluke again, that the book had attracted attention only because of its controversial nature, that in fact it was the biggest botch that had ever come into prominence in Aus[tralian] Letters.[24]

The reversion to the language of the schoolroom is significant. 'I had not passed on my merits.' We can hear all the old hurts rising up again. Though for a first novel *Capricornia* was a great success, was widely praised and had won a prize, none of that was enough. Because no praise is ever total. There will always be qualifications, and in those qualifications, however small, Herbert heard the voice of Grassopple.

'There are two types [of novelists],' Herbert once wrote, 'those who want to overcome their self-doubting with a Litt.D.(Hons.) and those incorrigibles like myself'.[25] The claim is not borne out by the facts. The real truth was that, far from being one of the 'incorrigibles', Herbert took every opportunity that offered to angle for honorary doctorates.[26] For all his disclaimers, he was as eager as anyone for marks of critical recognition and was quick to resent perceived slights. Take, for instance, his response to Manning Clark's letter of condolence on the death of Sadie. The subject was purely personal; the intention sympathetic; the response—bitter!

> It is a curious thing that these flattering posts of yours
> invariably follow some dissertation, either in writing or
> speech, in which you have dealt with Australian history
> and those who have had a special part in it particularly in
> writing but never, never, never with a mention of me. As
> I feel sure that you don't incline to insincerity ever since
> 1978 (before which I had assumed that you were part of
> that large band of Aust. Literati whose opinion of me was
> aptly summed up by one of them thus: 'Herbert has
> genius, Don't give me the shits!') [...] Thank you again for
> your clever little pretences.[27]

Nothing rankled more than that comment, made by someone early in
Herbert's career—'Herbert has genius? Don't give me the shits'. It
appears again and again in his letters. Incensed at one point, for
instance, by a perceived slight from Patrick White, he responded
thus:

> My first novel CAPRICORNIA which for all its faults (and it
> has so many that long ago I repudiated it as 'my Bastard
> Son') is an Australian 'Classic' [...] The repudiation of it as
> such by the Literati in the past was generally with the
> expression 'Don't give me the shits!' [...] If you don't
> accept me as a sensitive and talented novelist then you
> are either an ignoramus (ignorant of my work) or a
> ponderous ass. I'm pretty sure you are amongst the legion
> to whom I give the shits.[28]

This is not the letter of a man loftily above the response of the
establishment but one obsessed by its injustice to him. If he railed
at the literary establishment for most of his life, it was because, for
most of his life, it refused him the acclamation he desperately
wanted.

The difference between real unconcern for the plaudits of
the academy and Herbert's pretended unconcern is seen in an ex-
change of letters between Herbert and Patrick White following the
publication of *Poor Fellow My Country*. Revelling in the favourable

attention he was at last getting from at least some academics, Herbert had written to enlist White's support for the literary journal edited by his foremost supporter. White replied coolly:

> Years ago I saw a couple of issues of *Australian Literary Studies* and found them full of the most futile kind of academic cerebrations. I can't see that its death would be a great loss [...] I must say I am astonished at your reverence for the Australian academics. With a few exceptions they are a sterile lot.[29]

It had, of course, never been their sterility that bothered Herbert but their failure to acknowledge his worth. Now that some at least were doing so, he could not speak highly enough of academics. In his reply he described one of them thus:

> I was astounded by the man's sheer dedication to his task and the love he showed for both work and author. Again there was this warmth and homage in the discussion.[30]

Capitulation to the old enemy is complete. 'Homage'—that was what he could not resist. The force of his scorn was seen now for what it had always been: a serious case of sour grapes. Easy enough, Herbert must have thought, for Nobel laureate White to scorn the establishment. For Herbert, the fruits he had for so many years desired were irresistible. He did his best to pretend unconcern, but he knew the pretence had become threadbare. Writing to White from Queensland University, he says:

> From the heading you will judge me incorrigible. However it's God's truth I tried to get out of it [...] Unfortunately as I am by nature something of a creep (wanting to be friendly with people rather than otherwise) I didn't do much of a job of it. [...] I have to go South towards the end of the month to be embarrassed by awards I'd rather be without.[31]

The shows of reluctance could not hide a reality plain to see. Tiring of the charade, White, some years later, wrote a letter blunt enough to sting Herbert into the following response:

> You begin your tirade by saying that I amaze you for calling myself a revolutionary—'When here you are sucking up to the establishment and accepting honorary doctorates' [...] Despite my acceptance by people like Harry Hesseltine, Laurie Hergenhan, Ken Goodwin, I did not ever acknowledge their existence until finally I was thrust into their company. Such a one for 'sucking-up' to established folk am I.[32]

But White was right. For all his protestations, Herbert was one for 'sucking up'. The pattern was again set early, in response to the first group that rejected him. It was the coping mechanism he developed in response to family rejection that provided the model for his later response to literary critics. Desperate for acceptance, young Herbert fell into a pattern of behaviour he later described thus: 'I mostly truckled to them. The very inconsistency of mostly truckling and then of blazing into indignation when my humility was too grossly taken advantage of was surely cause for misunderstanding and strife'.[33] Outside the home, too, this mixture of 'truckling' and 'indignation' became, for Herbert, the norm when faced by rejection.[34] It was wholly natural, therefore, for him to kiss the rod in an attempt to placate his critics and then blaze into indignation when they did not respond favourably.

All this explains Herbert's attempts to win critics over in the fifties by giving them what he thought they wanted. It does not explain why he so badly misjudged what they did want. There were a number of reasons. First, his thinking was less than profound—on writing as on everything else. Had it not been so, he would have based his experiment in style on more secure foundations than the simplistic equation 'novelty equals originality' and the spurious logic of 'a paragraph consisted of an entity of the whole composition that was self-contained and hence could have but one initial capital and one concluding stop'.

But if the fallibility of his thinking led to the misguided experiment, it was the fallibility of his taste that compounded the problem. Had his taste been more trustworthy, he would have recognised the negative effects of his experiment before too much harm had been done. But Herbert's taste was an unreliable guide. He found it very hard to distinguish between the good and the bad in his own work. 'The scene between Clancy and the fat Clerk of Courts is, I believe, a masterpiece'[35], he said on completing one of the less memorable scenes in *Poor Fellow My Country*. It was proof that he had 'arrived at the peak of [his] power'[36], he wrote of 'The Little Widow', undoubtedly the worst book he ever wrote. Such lack of critical judgment left him desperately vulnerable. Like a famous chef with atrophied tastebuds and no sense of smell, he never knew whether the next banquet would receive five stars or end up in the bin. The mixed reaction to *Capricornia* left him 'utterly confused about the value of the book...called botch by this one and a masterpiece by that one'. The adverse reaction to his experiment with style left him even more confused.[37] His confidence, already shaken, received the final devastating blow when he submitted 'The Little Widow' for publication. This was the book he thought would prove his genius beyond doubt. To be told that Angus & Robertson would publish if he insisted but that its poor quality would damage his reputation was the last straw.[38] Outright rejection would have been less humiliating. His confidence in tatters, he wrote sadly back to Beatrice Davis:

> It took me a good fifteen years to get over the [*Capricornia*] failure. [...] I knew all the while that the test would be with ['The Little Widow']. I kept saying to Sadie that if it was acceptable I had arrived at the peak of my power [...] no, what am I talking about. I simply said that I could have 'arrived'.

Again that phrase. How important it is to him. It is acknowledgment he wants. Without it, he sees no point continuing:

> I can't go on with it. [...] I've just failed to do what I wanted to do in respect of being a big fellow. I'm only a

little fellow. [...] I don't [want] to write any more. [...] I guess I could only write one book, the thing I despise, the old botch of my youth.[39]

The decade ended with Herbert in total confusion. He had done everything he could to win the critics over, to prove he could write proper 'literature'. He had sacrificed on the altar of their taste his first child, *Capricornia,* learning to call it 'my bastard son' and 'botch', hastening always to be first to speak of its 'many faults'. He had laboured for years to write a novel that would please the critics; and not only did they reject it but, adding insult to injury, they compared it unfavourably to *Capricornia.* How galling must have been the following well-meant and kindly advice from Tom Inglis Moore, a critic who had always treated Herbert's work sympathetically:

> You should never have believed the silly coots who said *Capricornia* was badly written. [...] It was a bloody tragedy that you laboured to change your style into something which didn't fit your natural gifts. [...] You ask what in the hell is 'literature'. The answer is easy, old man— *Capricornia!*[40]

The following, from novelist Hugh Atkinson, must have been equally frustrating:

> In your letter you spoke about the difficulty of knowing where 'originality' lies. [...] I think the great writer is great because of his *attitude,* the sensitivity of which he is capable—the style is the sport of the moment, the fashion or the unfashion. You made the mistake of listening to the pundits and trying to write it out their way.[41]

The only thing wrong with these eminently sensible pieces of advice is their blame of 'the pundits'. The 'silly coot' was Xavier Herbert, not the critics.

Flawed as his own judgment was, it would have helped if Herbert had been able to make effective use of the judgment of others. If only, instead of reacting irrationally to critics, he had been able to listen sensibly to the advice of the people who could have helped him—his editors, for instance! Unfortunately, while his early experiences made him abnormally sensitive to criticism and desperately keen to get critics 'on side', they also, paradoxically, made it almost impossible for him to take advice from those who were already on his side. He hated to be questioned, was easily offended, and took adverse comments very personally.[42] Not surprisingly, he was an impossibly difficult writer to edit effectively.

The problem was that any suggestion for improvement involved criticism, and Herbert simply could not take criticism, however tactfully offered. His response was always extreme, his morbid sensitivity making him see suggestions from editors as personal attacks. No-one was kinder, more patient, more helpful, and more churlishly rewarded than Angus & Robertson's Beatrice Davis. Throughout the difficult birth pains of *Soldiers' Women*, she was enormously supportive. When, after reading the completed manuscript, she had to tell him it could not be published as it stood, she did so as gently as possible. First she sent him a personal letter in which she mixed praise with gentle analysis, doing her very best to soften the blow.[43] She followed this up three days later with an official letter in which she dealt with specific weaknesses such as:

> The details about clothes [...] become extremely tedious.
> [...] Repetition of the features and appearance of the
> characters is overdone. [...] The overwriting and carica-
> ture seem often in bad taste [...] the heavy satire, the
> grandiose phrases sometimes exaggerated to the point of
> artificiality.[44]

All valuable criticisms—if only Herbert could have treated them objectively. He couldn't. To him the letter was a treacherous, personal attack. His reply opened with all guns blazing:

> How am I to approach you now that I find there are two of
> you, Beatrice my Patroness, who taught me to fear the

criticism of none, and Miss Davis the Editress, who presents
me with four close typed pages of tabulated contempt.[45]

Tactful, kind, constructive and accurate though her comments were, to Herbert they were simply a personal attack—four
pages of tabulated contempt! He could not take, and did not want,
criticism, however constructive. What he wanted, as his books took
shape, was not the help of an astute reader but the support of an
uncritical admirer whose job was to believe in him, boost him with
praise, and give him the confidence to continue to the end. The role
of 'patron', as Herbert called it, was first played by Sadie when she
presided over the birth of *Capricornia*. He was never again to find
a patron so suited to his needs. Interested in Herbert, not literature,
she did not question his judgment on matters to do with his writing.
And that was important. The patron's task was to admire and
encourage, not criticise—which was what made Beatrice Davis's
task so hard. Herbert was happy for her to be 'my Patroness', but
she was paid by Angus & Robertson to edit, and as soon as she
tried to do so Herbert felt betrayed. His response was mean-spirited
and unjust. Unwilling to accept the message (that *Soldiers' Women*
and 'The Little Widow' were deeply flawed books), he preferred to
shoot the messenger. His later treatment of Beatrice was shameful.
When in 1973 Angus & Robertson sacked her after years of
dedicated service, he refused to join in contributing to a book of
personal tributes compiled by eighty-two of the authors she had
helped. When in 1974 *Poor Fellow My Country* was launched, he
publicly snubbed her by refusing to invite her to any of the
functions.[46] And when she responded with a letter telling him how
hurt she was by that treatment, his reply was unpleasant. 'What a
relief', he began, 'after all the years in which I've resented it as an
imperious imposition—not to receive that Xmas Card endorsed in
that female-spidery hand: Beatrice'.[47]

It was Beatrice Davis's misfortune that, of the four novels
Herbert wrote, she was stuck with the two bad ones, the ugly
ducklings that no editor, however good, could have turned into
swans. She could, though, have helped him make both books a lot
better if only Herbert had been willing to listen to constructive

criticism and advice. 'You are too much alone in your writing world', she counselled at one point

> and the taking of advice (if you do agree with it) can be a help—it certainly does not mean that you are relying on anyone else, or that the book that results will be anything but your own work.[48]

What sensible advice. But Herbert was incapable of taking it. And that was that. Other ways had to be found to avoid the problems of the fifties. What those ways were is the subject of the next chapter.

PART IV

POOR FELLOW
MY COUNTRY

CHAPTER 9

The Rule of Old Zave

AFTER the failures and disappointments of the fifties, it must have been hard for Herbert to nerve himself for another attempt, but in 1965 he was ready. On Tuesday 23 August his writing log contains the entry 'Yesterday marked the beginning of the book properly'.[1] The great work had begun. On 25 September he calculates, 'say I average 500 words a day, I have a book [of 150,000 words in] 300 days. It's thus about a year's work to do the first draft. So we can say this will take 18 months'.[2] How wrong he was. It was to take nine years and 850,000 words before 'the opus' was finally completed.

Considering the trouble he got into in the fifties, one might have expected Herbert to have sought advice early and often during the writing of *Poor Fellow My Country*. But no. He was, if anything, more determined than ever to take advice from no-one. No more would he submit work in progress to an editor. He would do his own thing without interference, and if critics and publishers did not like it at the end, so be it. He simply wrote on, year after year, with no-one but himself ever seeing what he had written. And as the years went by, and the book got longer and longer, he must sometimes have wondered whether he had got it right this time.

He was horribly vulnerable. He knew now how fallible his taste was. It had betrayed him in the fifties and could do so again. How could he be sure *Poor Fellow My Country* was not another 'Little Widow'? How could he be sure his delight in this most recent and lengthy of his works was not as misguided as the equal delight he had felt in the failed novels of the fifties? He could not be sure, and the closer he got to completion, the stronger must have become the fear of finding out. In late 1970, he expressed this fear to Laurie Hergenhan, an academic who, having recently won Herbert's trust and approval[3], was the first to be allowed to read the manuscript. 'This thing I'm doing could be a complete botch', he writes. 'My only real achievement may be *Capricornia* which I abominate myself.'[4] Hergenhan's response lifted a burden from Herbert's shoulders. He gave the novel an enthusiastic thumbs up, and Herbert was able to continue with renewed confidence. So happy was he that, overcoming his mistrust of editors, he suggested Hergenhan take on something of that role:

> I, who couldn't accept an independent editor, could accept a trusted person as co-editor. A great peace has descended on me—the effect of giving myself into your hands [...] I'm sure I shall express myself more naturally knowing that there is someone to check it whose understanding of my needs I can trust. The fear has gone out of me. I am saying to myself: This is the way I want to say it. If it's silly, L.H. will help me out.[5]

Why, one wonders, if it brought such peace now, had Herbert not sought this kind of help earlier? In the event, *Poor Fellow My Country* turned out well, but it seems, at first sight, the height of foolishness for him to have waited so long to confirm he was on the right track. However, behaviour that commonsense might judge foolish seems, in retrospect, to have been the right way for a writer with Herbert's particular strengths and weaknesses to get the best out of himself. The blocking of advice during the writing stage seems to have been an essential condition for his best work. He worked by instinct, and if that instinct played him false in the fifties, it was because he contaminated it in two ways: first, by paying attention to the advice of outsiders; and second, by listening to the advice of his own conscious mind. He wrote best when he shut his ears to both and listened instead only to the inner voice, the voice of his subconscious, the voice he called 'Old Zave'. While writing *Poor Fellow My Country*, Herbert always paid heed to that voice. And one thing it told him very firmly was to stop trying to direct and control the development of the story. One night, for instance, he dreams of an old man working in a pigeon loft:

> When he saw me he stood very still [...] I guessed it meant those inner processes of [mine], the subconscious self I call Old Zave [...] This was a good lesson in *Let it Do Itself*. The fact of seeing Old Zave stop and not budge while I was looking should teach me once and for all.[6]

To tap the wisdom of Old Zave, Herbert followed a writing routine whose effect was to shut down the conscious mind and allow the unconscious greater freedom to work. First came two or three miles of hard running. 'Running', he said, 'is a means of letting the psychic force outflow into consciousness'.[7] It induces 'a sort of trance-state in which I would have vision—word pictures—of what I wanted to do in the next session'.[8] 'It's during that exertion', he said, 'that I get the *inspiration* and at no other'.[9] Thus it was that when, one day, 'an idea began to form' as he was out driving in the mountains:

> I stopped at the first turn-off [...] Of course I must run to get my opening lines: So I changed into shorts and boots and ran—about 1½ [miles] while all the time the ideas gathered. When I got back to the car, it was all ready to jot down.[10]

It's a glorious picture. The great writer, driving along the road, suddenly feels a touch of inspiration coming on—too precious to waste, but impossible to use unless the proper method is followed. So. Off with the ignition. On with the running shorts. And the grand old man of Australian letters pounds up the road to get the subconscious working.

Running began the process. It gave access to the new creation forming beneath the level of conscious thought:

> All I've had to do is run a couple of miles and there it is, the gleaming thing, like an underground stream glimpsed for a moment in sunlight. Take the glimpse and put it into some rough order. Go to bed. Get up and cast it into gold.[11]

The purpose of going to bed, the next and perhaps most important part of the routine, was not to rest—but to dream. Ideas glimpsed during the running must be properly developed and that was a task beyond the conscious mind:

> It's the spell of subconscious gestation that's all important [...] You conceive the scene vaguely, might even seem to see it (mostly do) very vividly—but the facts of it will be blurred. You'll have characters acting out of character, saying the things they wouldn't. It has always to be slept on.[12]

It has always to be slept on because it has always to be dreamed on:

> Have [got] another short piece sketched, but can't say yet if I can do it. These things have to be dreamt over. Maybe after a little sleep at midday...don't usually have one but I've found they are productive when I do.[13]

Whenever he is not sure he is taking an episode in the right direction, or is uncertain how a particular character should behave, or when he simply runs out of ideas altogether, Herbert shuts down the workings of the conscious mind and leaves it to his dreams to work things out:

No taping this morning. Just couldn't think of an opening to the piece. Maybe it's too complicated for just barging into and has to be given a lot of dreaming over.[14]

And so, finally, to the writing. The subconscious has done its work. It's all there in the mind; all Herbert has to do is let it flow:

Again the miracle—so different from my conception of it yesterday. I did most of it [i.e. taping the next piece of the story] while walking about [...] making porridge [...] it is even good to have something to do with your hands while the stuff flows. Now to bed again to dream over the lovely thing some more.[15]

The guiding force of *Poor Fellow My Country* is not the planning of the conscious mind but the working of the subconscious. 'It is going *perfectly*', Herbert said early in 1968, 'by being left to do itself'.[16] Later that year he told Sadie, 'I never know, never will know *how* it works. It is enough to be blessed by its incessant *working*'.[17] About this aspect of his writing he is, at last, quite clear. He knows now what went wrong in the fifties. 'The Little Widow', he now sees, 'failed to get into print because it was the work of a man whose talent is expression of the exuberance of life trying to tie everything up tidily with simple meaning'.[18] He understands now the importance of bypassing his dangerously limiting reason and tapping the rich depths of his subconscious. 'Sometimes I wonder', he said, 'what I'm really "at". But it must be done the way the voice dictates, even if it has to be undone later'.[19] He records a typical day's work as 'lovely work (I think—I never read it over) and quite different from what I'd planned. That always amazes me. It seems as if a part of myself thinks the other part silly—quite right too'.[20] He understands now which is the wise, which the silly part, and though it is natural for the conscious mind to plan and organise, its planning must not now be allowed to interfere with the dictates of the wise part. The work must go in the direction Old Zave determines.

To prevent the meddling brain spoiling things, Herbert kept it on a tight rein. As he reflects on each day's writing, he can't help exploring the implications of the symbolism contained within the characters and events, but he knows it is dangerous. At one point he wonders 'if it will be spoilt [...] by my becoming conscious of what I am doing'.[21] At another he speaks of 'a feeling of being rushed along by the story' and says 'that is what I want at this juncture'.[22] His busybody mind must not, this time, be allowed to rationalise and turn complexity into simplistic moralising. On the character of Rifkah, for instance, he muses, 'I've given so much to this odd girl—why?' He embarks upon an answer, 'Of course as a symbol of woman', but then cuts himself short with a firm 'No don't let me analyse'.[23]

It helped that there was plenty to keep his conscious mind occupied. What Herbert called 'the tin-tacks of plotting'[24] was no simple task in a novel as long as *Poor Fellow My Country*. How to get Pat Hanahan involved in Rifkah's escape and then, his part played, how 'to get rid of him', since 'he isn't going to give Rifkah up easily'? How to provide dramatic interest during Rifkah and Clancy's trip to Darwin when their 'personal drama is something to be expressed only in silence, shyness, even bewilderment'?[25] How, also, to maintain consistency in a plot so long and complicated, written over so many years and subject to so many changes. 'Oh dear,' Herbert says at one point, 'so many irons in the fire!'[26] It didn't make things any easier that Old Zave's directions were not always clear. There were mis-readings of the oracle along the way, leading to wrong turnings and dead-ends.[27] There were also new insights, vouchsafed at later stages in the composition, that caused Herbert to 'go back and change everything done to fit what develops out of better understanding of the job as it progresses'.[28] Keeping track of all the changes and making sure that nothing in what had previously been written was inconsistent with the new vision must have become, as the book progressed in size, a more and more demanding task. It was a task Herbert fulfilled admirably. *Soldiers' Women*, he said, taught him how to plot a really long novel effectively, and the results are evident in *Poor Fellow My Country*. For a book so long, and written over so long a period, it is amazingly free from inconsistency and incredibility.[29]

As well as ensuring consistency and credibility, the time he had to spend sorting out 'the tin-tacks of plotting' kept the prosing old bore who ruled Herbert's head busy enough to prevent him interfering in the deeper levels of the creative process. That left Old Zave free to give the really important directions, and it was under his guidance that Herbert's story developed its complex and richly ambiguous meanings. With Old Zave in charge, all Herbert's experiences, all his thoughts and feelings, all his passions and prejudices, all his knowledge and ignorance were able to rub shoulders down there in the dark, connect, split up, reshape and finally join in the dance upwards into consciousness and onto the printed page. 'The poet's mind', T. S. Eliot once wrote, is 'a receptacle for seizing and storing up numberless feelings, phrases, images, which remain there until all the particles which can unite to form a new compound are present together'. Poetry, he continued

> is a concentration, and a new thing resulting from the concentration, of a very great number of experiences which to the practical and active person would not seem to be experiences at all; it is a concentration which does not happen consciously or of deliberation. [...] Of course that is not quite the whole story. There is a great deal, in the writing of poetry, which must be conscious and deliberate. In fact, the bad poet is usually unconscious where he ought to be conscious, and conscious where he ought to be unconscious.[30]

For too many years Herbert had been conscious where he ought to have been unconscious. He had tried to control 'meaning' and in so doing had limited it to the narrow constraints of a less than profound capacity to reason. During the writing of *Poor Fellow My Country*, he reverted to the methods of *Capricornia*[31], ceding control of the deep centre of the book to his subconscious, while using the conscious mind for what it does best, tying up loose ends, organising details, checking for inconsistencies and so on—all the worthy Martha-like, novelistic housekeeping that is, Eliot implies, the proper task of the poet's conscious mind.

The reason we can speak with certainty of the way Herbert wrote *Poor Fellow My Country* is that for a crucial stage of its writing, there exists a detailed, day by day record of what he was thinking and doing as he wrote the book. That record owes its existence to Herbert's stint, in 1968, as relieving pharmacist at Innisfail Hospital. He had taken the job reluctantly. Well into the novel by then, he feared that with a day's duties to attend to, he would not find the time and peace he needed to write. But find them he did. At the end of each day's work, he went straight to a nearby playing field for his run, then back to his room for a light meal and then sleep. At about midnight he woke, the dreaming done, ready to write. But as a precursor to the real writing, he warmed up with a longish letter to Sadie, much of which was devoted to an analysis of the work in progress. Through these letters we are able to see how, in response to the prompting of his subconscious, ideas that initially are as limited as those in *Soldiers' Women* gradually acquire more complex, ambiguous and elusive meanings.

A good example is the gradual development of Rifkah, a character who first arrived on the scene during his time at Innisfail. Herbert describes her arrival thus:

> I started off [...] simply by having a Jewish cinema-tographer like Kurt Sternberg, and his girl-friend, come to the races, while photographing for a scheme like that mooted in 1935 [...] for settling refugees in n.w. W.A. You know I had the Australia First business represented in an anthropologist named Fergus Ferris. [...] The idea of Kurt was to have a Jew for Fergus to try to score off. [...] But the Jewish lady got into it—and you know what they can do! Apart from the girl's personality and beauty, there is her sheer desperation as a refugee. I had suddenly conceived the despair of the Jews of that period. It was, of course, terribly unvalued (the real thing, I mean) by Communism, the Coms taking advantage of the desperate-ness of the Jews to gain their own ends [...] I saw the opportunity to deal with it here, along with the terrifically human story of two dispossessed and desperate people.[32]

This is the conscious part of Herbert's mind at work. It is this that initiates characters and actions. The way they develop is left to the agency of dreams and the unconscious, but the starting point is a decision in pursuit of one of his conscious aims, in this case the aim of making *Poor Fellow My Country*, on one level, into a microcosm of mid-twentieth-century Australia. He had created Fergus Ferris to represent the fascist Australia First movement and needed a Jew to represent the Jewish refugees of the period. By making that Jew one involved with the 1938 settlement scheme and with the Communist Party, he could fit two more pieces of Australia's history into the jigsaw. Casting about for a real-life model, he remembered Kurt Sternberg and his girlfriend, and thus arrived one of the most important characters in the novel, towed in on the heels of Herbert's Jewish exemplar.

Once Rifkah has arrived it is, predictably, not long before Herbert is exploring the psychological possibilities she presents.

> [Prindy] has been young enough to *need* a mother to this moment—but being what he is, he had to have possession of his mother not vice versa. The trouble with his own mother was her stupidity. She knew she had something special in her son, but was not perceptive enough to understand it and serve it. [Rifkah] saw his genius and encouraged it. He wanted to do with her what he couldn't with his mother, take her into the wilderness to charm her with his interpretation of it [...] He wanted a woman to show off to. Is that so? But a woman of the first perception. Is that the case with me and you? Are you first of all my audience? Do you first of all bow down to my genius? That's it I think. The nurturing is secondary.[33]

The idea of using Rifkah as an exemplar of his psycho-sexual theories clearly appeals to Herbert. But he is no longer, as in *Soldiers' Women*, simply using characters to demonstrate a thesis and, interested though he is in the psycho-sexual possibilities of Rifkah's situation, he is not sure whether that is the direction in which he should take her. We see that in the tentative tone of 'Is that so?' and 'That's it I think'. The tone intensifies as he explores the psychological issues further:

> I have [Prindy] and [Rifkah] in the cave, with the fire lit. [...]
> I want to show how they spent the night briefly but with
> great effect to show the new condition of their existence.
> This is actually the climax of their association. To me it
> seems that there is always a climactic quality in human
> relations and perhaps more truly it is a series of climaxes
> coming to a grand one. Where—what? I don't know yet.
> Maybe this is the purpose of this piece. Let's look ahead.
> When R becomes Clancy's wife P drops her. He can't share
> her with anyone except his grandfather [...] He loves R. It is
> true love of two people—nothing much to do with sex.
> P being an artist can renounce love when it fails him.[34]

'I don't know yet' and 'Maybe this is the purpose of the piece'. As he
involves Rifkah more and more deeply in the plot, Herbert becomes
less and less sure of what he should be doing with her:

> The work is troubling me [...] The Rifkah thing is *not*
> elucidated. I have been *swept* to this point. I rely so much
> on my instinct to guide me...I have to...but I've got to be
> wary of its fallibility.[35]

The 'Rifkah thing' is 'not elucidated' because she is moving
beyond the more easily explicable reach of his historical thesis and
his psychological theories. Something of both remains, but she is
being drawn now into the core of symbolic meaning that is the real
heart of *Poor Fellow My Country*:

> Remember I was asking how did Rifkah and Clancy fit
> into the future of the story, or rather into its general pat-
> tern. No one must become a major character without deep
> purpose.[36]

The deep purpose he refers to here is the central purpose of the
book: to express allegorically Herbert's tragic vision of the Australian
experience. It is Rifkah's relation to this purpose that Herbert now
struggles to understand:

So we must show it on this strange night in this strange place, this utterly alien and quite lost girl (the perfect character because of her race and its ancient tragedy) with a little boy who belongs to it so much that he believes he has been re-incarnated, has been in the belly of the Rainbow Snake and to heaven and back, not a primitive black boy, but one of the new and strange and odd race so much belonging, too much belonging to last in a land doomed to have its ancient wonders blasted away before they can be established—more and more complicated. But there it is. That is the lovely truth of it, that is the essence of the book, the mystique that has captured me. Here this night in this cave must be shown something of it, as they lie together under blankets in the sand, arms about each other, mother and son, lover and lover, two primitives in a land to which neither quite belongs [...] watched in the firelight by the symbols of this alien ancientness as if guarded as belonging by the creatures taking refuge with them [...] Is it mad? I'll leave it for you to decide while I go to make porridge. [...] Don't forget this is *all* a tragedy.[37]

Is it mad? The question is only half-joking. He is not in control of these ideas as he was of the ideas in *Soldiers' Women*. These ideas grow and develop on the edge of consciousness—in his dreams. They are at work in his subconscious long before he consciously explores and develops them.[38] He knows they are 'the essence of the book'. He glories in their 'lovely truth'. But the way he develops them is a matter of intuition, not logic, and he cannot always explain why he does one thing rather than another. He senses a link between Rifkah and Prindy. His intuition is that her presence adds a new dimension to Prindy's meaning, but when he tries to explain why that is so, there is none of the simplistic logic of his psychological theory. It has something, he feels, to do with a connection between the ancient tragedy of her race and the ancient, doomed land that is Prindy's. It has something to do with not belonging: she an alien in a land alien to her; he a new birth in his own land; both of them 'primitives in a land to which neither quite belongs'. The explanations slip into paradox, the currency throughout the centuries of those who attempt to explain the inexplicable. Prindy does not belong because he belongs too much. Though neither he nor Rifkah belongs and the land is alien, they are 'guarded as belonging' by 'this alien ancientness'.

In another letter, Herbert continues to search for the meaning of what Old Zave has led him to create:

> I've given so much to this odd girl—why? Of course as a symbol of woman. [...] There is basically the country and the thrall of it, the witchery of life in it, the wonder of it all, ultimately destroyed by the lack of most people to accept the wonderful—perhaps it is exposure of the development of man from a sensitive child to a pachyderm-brute. [...] I have to keep the wonder of life before us. It is expressed by our aboriginal characters [...] Oh how deeply I do understand such things! Such wonderous [sic] things, where possums peep out of trees in the moonlight watching and there is the background of the corroboree chant and the click of the music boomerangs. *That* is my story. Rifkah is a part of it.[39]

The suggestive vagueness of the analysis testifies to the working of something beyond the control of Herbert's conscious mind. The writing now resists intellectual analysis. He knows it has something to do with the country and with wonder—and that is as far as he can explain it. He toys with psychological explanations ('symbol of woman', 'development of man from sensitive child to pachyderm brute') but the dismissive 'of course' and tentative 'perhaps' show Rifkah has moved far beyond the trite psychologising of *Soldiers' Women*.

Two weeks later he is still feeling his way:

> We mustn't lose sight of the fact that the centre of all the drama is the boy Prindy. I'd had [Rifkah] as an alien thing somehow finding identity with it all, as no other breed of

person could (God knows why I've picked a Jewess—but it must mean something) and in the end [...] I was going to bring her back, when all the others had gone, to cry over the lost dream of it all [...] But that now seems quite wrong. The last person on the stage must be he who took the first bow, Prindy. At first we see him as the strange golden savage playing with a painted python. At the end we have to see him go out as a victim of what dominates it all, the power (perverse) the Rainbow Serpent. Let's never get too far from Old Tcharada [sic], the Snake, who is, of course, the Devil and the Spirit of this Land. [Rifkah] was intended to die, lured by old Charada [sic] into the Rainbow Pool—actually went in to follow Darcy[40] who [had] gone in to get away from the futility of his existence. But what of the living symbol of the Snake—Prindy, who'd excited so much interest from both black and white, the Enchanted Boy—[Isn't] it more likely that *he* will lure both of these people who loved him and whom he loved in his negative way, to be victims of his master, Tcharada. Never let us go too far from the fantasy.[41]

This is no longer the allegorising of the fifties where Herbert maintains tight control and everything is 'tied up tidily with simple meaning'. Herbert is content now to travel blind, able only to guess at the purpose of the journey ('maybe this is the purpose of this piece'), forced simply to trust in the higher wisdom of his subconscious, even when his rational mind cannot fathom that wisdom ('God knows why I've picked a Jewess'). He is doing what *feels* right, what intuition rather than reason tells him ('That now seems quite wrong'). He is feeling his way ('Isn't it more likely that'). And finally, unlike *Soldiers Women*, there is a strong sense here of commitment to the integrity of the story ('Never let us go too far from the fantasy'). If it is 'more likely' for a character to do one thing, he or she must not be made (as in *Soldiers' Women* characters were[42]) to do another, simply to make the intended message clearer. There the plot was manipulated to serve the message. Here the meaning evolves as the plot evolves. It is discovered, by the author as much as by his readers, through the telling of a story whose characters and events first play out on the stage of Herbert's subconscious. 'I get amazed', he says, 'when I see how things suddenly work themselves out. [...] I create [characters] for a purpose, and as soon as life is breathed into them they up and off and do something entirely on their own'.[43]

E. M. Forster once distinguished a class of novelist he called 'prophets'. 'The prophet', he said, 'has gone "off" more completely than the fantasist, he is in a remoter emotional state while he composes'.[44] The description fits the Herbert seen in letters like the following, written on consecutive days in October 1968:

> I glimpsed the sheer genius of my Rainbow Snake idea, and saw how Rifkah becomes the victim of it [...] I saw how Prindy was caught in it in that very first scene of the story, when he found the painted baby python, and was revealed to that strange old devil, Bobwirriki [sic], as a part of himself and of the Rainbow Serpent (better than snake) the force of Negation—and Negation as the nemesis of Australia Felix—oh, what a masterpiece of symbolism it will be when complete! [...] I am much of the Welshman in my religiosity, with the Dragon in the mountains as the dominating force of my existence— what an odd thing to say![45]

> Primarily I want to show the great Negative Force that grows up to destroy the Dream of Australia Felix—the Rainbow Serpent. Hence all my chief characters, black, white, brindle must fall victim to it—except one, the genius. I myself am the genius—and I myself will be the one person [...] who will benefit from this extraordinary thing. I shall disappear like Prindy with old Bob Bobwirriki [sic] into the sky, into that Black Hole at the end of the Milky Way, which has fascinated me *all* my life, as it has the blacks.[46]

The Herbert who can say 'I shall disappear like Prindy into the sky' and 'the dragon in the mountains [is] the dominating force of my existence' sounds like a writer who has moved into the 'remoter emotional state' of the prophet. It was a state that served him well in writing *Poor Fellow My Country*. The trust he placed in Old Zave proved to be trust well placed. Content this time to listen and learn, to serve rather than direct his muse, Herbert opened the way for his strengths as dream-maker and symbol-thinker to work as never before. Thus it was that he finally learned to take the themes of *Capricornia* further—by leaving his ideas on Australia to develop below the surface of consciousness as a never fully articulated but fully felt and fully dreamt core of feelings, beliefs, symbols and intuitions that found expression not through logical propositions but, as is the way of all dreams, through scenes, actions and characters. Wisely refusing to attempt detailed analysis, it is enough for him to know, intuitively, what the core consists of: the land ('There is basically the country and the thrall of it'), the wonder of life ('I have to keep the wonder of life before us'), the tragedy of Australia ('Don't forget this is all a tragedy'), the 'awful invading alienness', and the negativity and 'perverse' power of the 'Devil and Spirit of this Land' ('Let's never get too far from Old Tcharada'). He knows these are the centre of his book, and all major characters must come into relationship with this central organising vision. But they do so in a region beyond his conscious understanding. '[Prindy's] character has developed', he says

> without my really being aware of what I (I?) have been
> doing in it. [...] There was the thing inside me pointing
> the way while I was striving to go another—altho, of
> course, only too well aware I must go where that finger
> points, no matter.[47]

Where, precisely, that pointing finger finally led Herbert is the subject of the remaining chapters.

CHAPTER 10

An Anatomy of Australia

A ND so we come to Herbert's most important work, the book in which, through an adventurous mixture of genres, he created a comprehensive portrait of Australia's past, present and possible future. To picture the past and present, he used the conventions of anatomy, confession and romance. Anatomy provided an efficient way to convey a mass of factual information about Australia. Confession allowed him to express his personal views on the significance of that information. Romance added complexity and imaginative force to those views. Against this background of Australia's past and present are played out the two stories through which Herbert explores alternative possibilities for the future. Using the conventions of novel and confession he paints, in the story of Jeremy Delacy, a pessimistic picture of the likely future. At the same time, using the conventions of romance, he presents in the story of Prindy his vision of a better future towards which Australians might, if they chose, aspire.

The conventions of anatomy were well suited to achieving part of Herbert's purpose in *Poor Fellow My Country* but, in using them, he ran the risk of being misunderstood and undervalued. Anatomy is still not well recognised as a genre in its own right, even though Frye's argument for acknowledging its existence is compelling:

> We remarked earlier that most people would call *Gulliver's Travels* fiction but not a novel. It must then be another form of fiction, as it certainly has a form, and we feel that we are turning from the novel to this form, whatever it is, when we turn from Rousseau's *Emile* to Voltaire's *Candide*, or from Butler's *The Way of all Flesh* to the Erewhon books, or from Huxley's *Point Counterpoint* to *Brave New World*. The form thus has its own traditions, and, as the examples of Butler and Huxley show, has preserved some integrity even under the ascendancy of the novel. Its existence is easy enough to demonstrate, and no one will challenge the statement that the literary ancestry of *Gulliver's Travels* and *Candide* runs through Rabelais and Erasmus to Lucian. But while much has been said about the style and thought of Rabelais, Swift, and Voltaire, very little has been made of them as craftsmen working in a specific medium, a point no one dealing with a novelist would ignore.[1]

As with Swift and Rabelais, so with Herbert. Little attention has been given to the skill with which, in *Poor Fellow My Country*, he works within the medium of anatomy. Instead of examining his use of anatomy conventions in terms of their appropriateness to his purpose and his skill in their deployment, critics have more often condemned their use out of hand, basing their objections on grounds more appropriate to 'novel' than anatomy. Once the prejudice in favour of 'novel' is overcome, a fairer assessment of Herbert's skilful use of anatomy becomes possible.

Anatomy, says Frye, 'deals less with people as such than with mental attitudes'. It 'presents people as mouthpieces of the ideas they represent'.[2] Using this convention, Herbert was able to create a detailed picture of the social, political and intellectual life of Australia. For each significant group and ideology, he provides a mouthpiece. Lord Vaisey represents foreign ownership, Monsignor

Maryzic the Catholic Church, Lydia Esk British fascism, her father British imperialism, Kurt Hoff European communism, Fergus Ferris the Australia First movement, and so on.[3] Nor is it only what they say that is significant. Characters also exemplify social and political trends through what they do, and what is done to them. The policies that created a 'Stolen Generation' of Aboriginals are exemplified in the story of Prindy.[4] The unholy alliance of police, communists and British business interests that kept the meat industry running smoothly is seen in the treatment Delacy receives on his visit to Port Hartog.[5] The circumstances surrounding Rifkah's arrest are used to exemplify the power struggle between the Australian Government, the Communist Party and the Catholic Church. The scene in which she is taken prisoner becomes a graphic illustration of the anti-communist policies of the government and the fiercely anti-libertarian powers that were brought to bear to enforce those policies. Subsequent attempts to save her illustrate the relative power of the Catholic Church and the Communist Party. The ruthless pragmatism of communism appears in the plan 'to marry Rifkah off to beat the law'. The political influence of the Catholic Church is demonstrated when Cardinal Maryzic manages, because 'Ve haf our man at Head of Government', to secure her citizenship.[6]

Another feature of anatomy whose influence is seen in *Poor Fellow My Country* is its robust ridicule of pretension. Writers of anatomy relish the opportunity to cut the pompous and the powerful down to size. 'Ridicule of the *philosophus gloriosus*', or 'learned crank', and '*miles gloriosus*', the puffed-up military figure, was, Frye tells us, common in early anatomies.[7] In *Poor Fellow My Country* this strand of the tradition is evident in Herbert's descriptions of political and military leaders. Prime Minister Billy Hughes is a 'Cockney runt', King George VI 'that inoffensive, stuttering, in-bred, German-Danish-anything-but-English, young Englishman', Winston Churchill 'a podgy little Englishman [...] who thought he was a military genius' and his opponent 'that fat-arsed old Sultan of Turkey'.[8] The tone comes from the more crudely irreverent traditions of satire, those that prefer bludgeon to rapier. International affairs are described in language more usually applied to schoolyard bullies and common criminals than political leaders. The founding of Australia becomes

'Cook's bit of petty thieving [...] for the Royal Crook who employed him'. The Munich Agreement is mocked as 'giving the blessing of half the world's lunatics to Hitler to indulge his frankly mooted wholesale homicide, while the other half cursed and spat upon the first'.[9] This type of description has two effects. First, it reinforces the book's view that its leaders have failed Australia by sacrificing it to foreign interests: the unflattering descriptions of Australian politicians emphasise their failure; those of foreign politicians imply the unworthiness of the ambitions for which Australia's interests have been sacrificed. The belittling descriptions also convey a sense of how ordinary Australians experienced the events of the period. This is not the history found in history books. This is a view of events as seen by ordinary men and women. It is a simplistic view, as such views often are. It is cynical and jaundiced, as the common man's view of politics and politicians often is.

This sense of 'the ordinary Australian's view of politics' is reinforced by the techniques Herbert uses to introduce information on national and international affairs into *Poor Fellow My Country*. Some of it enters the book as it would have entered the lives of ordinary Australians—in the form of radio news bulletins. Alfie, for instance, hears one night that

> Italy was sending troops into Spain to fight against the Republicans with the insurgent General Franco, while the British Government, under Prime Minister Baldwin, was preventing even the passage of volunteers to go to help the legitimate Spanish Government.[10]

Information also enters the book in the form of conversations between ordinary Australians. Sometimes this conversation is the uninformed chatter of the politically naive:

> Talk of bringing Reffo Jews into the country and settling them in a sort of New Jerusalem—Sheenies in elastic sides—did you ever 'ear anything so bloody silly? [...]
>
> This Munich business. You didn't hear anything else but that now. Everybody arguing about it [...] and not merely

> arguing, but fighting over it [...] violence in Finnucane's
> bar, with bottle throwing and yells of Commo Bastards
> and Fascist Shitheads [...] Strike me lucky, what was the
> country coming to?[11]

Even more frequent are conversations that present the views of politically sophisticated Australians. These take the form of discussions between Jeremy Delacy and a succession of new acquaintances. With Bishoff he discusses the position of Aboriginals in Australia, with Lydia the role of British fascism in European affairs, with Esk the effect of British foreign policy on Australia, with Alfie issues of Australian nationalism, and so on.

Symposium discussion, described by Frye as 'a dialogue or colloquy, in which the dramatic interest is in a conflict of ideas rather than of character'[12], is one of the most recognisable of anatomy conventions. Having experimented with it briefly in *Capricornia*, and more often but with less success in the books of the fifties, Herbert used it extensively[13] in *Poor Fellow My Country* and with a skill that is rarely acknowledged. It is hard to recognise how effectively Herbert has mastered his craft in this respect if his achievement is judged by the wrong criteria. It is only when we stop treating symposium discussion as a failed attempt at naturalistic dialogue that we can begin to see how well it suited his purposes, and how much skill has gone into making it as congenial as possible for readers more used to 'novels' than anatomies.

Symposium discussion was appropriate to Herbert's purposes because it allowed him to convey a great deal of information swiftly and economically. From the lengthy first discussion between Delacy and Bishoff, for instance, we learn much about Aboriginal traditions, beliefs, myths, cults, kinship systems and language. We learn much about the civil rights abuses Aboriginals suffer: about their lack of legal status and their mistreatment by police. We learn much about Australian history: about the development of the pastoral industry and the meat trade, about the building of railways, and about the part Australia played in World War I. We also learn Herbert's views on all these things: on the value of Aboriginal culture, on the attitude of Aboriginals to their situation, on the failures of white Australia, and on the relations between Australia and Britain.[14] The convention of symposium discussion, here and in many other places, allows Herbert to deal with far more than would have been possible using the conventions of the novel. The constraints imposed by naturalistic dialogue would have allowed him, in the same space, to deal with only a tiny fraction of all this.

Useful, however, though symposium discussion is for a writer with Herbert's purposes, it is not an easy one for a twentieth-century novelist to employ. Though naturalistic dialogue is no less conventional, and only sounds more 'natural' to twentieth-century readers because they are used to it, the fact remains that they *are* used to it. Conversely, they are not used to dialogue that is overtly didactic, goes on for a long time, is very one-sided, and contains a heavy load of information and opinion. Until they do become used to it, it is bound to sound less 'natural'. The technical challenge for a writer, therefore, is to find ways to help readers adapt to a type of dialogue that is new and strange to them. It was a challenge Herbert met very well. He could do nothing about the length or didacticism of these discussions. Both are essential to their purpose. What he could, and did, do was organise things in ways that would help readers accustomed to the 'naturalistic' dialogue of the 'novel' cope more easily with that length and didacticism.

One thing he did was to set the discussions within a narrative framework that made them seem 'natural'. The framework was what we may call the 'stranger in a strange land' plot motif. It is a motif often found in anatomies. Swift uses it in *Gulliver's Travels*, Butler in the *Erewhon* books, Huxley in *Brave New World* and *Island*. In all these books a stranger finds himself in a radically different society from his own and gradually learns about it through extended discussions with a friendly native. In the texts cited there is a single stranger; in *Poor Fellow My Country* the 'friendly native', Jeremy Delacy, guides a procession of 'strangers' (Bishoff, Lydia, Alfie, Rifkah and Esk) through the 'strange land' of Australia.

The value of this plot motif is that it provides a good reason for supplying a great deal of information in a short space of time. It is natural for the friendly native to take the strangers to see everything of interest, and to explain anything they do not understand. It is natural for the strangers to ask questions and prompt more information. In *Poor Fellow My Country* Herbert also finds a further use for the motif, demonstrating in this how creative and skilful a craftsman he has become in his use of anatomy. As well as using the 'stranger in a strange land' motif in the traditional way as a 'natural' framework for symposium discussion, Herbert also uses it, very cleverly, to reinforce one of the book's major themes—the failure of white Australians to become truly a part of the land they occupied. The fact that Bishoff and Alfie, though born and bred in Australia, are as much 'strangers in a strange land' as the foreigners, Lydia, Esk and Rifkah, is a neatly ironic, and deftly understated, reminder of that failure.

Another way Herbert made symposium discussion sound more 'natural' was to make the key figure in these discussions a man whose nature it was to pontificate. Delacy is a man who likes showing off his knowledge. In his mouth, lengthy, didactic speeches sound perfectly natural. Their patronising tone is also just what one would expect from a man like him. Thus, and again cleverly, Herbert turns a potential negative into a positive, since any irritation readers feel as they listen to Delacy's lectures is a perfectly appropriate response to the character Herbert has created. Clever, too, is the way his confessional connection with Delacy allows Herbert to indulge his own love of dogmatic pontificating to the full without in any way spoiling the novel. Expressed by Delacy, Herbert's ideas, however dogmatic, are offered in a non-authoritative way that leaves readers free to decide for themselves which are insightful, which wrong-headed.

To make the didacticism even more palatable to 'novel' readers, Herbert is careful to include in these discussions as much purely narrative interest as possible. During the first discussion, for instance, two aspects of the immediate plot provide interest: the conflict between Clancy and Martin over Nelyerri, and Delacy and Bishoff's search for the elusive Bobwirridirridi. Throughout the discussion, the reader's attention is periodically drawn to the development of both these narrative strands. Adding further interest are the two stories Delacy tells Bishoff during the discussion. The first, the story of Bobwirridirridi's exploits, provides a good reason to talk about Aboriginal culture. The second, of Delacy's early life, leads naturally to a discussion of white Australian history.

The final thing Herbert did to help readers adapt to symposium discussion was to make it seem less lengthy by breaking it up. The first discussion is broken into four sections of about seven pages each. Between each section Herbert provides a bit of straight narrative to give readers a rest before he launches into the discussion again.[15] He also breaks each section up by keeping Delacy and Bishoff on the move and interrupting their talk at regular intervals with references to that movement.[16]

Once you stop treating symposium discussion as a botched attempt at naturalistic dialogue, it becomes possible to see how well it achieves Herbert's purposes and how much care has gone into its construction. If they are looked at without prejudice, the same care and effectiveness can be seen in his deployment of other conventions that will, at first, seem strange to readers unused to anatomy. The anatomist, says Frye:

> shows his exuberance in intellectual ways, by piling up an enormous mass of erudition about his theme [...] The tendency to expand into an encyclopaedic farrago is clearly marked in Rabelais [...] The encyclopaedic compilations produced in the line of duty by Erasmus and Voltaire suggest that a magpie instinct to collect facts is not un-related to the type of ability that has made them famous as artists [...] digressing narrative [and] catalogues [...] are all features that belong to the anatomy.[17]

Digressing narrative, encyclopaedic detail and displays of erudition all attract criticism from novel-centred commentators. Again, it makes better sense to judge the conventions on the grounds of their effectiveness in achieving Herbert's purposes.

The way Delacy tells the story of Bobwirridirridi provides a clear example of Herbert's use of digressing narrative. It takes him twenty pages.[18] A study of two gives the flavour of the whole. On page 39 Delacy resumes the story with 'I spoke of Wirridirridi's return to civilized ken as contemporary with those unemployed riots at Beatrice'. This sentence is as far as the story gets for the moment, since mention of the riots triggers a digression on their causes, and that in turn leads to a digression on the decline of the meat trade. A description of the meat workers' strike prompts a digression on the abortive attempt to construct a north–south railway. In passing, Herbert slips in a digression on sexual relations between whites and blacks. And so back to the story with: 'That's how things were when Bobwirridirridi reappeared. But I must take you back to what he was doing earlier'—which was, we are told, establishing the Snake Cult on a station left in the care of Queeny Peg-leg. This prompts a digression on the 'booze, opium and prostitution' rackets Queeny now runs and her exploitation of young black prostitutes. 'I'm diverting again', says Delacy, in order 'to give you the picture complete'.[19] Taking up the story again, Delacy describes how Queeny ran Bobwirridirridi off the station and he, in turn, lured her to 'the sacred initiation ground, the Ring Place'. The telling of what happened to her there, though, must wait as Delacy deals with the role of Ring Places in Aboriginal cultures. Following that, he feels he 'must digress again to explain an oddity about this Kurrawaddi or Koonapippi business', which is that, though a masculine cult, it derives from women's secret business. This leads to a digression on the matrilineal organisation of Aboriginal cultures. The harsh treatment of women who trespass on sacred ground is mentioned and this leads to a digression on the nature of humanity in general. He has, he says, a 'hunch that some degree of diabolism is essential in human behaviour' and wonders 'if our propensity to murder, with which I include war, isn't due to this'.[20] He follows this with 'I hope these philosophical digressions don't spoil my story'. It is a matter to which we will return.

Closely associated with digressing narrative are the encyclo-paedic detail and displays of erudition typical of anatomy. Both are evident throughout *Poor Fellow My Country*. The arrival of a train, for instance, is reason enough for Herbert to specify that it

would be scheduled in the Train Notice as Dep. Beatrice
R. 7.00 a.m.

that it had spent the night

> in the little engine shed, into which she was run always of
> nights, not so much for shelter as for the facilities there for
> ash-dropping and tube-blowing

that it

> comprised ten ballast hoppers and two small flats packed
> with the gear the fettlers had been using in their repair
> work, two passenger coaches in which the men had
> travelled and camped, and the brake-van

and that the coaches

> were of the single type used locally, old-fashioned things
> like everything else on this railroad, each consisting of
> two compartments, with wooden seats running length-
> wise so that one sat with one's back to the windows and
> looked out through those opposite, the compartments
> divided by tiny lavatories, one on either side, with a
> swinging door between, and with platforms at either end.

Nor does it stop there. Before the main narrative can resume, the
reader must be given detailed descriptions of the couplings, the brake
and, finally, the safety chains:

> a brace of chains on either side of the couplings of each
> vehicle, these to hold the train together in the case of
> breaking of the couplings proper for long enough to bring
> the train to a halt and, if possible, rectify the damage. Spare
> hooks and pins were carried in the van. However, there
> was no roadside way of repairing broken safety chains.[21]

The book is a mine of information, some of it relevant to the narrative, some of it demonstrating simply the anatomist's 'magpie instinct
to collect facts'.

Delacy justifies 'diverting again' from the story of Bobwirri-dirridi on the grounds that in so doing he is able 'to give you the picture complete'. In the wider context of the book, the same justification applies. Without the digressions and encyclopaedic detail, the picture given of Australia would be far less rich, far less full and far less accurate. The mass of detail results, for instance, in a marvellous evocation of life in country Australia. The milk made from powder. The role played by mail order catalogues. The way flies appear the moment you get out of your car. The wares Barbu peddles round the stations: the fly whisks made from dead cows' tails, the fly-proof sunglasses 'with tiny screens of gauze to keep out the pests'. The arrival of the Flying Doctor. The mass held in the Dance Hall.[22] In these, and a multitude of other details a less encyclopaedic text would omit, Herbert builds a picture of bush life in mid-century Australia that is comprehensive and powerfully evocative.

The digressing, encyclopaedic tendency also ensures a richly detailed picture of Australian cultural mores. Its attitude to social class, for instance:

> Now, where Lord Vaisey got the idea that class distinction meant nothing in Australia would be impossible to say. [...] But there it was in full sway at the Princess Alice Hotel also—second-class-distinction to be sure, but no less strict, even for being merrier through being less stiff. There had been a grand dinner at which those of social eminence insufficient to get them a place at the Big House table had been guests of old Shame-on-us—people like Eddy McCusky, the two Police Inspectors, Mr and Mrs Bishoff, Col Collings the Station Master, other lesser silvertails and business men from Town, some squatters lacking the gentility to be classed squattocracy in a social sense [...] Hock had been the drink. Champagne would be reserved for the Cup Dinner [...] The festive board, made up of table sections of special design, had occupied all one side of the large dining-room, and the feast partaken of in the presence of the other diners; that is the lesser ones with the lesser fare that they had to pay for

[...] meaning everybody qualified for admittance to the dining-room at this season, which was certainly not anybody.

This is a class system that is clearly stratified and well understood, albeit not openly acknowledged. The levels described all know their place, excluded from the level above, excluding the level below in the time-honoured fashion of class systems. As the description proceeds it takes in two more levels, and demonstrates that the rules of inclusion and exclusion are no less rigorously policed for being unstated:

> But when the dinner was over, it was everybody from the dining-room who trouped outside to the colourfully lit courtyard to take part in the fun and games there. Outsiders of the proper kind were also admitted here, people from the camps mostly, the train crews, [...] the lesser policemen [...] and some soldiers from the garrison [...] Occasionally someone from the packed bars up front [...] would wander in, usually with shirt-tail out if he were a ringer or fly half-gaping if he were railway fettler, fencer, well-sinker, but always to be gentled out again by Shamus and his blarney [...] Here was no real trouble at all with intruders, as if in this famous egalitarian society everybody knew their place quite well.[23]

The leisurely pace, the interest in details as small as the 'table sections of special design' and the 'shirt-tail out'—it is these that create in *Poor Fellow My Country* an infinitely richer and more human picture of Australian culture than any to be found in sociology texts.

It is easy enough for unsympathetic critics to make a case against the usefulness of this or that digression. Is it really necessary, they might ask, for the precise workings of the dunnies in the 'Halfcaste Home' to be explained, or the economics of the indenture system in the pearling industry analysed, or the full history of an anti-Semitic pamphlet given?[24] In similar fashion, critics of *Les*

Miserables might complain of that book's digressions and encyclo-paedic detail.[25] But it is precisely because Hugo and Herbert allow themselves freedom to explore the byways as well as the highway of their narrative that the picture each gives of his country is full and accurate in a way no process of more ruthless selection could possibly have produced. A passage like the following, for instance, would never be allowed in a text disciplined by the rules of the novel. Yet it is precisely the inclusion of such quirky little socio-logical scraps that makes the picture of Australia given by *Poor Fellow My Country* so richly comprehensive:

> Perhaps Jeremy was thinking of the Australian pre-occupation with what was called The Bayonet with a kind of reverence. Australian troops claimed to be the Best in the World With The Bayonet. Speaking now of the War of 1914–18, currently referred to as The Last Turn-out, to say, 'We got to 'em with The Bayonet,' was tantamount to declaring, 'The Victory was Ours.' Old enemies were honoured or despised according to their readiness to be disembowelled: ['Johnny Turk was a great fighter...met you with The Bayonet man to man. But Fritz didn't like cold-steel. He only had to see The Bayonet...and up'd go his hands and *Kamerad*!' The preoccupation is to be seen in the Australian Military Emblem, the so-called *Rising Sun*, introduced with the establishment of the Australian Military Forces along with semblance of nationhood, which in fact is a semi-circle of Bayonets cropping out of a Crown. Yet so far are Australians from having a propen-sity for gut-slitting in normal life that their chief dislike of non-British immigrants is their readiness to use a knife in violent disputation. Judges and Magistrates continually rant: 'We will not tolerate use of The Knife in this country.' The bottle, the axe, the gun, the boot...but never the foreign Knife.[26]

It is time now to switch genres and consider the contribution confession makes to the picture of Australia given in *Poor Fellow My*

Country. What it most obviously does is foreground the fact that this is not a coolly objective picture of Australia. This is Australia seen through the opinionated eyes of a particular Australian. In confession, Frye tells us, 'theoretical and intellectual interest[s]' are often explored through the creation of 'a "mental history" of a single character'.[27] In *Poor Fellow My Country* that character is Jeremy Delacy, whose ideas on Australia we learn through the many symposium discussions in which he takes part. Two aspects of Australia dominate his thinking: the condition of Aboriginals and the ethos of modern Australia.

On the condition of Aboriginals, Herbert's thinking has developed considerably since he wrote *Capricornia.* While still attacking the mistreatment of Aboriginals by individuals[28], he now understands that the worst civil rights abuses are those created by official policy. The state, Delacy explains to Bishoff during the first symposium discussion, treats Aboriginals as non-persons. They have no birth or death certificates, are entered on no electoral roll, receive no mention in any census.[29] Refusal to recognise their existence, however, does not prevent the state from exerting the most ruthless control over Aboriginals. The ironically titled 'Protector of Aborigines', says Delacy, has the power to 'do what he likes in respect of his lawful assignment of protecting Aboriginal persons'.[30] It is 'an offence under the Aboriginal Act' for an Aboriginal person to travel, to do business or even to be out after sunset 'without the permission of a Protector'. And it is by the authority of the Protector that children are taken from their mothers and sent away to learn the ways of the white man.[31]

Through Delacy's fierce criticisms of the system, Herbert gives a passionate and detailed exposé of the way government policies, for years, oppressed Aboriginals and denied them civil rights. But, shocking though the civil rights abuses were, they were not, *Poor Fellow My Country* suggests, as serious in their long-term effects as the destruction of Aboriginal culture. In 1962 Herbert wrote an article for the *Bulletin* called 'A Town Like Elliott'[32] in which he expressed his views on this subject. At one point during his visit to Elliott, he recounts, he asked an Aboriginal resident of the town why his people still lived in squalor when a lot of government money had been spent on providing better conditions for them. The man replied, 'I reckon that's what's wrong with us blackfellers. We lost all that, all the sort of thing we only want—our own way of living'. In *Poor Fellow My Country* Rifkah teaches Delacy the lesson Herbert learned in Elliott. 'For Jew to give up beingk Jew', she tells him, 'is like blackfellow give up Dreamingk for viteman vay...it only mek him what blackfellow call Bloody Nutching'.[33] His eyes opened by Rifkah, Delacy finally understands that an Aboriginal 'like the Jews, [...] wants to be what he is, what he's proud of being'. 'I've raged', he says, 'against their ill-treatment [...] but I've never wept over the rejection of them for what they are [...] nor had I realized that in their hearts there must be a great sadness on account of their rejection for what they are'.[34]

The problem, *Poor Fellow My Country* suggests, is that the dominance of white culture in Australia has made it impossible for Aboriginals to 'be what they are proud of being'. Instead they are presented with two choices, both unpalatable: assimilate and accept the cultural values of the white invaders or remain in squalor and poverty on the edges of white society. Herbert sees little difference, as far as Aboriginals are concerned, between 'assimilation' and 'integration'. The policy of assimilation is expressed, early in the book, by Dr Cobbity, who seeks to teach Aboriginals to 'understand the value of money and the nature of work and of contracting to work, so as eventually to be able to take part in the general economy of the Nation'.[35] The policy of integration receives a mention at the end when 'Government Welfare Officers' preach 'the millennium for the Aboriginal Race with the slogan: *Integration!*' But for Aboriginals, the novel implies, integration, in practice, still means 'learn to live like whites and you'll be saved'.[36] It still involves giving up Aboriginal culture. European cultural groups can be 'integrated' into, rather than 'assimilated' by, an Australia whose individualistic, materialistic core values they already share. Traditional Aboriginal cultures, however, have such radically different core values that expecting members of those cultures to be 'successful' in Australian society while remaining true to their core values is like expecting fish, deprived of their natural element, to function effectively on dry land. The only way, therefore, for Aboriginals to function successfully in modern Australia is to give up their core values and 'assimilate'. That is what the Aboriginal Rangers employed to protect the Painted Caves do.[37] Having lost their Aboriginal culture as a result of white invasion, they have learned to live like whites, 'only pretending to be Aboriginal ven it suit zem'.[38]

But what of Aboriginals who do not want to give up the core values of their culture? For them, Herbert thinks, the future is bleak. The only alternative he sees to assimilation is the kind of life he describes at the end of *Poor Fellow My Country*. 'Social Service', he says, 'had become the blackman's livelihood since the acquirement of citizenship' but 'was barely enough to keep in booze such booze-artists as the Aboriginal Race had proved to be with the lifting of restrictions'.[39] Aboriginal housing, 'despite tremendous efforts on the part of experts of all kinds [...] had quickly degenerated into a slum, and not only as regards domestic squalor, but social', since its occupants 'in trading on the guilt of the *kuttabah* were never much concerned about their behaviour these days'.[40] Statements like this are unlikely to endear Herbert to fellow supporters of the Aboriginal cause, but before rejecting them out of hand it is important to be clear on what he is saying. The point he is trying to make is easily misrepresented and misunderstood.[41] He is not criticising Aboriginals. What he is trying to show is that money cannot solve problems that are cultural, not material. Misunderstanding of his position arises when readers see no further than his deliberately confronting descriptions of a degraded way of life and pessimism about future improvement. For Herbert, though, to minimise the awfulness of the situation and exaggerate the possibilities of improvement is to allow white Australia to avoid acknowledging the guilt it bears for what he sees as the irreversible damage it has done to Aboriginals.

One of the most important passages in the book for understanding Herbert's position is Delacy's defence of Aboriginals who live in degraded conditions:

> Even those few people truly sympathetic towards them
> think of them as lowly creatures to be raised to our own
> exalted way of life. You'll find these good people mildly

voicing the same objection to the blackfellow as drove the
pioneers to destroy them in rage...that finally they're
useless, because they won't give up their simple savage
freedom, even if that amounts at last only to living like
animals on the edge of the conquerors' towns [...]. What
you'll see of the blackfellow mostly will make you feel
he's pretty low. I'd like to put the idea into your mind
that he's like that because he never gave in...for all the
bullying, the sheer brutality and the pretended brotherly
love, he has never, never given in. That's why I want to
tell you the story of Bobwirridirridi.[42]

The passage contrasts two views. Those holding the first would
argue as follows. Point one: Aboriginals are living a degraded life.
Point two: they have been given plenty of assistance to lead a
purposeful and non-degraded life. Ergo, point three: it is their fault.
Concluded by people of goodwill with reluctance, by racists with a
triumphant 'I told you so'. But concluded by both in the same way.
And concluded wrongly according to this passage, whose implicit
argument runs as follows. Point one: whites have destroyed, irrevo-
cably, the conditions under which the traditional Aboriginal way of
life could be lived. Point two: Aboriginals who want to continue
living their way of life rather than acquiring white ways no longer
have the conditions for doing so. Point three: the only alternative to
learning to live like whites is to carry on as if nothing has changed.
But everything has changed. The meaning that traditional cultural
practices gave to life has disappeared. The cultural practices
themselves have disappeared. And the inevitable result is a social
vacuum within which the rootless existence of Aboriginals who do
not wish to assimilate into an alien, individualistic, materialistic
culture becomes inevitable. Point four: to blame Aboriginals for
living like this rather than learning to live as materialistic indi-
vidualists is to blame the victims for the results of the crime that has
been committed against them. Point five: instead of looking down on
them, one should admire Aboriginals who refuse to capitulate to the
alien, conquering culture, even though that refusal can only find
expression in an outwardly degraded way of living.

The convention of symposium discussion is sufficient to 'put the idea' of Aboriginal resistance 'into our minds', but something more is needed to fix it in our hearts. Herbert provided that 'something more' in 'the story of Bobwirridirridi'. Part of Bobwirridirridi's complex allegorical significance is to represent the strength and nobility of the dauntless resistance that lies behind the degradation that is all most whites see in the lives of Aboriginals who refuse to give up their culture. In passages like the following, Herbert, with great skill, pictures simultaneously both the disreputable old man Bobwirridirridi appears to untutored eyes and the man of dignity and power he actually is:

> Jeremy turned out at first light, to find Bobwirridirridi awaiting him, clad in khaki again, a scarecrow figure against the luminescent milky East. The top-knot merely nodded to Jeremy's greeting. However, there was a flash of tongue and a cackle for the bottle of brandy he carried. […]
> […] At length, when they came to a creek where water flowed through limey ropes, he pulled up, got out and said, 'Too rough ridin' in the back there, Pookarakka… more-better you come out in front, eh?'
> The scarecrow rose up from the canopy, then bent and hauled out spears and other gear. Jeremy said, 'Leave him.'
> The red eyes fixed him, then turned to measure the distance to the ground. Like a grey spider Bobwirridirridi clambered down, reached up and got his equipment.
> 'What you goin' to do, old-man?' asked Jeremy.
> 'Me go look-about.'
> 'What about you come station…I give you tucker.'
> 'By'n'by.'
> 'I want a yarn with you.'
> The top-knot nodded, while the eyes searched the irridescent [sic] water.
> 'You go look-about Snake Cave, eh?'
> With eyes still on the water, Bobwirridirridi went a few paces along the low bank, to a clear spot, where, looking like a crouching spider, he bent and drank deeply.

Rising again, he belched, then looked at Jeremy with a grin, cackling, 'Proper-lee...numberr-one!'
'Rainbow water, eh? Good for Snake Man.'
Another belch.
'What you goin' to do about soft tucker?'
'Me find him.'
'Spone you come station, I give you swag tucker, bring you back.'
Bobwirridirridi came back, bent to pick up his belongings.
'All right, I'll get along then, Pookarakka.' Jeremy thrust out his hand. The red coals met the grey eyes. '*Mummuk, yawarra.*'
Bobwirridirridi took the hand lightly, grinned: '*Mummuk, yawarra,* Mullaka.'[43]

It's a beautifully written piece. Bobwirridirridi, to untutored white eyes the underdog, the tramp cadging a lift, is shown to be quite the opposite, a figure of regal condescension, the one importuned, not importuning. He treats Delacy's overtures with crushing lack of interest, not even deigning to reply to Jeremy's offer of tucker and a lift back. It is Jeremy, not Bobwirridirridi, who is the suppliant here. To emphasise the symbolic significance of Bobwirridirridi's refusal to respond to Delacy's overtures, Herbert follows this scene with one in which Delacy takes supplies to a group of blacks at their bush camp. Like Bobwirridirridi's, their alien 'ugliness' (to white eyes) is emphasised. Like Bobwirridirridi, they respond to Delacy's offers of largesse warily.[44]

Bobwirridirridi is the epitome of Aboriginal resistance. Regularly the white world manages to hold down his physical body—but never his spirit. He flits in and out of *Poor Fellow My Country* as he flits in and out of the trees at Catfish Station in the first scene. Shadowy. Conferring with no-one except his acolyte, Prindy. Making no concessions whatsoever to the white world. The emptiness of white power over him appears in the contempt with which he treats its symbols: the police, the court, the prison. His trial progresses 'to the apparent boredom of the Pookarakka [...] who shut his eyes and dropped his hairless bony chin into the grey collar of his shirt'. Called on to testify, '[h]e may not have heard, so stonily did he sit with red eyes fixed on the last of the five-miles-long backbone of the Shade of the only master he recognized'.[45] In Bobwirridirridi, Herbert provides mythic expression to the dauntless resistance he sees where others see only degradation.

I said earlier that *Poor Fellow My Country* sees only two alternatives for Aboriginals: accept white culture, or live, dauntless but degraded, on the fringes of that culture. I should have said it sees only two realistic alternatives. Delacy does argue for a third option. In the words of his disciple Rifkah, it is for whites to

> Give back to ze blackman a vorthvile piece of ze stolen land, and let him live zere as he likes. [...] If ze *kuttabah* [...] get out and keep out, ze truly native people, if left alone, vill go back to old vay [...] Change moost come. But let ze blackman change himself. [...] Leave zem alone, and zey vill make a nation. Zey vill become proud people...like ze Jews now zey have ze dignity of owning again zere ancient land of Israel.[46]

The problem with this is its impracticality. You cannot turn back the clock. And Herbert knows it. He says as much through the death of Prindy, which marks the end of Bobwirridirridi's attempt to maintain Aboriginal tradition in a world dominated by whites. He says it in the brutal end Rifkah herself suffers for daring to voice these opinions. He said it in 'A Town like Elliott': 'There is no solution to the problem, at least no practical one'.[47]

Pessimistic though Herbert is about the future for Aboriginals who are unwilling or unable to assimilate, that does not mean he is against white Australia doing everything possible to ameliorate a situation for which it, and not Aboriginal Australia, is responsible. Again his views are open to misinterpretation. At the end of *Poor Fellow My Country*, he mocks 'emissaries of the Communist Party' who tell Aboriginals that 'Karlmarkus would soon be putting them back on the stations as bosses, provided that on every possible occasion in public places they shouted the slogan: *Land Rights*'.[48] It is important to understand that Herbert is not against land rights; what he is against is facile sloganeering and the false hope it offers. Far from being against land rights, Herbert pictures his hero going a great deal further than mere land rights in proposing 'a tax put on all property owners, according to property owned, and a percentage taken from transfer fees and such'[49]—all of which money to be given, without any conditions attached, to the Aboriginal people. It is not just a matter of justice; it is a matter of repentance. 'We stole this land', says Delacy:

> with murder and mayhem and about the lowest forms of meanness a human being could stoop to…and we have to reconcile the matter someday, either by acknowledging the fact that we're bloody-handed thieves and being proud of it, or giving back what we stole, and not as an act of charity, but of downright humility.[50]

In proposing such a policy, Delacy is interested at least as much in the condition of Australia as he is in the condition of Aboriginals. A community of thieves cannot become a nation until it repents of its crimes and does what it can to right the wrongs it has committed. What it can do will never be enough to pay for the crime, will never give back to Aboriginals the life they had before white settlement, but it may do something to help Australia become the nation Delacy believes it should have, and did not, become. Which brings us to the second of the two aspects of Australia that dominated Herbert's thinking in *Poor Fellow My Country*—the ethos of modern Australia. What the book has to say on that subject is explored in the next chapter.

CHAPTER 11

Colonials and Carpetbaggers

B Y the time he wrote *Poor Fellow My Country*, Herbert's view of Australia was bleak. Commenting on the panic evacuation of Darwin, Judge Bickering says:

[I]s it conceivable that an Englishman born in Birming-ham would run away from Dover if it were attacked? God Almighty, if these people are representative of the Nation as a whole, then none of us is less alien to the soil than a Greek or Chow and no more right to tenure to it [...]

The raid on Darwin, says Bickering, was a test

of the worth of this social entity we call Australia. What is a nation but a great family, bound together by a special identification? [...] The family that breaks up at a threat to its identity, that cries *Every Man for Himself*, is not a true family at all, but a gathering of rabble [...][1]

Accosted in Sydney by 'booze-reeking beggars' and a 'battered young prostitute', Jeremy Delacy mourns the 'end-point of one hundred and seventy years of the greatest chance for social advancement ever offered mankind', the loss of 'the God-given opportunity for *Australia Felix*'.[2] Gone are his hopes for 'a Nation I could be proud to belong to [...] a grouping of people who by the example of their own honest and dignified living could be an inspiration to the world'.[3] Delacy's hopes were the hopes that inspired patriots in the 1890s and the years following federation. In *Poor Fellow My Country* Herbert mourns the death of those hopes, expressing his views on the causes of that death through symbolism associated with the land and with Aboriginals.

Herbert connects the failure of the high hopes of federation with a failure in the way Australians feel towards their country. He highlights that failure as he did in *Seven Emus*, by contrasting it with the spiritual bond between Aboriginals and the land. Aboriginal myths, so many of which are told in *Poor Fellow My Country*, function as a constant reminder of that bond, and none more so than the creation myth of Koonapippi and Tchamala:

> The Ol'Goomun-Ol'Goomun came out of the sea, carried on a white cloud, the spirits of which she made into *booroolooloogun*, the nutmeg pigeons. She created the *mukkinboro*, the banyan trees, with their figs for the pigeons to feed on and their leafy branches for roost. She went on inland, followed by her dog, Wanjin, who pissed on everything she made [...]. Thus were the rank swamps made. It was then that Tchamala came out of the sea. He came as the rainbow, and landing, peeled strips off himself to make his pythons. These he hung from the branches of the banyans to look like the aerial roots of the great trees, telling them to wait till night, then crawl up and gobble the roosting pigeons. What birds survived fled to the islands just off the coast [...] and camped there in the jungles and made their nests, coming over to feed in the banyans only in daylight. [...]
>
> The pigeons could fly inland to feed by day, but not back and forth continuously to bring food to their nestlings,

which began to die of hunger. Then old Googoowinji the Cormorant [...] came to the rescue. He showed the pigeons how to stuff food in their gizzards as he did for feeding his young. Thus were the pythons outdone. Still, Tchamala made things hard for the *boorooloologun*. He created the South-East wind to blow them out of the country, which it did every time it came up at the end of the wet season, when the squabs were mature. But there was always Koonapippi's nor'wester to blow them back again with the rains. The trouble was that those that returned were the squabs of last season which must be taught Googoowinji's trick all over again. This was done now by the people of the Cormorant Dreaming, who held a great coroborree here every year when the pigeons returned, and instructed them in song and dance.[4]

In contrast to Christianity's picture of a fairytale garden long ago and far away, the Aboriginal myth is localised and specific. Each plant, each bird, each hill, each valley, the behaviour of snakes, the rank smell of swamps, the offshore nesting of pigeons—everything has its explanation in the actions of the spirit figures of the Dreamtime. Wherever Aboriginal eyes turn, therefore, they see reminders of the historical and spiritual links between themselves, the land and its creatures. The kinship system further deepens their sense of relationship with, and responsibility to, the land and its creatures. The men of the Cormorant Dreaming are responsible for teaching each new generation of pigeons the lesson their Dreamtime ancestor taught the very first pigeons.

Against this picture of Aboriginal connectedness and spiritual relationship, Herbert sets, again as in *Seven Emus*, the situation of the 'bloody nothing'. Being 'a Bloody Nothin'', says Billy Brew, is 'thinking you're a bit white anyway, and hatin' the black in you so's to justify the white'.[5] The position of the 'bloody nothing', caught between two cultures and at home in neither, symbolises the alienation Herbert sees in white Australia. 'A Bloody Nutching', he says early in *Poor Fellow My Country*, is 'what the average white person is, if you look into him or her deeply enough'. Cut off from the cultural certainties of their countries of origin and constantly 'trying to find roots in a land where [they] are forever alien', they too have 'lost their Dreaming'.[6] That 'loss of Dreaming', the spiritual emptiness Herbert now finds at the heart of Australia, is pictured at one stage of *Poor Fellow My Country* in a superbly written description that sets the present against the past in a manner reminiscent of Canto 2 of Eliot's 'The Waste Land'.[7] In the quotation below, which consists of extracts from a much longer passage, we hear, in the foreground, the tawdry, frenetic attempts of the 'bloody nutchings', white and black, to fill the spiritual void that is their life. In the background, semi-stifled, the 'ancient chanting' still speaks of the wonder of the Dreamtime, but speaks to deaf ears:

> They were stopped amidst a sea of white faces, in a reek of grog and *kuttabah* and the babble of *kuttabah* speech— Happy New Year, Bill—same to you, Harry—Happy New Year...Happy New Year All! [...]
>
> But for the sound of the motor they might have heard the old familiar click of the *minga-minga*, the drone of dijeridoo, a stanza or two of the ancient chanting, sadly, from those who still remembered, or the whoops and squeals of those who had learnt to forget—with the grog. [...]
>
> '[...] You like lil bits, Nelly...cujin Nell?'
>
> They produced the bottle and pannikins and cake.
>
> Over at the residence they were whooping it up: *Roll out the barrel, We'll have a barrel of fun....*
>
> The *minga-mingas* were clicking all around, the chanting voices raised: *kah-kai, kah-kai, imberrunni kah-kai... Brau, brau, brau!*
>
> The black drunks were yelling, screaming: *Bloody puggin bastard!*
>
> The white drunks bellowing, shrilling: *Show me the way to go home...*
>
> Then the tooting of cars and banging of cans and a bang or two of explosives from near and far, the giant's dijeridoo of the steamer at the distant jetty—*Boomb*—

boomba—booooooo! and the crowd with Mr. Turkney
bellowing and shrilling to beat it all: *Should auld
acquaintance be forgot and never brought to mind...
should auld acquaintance be forgot in days of auld lang
syne...Happy New Year everybody...Happy New Year.*
It dwindled away to silence—to silence over which
Igulgul rose, misshapen almost unto death.[8]

In 'The Waste Land' the confidence and coherence of Elizabethan
civilisation is set against the fragmented neurosis of modern civilisation. In *Poor Fellow My Country* the spiritual certainty of Aboriginal
culture is set against the spiritual emptiness, as Herbert sees it, of
modern Australia. 'Show me the way to go home', shrill the white
drunks, unconsciously revealing the cause of their malaise. The
home their hearts are set on is half a world away. They are colonials
still, never having learned to make the land they now live in truly
their own.

And how foolish they are, Herbert's descriptions imply, for
this is a land with so much to offer. Here, as in earlier books,
Herbert's descriptions of the land are full of a sense of its wondrous
beauty and pulsating life: the billabongs 'blue with the sky and
electric heliotrope with masses of floating lilies'; the sea 'an expanse
of blazing silver', the hills 'bright emerald with sweet pickin' [...]
where silver rocks spouted fountains that joined to become molten
red copper gushing under every culvert, drowning the grass'.[9] It is
also a land that gives richly to those who treat it properly. Again
and again, Herbert describes the successful hunter-gatherer activities
of his Aboriginal characters: the catching of geese, ducks, rock
wallabies, porcupines, catfish and crabs, the finding of turtle eggs,
cycad nuts and wild honey.[10] The methods are described in detail
and sound accurate, but if the techniques are realistic, the results are
not. There is never the slightest doubt of the outcome, never any
sense that the hunters may find no crabs in the mud bank or the
porcupines may choose not to appear. It is not realism Herbert is
aiming at here. The purpose is to create the sense of a promised
land flowing with milk and honey for those who approach it in the
proper spirit.

As well, though, as picturing its rich promise, Herbert also stresses the great challenges Australia presents to newcomers. He finds symbolic expression for those challenges in the cult of Tchamala. Descriptions of the cult's leader, Bobwirridirridi, stress the, to white eyes, alienating ugliness of the old man:

> It was of human shape, greyish, or blackish made grey with dust and ashes and ancient body hair, so as to appear kindred to the crawling roots. It had stick legs, [...] arms like a mantis, a tuft of grey hair sticking up like the crest of an angry bird out of a grubby ochred head-band, [...] an almost flat nose with slit septum dangling loosely from enormous nostrils [...a] scrub-turkey-like neck back and front.[11]

Bobwirridirridi is an incarnation of the ancient land and culture to which newcomers must adapt. The association with the natural world is insistent (dust, roots, sticks, mantis, crest of a bird, scrub-turkey). Association with the Dreamtime is also subtly implied in his kinship with 'the crawling roots', for these are the roots created when Tchamala hung his pythons from the branches of the banyan tree. To ensure readers make the connection, Herbert describes the banyans making 'the ruddy sandstone look as if crawling with grey snakes'.[12] The challenge to the reader's understanding and response presented by Bobwirridirridi symbolises the challenge Australia poses to newcomers. It is the challenge of adapting to a land utterly different from any they have previously known. That challenge is further emphasised by the brutal rituals of the Snake Cult. The confronting description of the ritual rape, mutilation and murder of Savitra is the most powerful expression of what Herbert once called Australia's 'awful invading alienness'[13], and presents in its starkest form the challenge Australia presents to newcomers.

It is a challenge, Herbert thinks, most have failed. Why they have failed is suggested allegorically through contrasting descriptions of the behaviour of three newcomers to northern Australia: Lydia, Alfie and Rifkah. The order in which each arrives is significant: Lydia, the first, represents the attitudes of early colonialists, Alfie, the second, those of modern Australians, while Rifkah, the third, represents an ideal future migrant. To encourage an allegorical reading of these characters, Herbert presents them in a series of parallel scenes whose similarities of detail prompt comparisons between their different responses to the land and its people. These scenes include the first visit of each to the Beatrice River Races, the Painted Caves and the Rainbow Pool, and their first encounters with Aboriginals.

On their first visit to the races, Lydia and Alfie behave in similar ways. Both assume that whatever they want must take precedence over everything else. Both foist themselves on Delacy when he clearly does not want them.[14] Neither is concerned that their behaviour offends local sensibilities.[15] Rifkah, in contrast, conducts herself with tact and restraint. Where the others led, she follows. Where they quizzed Delacy and demanded services, she answers questions and asks for nothing. Like Alfie, she is wearing an inappropriately 'mannish outfit'. Unlike Alfie, she defers to local custom as soon as she is made aware of it, allowing Nanago to get 'her something more appropriate'. Like Alfie, she joins the Lily Lagoons stable party. Unlike Alfie, she does not barge in but 'naturally as it were, became one of the strappers'.[16] These contrasts involve more than good manners. They demonstrate that Rifkah, unlike the others, approaches Australia with humility. She wants to learn and is willing to change to fit in with the culture.

The difference between the women is further explored in descriptions of their first encounter with Aboriginals. For both Lydia and Rifkah, the setting is a bush camp whose unlovely details Herbert stresses. Lydia's response is typically colonial. Asked what she thinks, she says, 'They seemed just animals'.[17] She has no desire for further contact. In one respect Rifkah's response matches Lydia's. She too was 'obviously disgusted, the way her beautiful nose was wrinkling'. But, unlike Lydia, 'doggedly she carried on with the inspection', refusing the offer to disengage, taking out her handkerchief to wipe the 'long candles of snot [...] hanging from [a] baby's nostrils'[18], preferring to stay and do what she can, however little, to help.

Alfie's first encounter with Aboriginals occurs in the 'Halfcaste Home' and in some ways she responds well. She is affectionate. She does what she can to improve their conditions. She fights for their rights. The one thing she does not do is treat them as equals. Herbert makes this clear later, in her relationship with Nanago. Alfie treats Nanago as she does the children in Port Palmeston, with easy, gushing affection.[19] But it is as hard for her to see Nanago as a real woman as it is for Lydia to see the bush camp Aboriginals as real humans. Though a guest in her house, Alfie makes no attempt to hide her designs on Nanago's husband. She assumes that being white gives her rights no Aboriginal woman, wife or not, could possibly deny and, when Nanago objects, she slaps the upstart who has dared question those rights.[20] If Lydia represents the arrogance and ignorance of initial conquest, Alfie represents the sometimes well-meaning, sometimes self-serving paternalism of later arrivals.

In contrast to Alfie, Rifkah is at first scared of Aboriginals. 'She made no pretense. She was simply not adventuresome in a strange environment.' She is not, like Alfie, arrogantly confident in the presence of Aboriginal Australia, but nor is she, like Lydia, repelled by it. She acknowledges the alien and her fear of it, and in so doing has taken the first step to an understanding neither Lydia nor Alfie seeks, or is capable of. This difference is expressed clearly when each woman first sees the paintings of the Painted Caves. Lydia finds the paintings 'bewildering'. Her voice rises 'hysterically'. 'I feel as if I don't belong in here...nor am wanted [by] the spirit of the place', she says and then 'rushe[s] back to the point of entry'.[21] 'There was no such drastic effect' when Alfie viewed the paintings. 'Pivoting for better angles of view on sharp-toed high-heel riding boots, her comments were mainly those of any knowledgeable art-gallery walker: "Hmm...striking, isn't it... primitive, but striking."' Commenting on Lydia's reaction, she says, 'She was a Pommy [...] an alien in the land...the strangeness frightened her'.[22] What she refuses to recognise is that she is no less alien. Indeed Lydia's passionate rejection implies a more genuine awareness of the 'Spirit of the Land' than Alfie's superficial praise. Mockingly, Delacy takes up her comment and points the lesson:

> 'You don't consider yourself an alien?'
> 'Why should I...when I'm second generation Australian?'
> 'You beat me. I'm only half a generation...'[23]

For half his life Delacy has worked at understanding Aboriginal Australia. Until Alfie does the same, she will remain an alien in her own country.

Rifkah's response to the paintings is like Lydia's in one respect. She too is frightened and leaves quickly. Asked what upset her, Rifkah replies, 'It vos so strange […] so strong vit' magic…and meaning I do not understand'.[24] In order to draw the most direct of parallels, Herbert has Esk ask Rifkah whether she felt 'rejected'. She replies:

> No. It is only I vont to help zese people. Like children zey seem to need help. Zen suddenly you see zey haf somezing you cannot understand […] somezing so strong and old […] like Jewish Ethos […] ze ritual of ze synagogue, ze household…it bring Gott to you […] I moost learn to feel like zat for Aboriginal zing, or my feeling is not true. So I get fright' lil bits ven I see zat strong Aboriginal-gott-zing staring down at me. […] You see, General, I am changing my religion. So far I am Proselyte of Gate, as Jews say, still outside. So…zat Burning Bush up zere…I moost go to it vit' my face cover up, and barefoot.[25]

This is how, Herbert implies, newcomers should approach Australia—as suppliants, not striding brashly in, assuming acceptance. They must take things slowly, doing their best to understand and adapt, not closing their eyes and ears and imposing their will.

If only all migrants had been like Rifkah, the dream of *Australia Felix* might have become reality. Instead, too few have had the desire, humility or patience to work at understanding their new country. In the symbolism of *Poor Fellow My Country* this unwillingness appears in the way white Australians have related to the land, and to its original inhabitants. As far as the land is concerned, it is not only newcomers like Lydia who look at it and see nothing but 'awful monotony […] a drab green-grey'. That is, says Delacy, 'the way most people see it…people born for generations in it'. If only, he continues, they had learned to look with the eyes of the 'truly native', they would see that far from being monotonous, 'no place on earth has natural variety in any way comparable with Australia', and far from being drab, it is 'filled with colour'.[26] Of course, if your eyes remain as untutored as they are bound to be on first arrival, you will never see Australia properly. Only when the eye ceases its search for the European spectrum of colour can the Australian colour burst forth. Only when it stops its yearning for oak and ash, rose and daffodil, will it see the fascinating variety of Australia's flora and fauna. Again Rifkah is the model. Eager to learn, she

> roam[ed] the neighbourhood [...] taking note of all that was shown her: the sprouting and budding, the shedding of old bark to reveal the wonder of what had been created in secret meanwhile, the frantic masonry of termites and engineering of ants.[27]

The attitude of white Australians to the land's original inhabitants is a further sign of their unwillingness to work at understanding Australia. Even those whose job it is to do so are unwilling to learn even the most basic facts about Aboriginal culture. McCusky has no idea why Prindy will not name his dead father. If, Herbert ironically comments, 'this man who knew Aboriginal minds and ethics so well that he [...] aspired to become their Number-One Daddy-o' had bothered to learn something about his charges, he would have known that 'before one could utter the name of a dead person a full year must elapse'.[28] Few whites in *Poor Fellow My Country* have the slightest knowledge of Aboriginal culture, and even fewer see that knowledge as an essential part of being Australian. Herbert deftly suggests the arrogance of their attitude through descriptions that contrast unlovely whites with the graceful Aboriginals they reject. The obese drunkard Piggy Trotters is set against the beauty of the boy he would never acknowledge as grandson.[29] The slatternly habits and gross body of Dotty O'Dowdy are contrasted with the loveliness of the girl she presumes to treat like an animal:

> Dotty looked [Nell] over as one would an animal, but without touching her. 'Are you clean' [...] She led the way in to her cluttered scent-reeking bedroom [...] and sat

before her dressing-table mirror, a heaving, blubbery mass of flesh.[30]

Instead of being willing to learn and adapt, most migrants, the symbolism suggests, come to Australia as carpetbaggers, interested in taking, not giving, exploiting, not loving. The attitudes of the carpetbagger are signified in images of a land laid waste and a people brutalised. As Prindy travels towards Aldinbinyah, the whole history of the destructive exploitation of Australia is exposed. Each stage of his journey records the effects of progressive waves of predatory newcomers. First the early settlers with their introduced animals destroying a previously balanced ecology:

Some of the first holes were damp enough to grow moss; but most were just hard-baked clay sterilized by rooting pigs.

Next the pastoralists:

The last of the billabongs were fouled with cattle dung and churned up mud out of which bleached bones and horns protruded. [...] No more knee-deep Flinder's grass growing on the little flats. [...] Every shady spot was now a dung heap.

Next the miners:

What had been done to the country they had passed through, by pigs and cattle, was nothing compared with what the gold miners of forty or fifty years before had done to the region they now entered. [...] All that grew [...] besides the weeds, the stinking-rodger, the castor-oil bush, the Chinee burrs, were the slow-decaying parts of the edifices erected by those who had brought Civilization into the land.

Finally the road builders:

Their progress towards civilization was soon to be measured [...] by the smell, the dust, the smoke of gasoline

> and dieseline and gelignite. [...] Now there was dust to be
> seen dulling the natural sheen of leaves evolved to reflect
> a blasting Sun and now tending to wither under it—dust,
> dust, dust—on everything. The guts of animals that ate
> the grass must be full of mud.[31]

Whereas the original inhabitants were its custodians, the newcomers
are a blight upon the land. As Jeremy flies in to Sydney, images of
disease proliferate: 'Townships pocked the plains, abcessed [sic] the
woodlands, carbuncled the hills, binding themselves to the host
they'd settled on [...] sucking of its substance'.[32]

Images of a land laid waste are reinforced by images of a
people brutalised. Aboriginal children with policemen's chains round
their 'slender golden neck[s]'[33] and Aboriginal girls raped by unlovely
white men are powerful symbols of the carpetbagger's destructive
attitudes:

> Nell stood under the streaming shower [...] in all the
> slender grace [...] of Australoid womanhood. Breathing
> heavily, Nobby [...] lifted the screen [...]
> She gasped, 'No-more...no-more!' But he flung himself
> on her, [...] put an arm on her throat when she tried to cry
> out, in a moment had her overpowered, got to her. It was
> over in seconds. [...] He got off her, reached for her hand
> to pull her up. She snatched it away. He scowled:
> ''Ere...that'll do you! Yo' me girl now.'[34]

Nobby's rape of Nelyerri symbolises the rape of Australia, his final
words an expression of the carpetbagger attitude. 'I've raped you,
therefore you are mine', rather than 'I've wooed you and I am yours'.
Thirty pages later, another rape, a different white man, an identical
claim of possession: 'Tha's bes' poke I ever 'ad. You goin' 'o be my
girl, eh? My girl'.[35]

Carpetbagging attitudes to the new country are one reason
for the failure of the dream of *Australia Felix*; colonial attitudes
towards the old country are another. Those attitudes are seen in *Poor
Fellow My Country* at all levels of society. On the one hand, the

Prime Minister himself speaks of Britain as his 'spiritual home'.[36] On the other, the ordinary folk of Beatrice River listen without protest as an Australian naval officer harangues them thus:

> Our grand old Empire is fighting for her life [...] Not long ago we heard a broadcast by our beloved leader, dear old Winny. [...] Now's the hour we British face our destiny.[37]

No-one queries the assumption that 'we' are 'British', 'our leader' 'dear old Winny'. Only Delacy and Finnucane see anything wrong in such sentiments. And Finnucane's objections come not from a sense of Australian patriotism but from an allegiance to 'ould Ireland' as wrongheaded as the British imperialism of the others.

The colonial attitude is also reflected in the British symbolism against which Delacy rails: the use of British placenames for Australian towns, the mountains and rivers named after British monarchs, the singing of the British national anthem at public gatherings, the picture of the British monarch on classroom walls. 'We live', he says, 'in a land the wonder of which, as damned and doomed Colonials, we've been unable to see. What wonder is in our lives is taken at second-hand, moth-eaten, only half comprehended, from our origins'.[38] We must, he argues, stop looking to the cultures from which we came for our symbols, and start looking to cultures native to Australia. Only then will 'the non-indigenous [...] come truly to feel at home'. While 'only true Aborigines' can 'feel at one with' Aboriginal myth[39], the rest of us can at least learn to value Aboriginal myth as an expression of the spirit of the land. 'Are the legends of the Ancient Druids', he says, 'any the less satisfying to the English because based on culture long ante-dating the coming of the people who became the English?'[40] By learning to respect the history and traditions of their country's first inhabitants, Australians will demonstrate they have stopped looking backwards to European origins and started building a new, Australian sense of self.

Australia's colonial attitude is further reflected in its acceptance of constitutional and economic ties, against which Delacy also rails. Australia is 'dominated by the British Parliament, and ultimately by British capital'.[41] Each state has 'its Governor, appointed by the

British Crown, living in regal isolation under the Union Jack and possessing all the privileges and prerogatives of the Sovereign, even to taking over Government if need be'.[42] Australia is 'still governed from Westminster to the extent of what [...] is called somewhat vaguely Function', and General Esk is sent to Australia in the same way he might have been sent 'to India, Burma, any such place still ruled from Westminster'.[43] The dominance of British capital meanwhile is seen in Lord Vaisey, 'the English landlord' who holds 'all the country worth a damn' and has 'in his pocket every citizen of similar worth'.[44] As for the unions, the Port Hartog unionists are as much lackeys of a foreign power (in their case, Russia) as the squatter who accepts an English absentee landlord as master. Australia, complains Fergus Ferris, has 'never been any better than a federation of British Colonies' and is ruled not from 'Canberra...but from Westminster, Moscow, Rome'.[45]

Another sign of Australia's colonial attitudes is its willingness to enter wars that serve British, not Australian, interests. World War I, says Delacy, prevented us 'establishing ourselves truly as a nation'. It 'decimated our manhood and bankrupted us'.[46] He is equally scathing about Australia's willingness to serve British interests in the European phase of World War II.[47] It is only when Japan enters the war that, with Australia itself now threatened, the situation for Delacy changes. 'War with Japan' offered a 'chance of true independence and nationhood' provided Australians themselves 'make the decision whether or not to fight them'.[48] He is furious when a new command is formed called 'ABDA [...] American, British, Dutch, Australian, in that order', remarking bitterly, 'It's a wonder they bothered to include us at all [...] seeing that in fishing round for a C-in-C for it they haven't made mention of a man of ours'.[49]

The problem, suggests *Poor Fellow My Country*, is partly one of leadership. The legacy of the convict colony remains. Rulers still rule not in the national interest but in the interests of their own sectional group. They serve the interests of the colonial power because in so doing they serve their own. In a statement published after the ousting of Whitlam, Herbert claimed: 'from the beginning we have been bossed from the outside—the alien masters have never been short of agents within to do their bidding, people who never came to love the land as was natural for most of us'.[50] In *Poor Fellow My Country* Lydia describes the Australian ruling class as 'colonial louts and toadies'. Lord Vaisey's leases, she reminds Delacy, were 'granted to him readily enough by your Government'. 'That's the pity of it...' he sighs, 'Australians are to blame'.[51]

The non-ratification of the Statute of Westminster is, for Delacy, the ultimate proof of the self-interested, colonial attitudes of Australian leaders. The statute empowered dominion governments to 'amend or repeal British legislation applying to them' but, unlike Canada, Australia chose not to ratify it, for reasons explained by General Esk thus:

> [Scullin] came back from Westminster to find one Lang, Premier of the State of New South Wales, in process of being sacked by the State Governor, one Game, an Englishman [...] a frightfully high-handed thing to do, evidently engineered by British banking interests, because this man Lang wanted to introduce some unorthodox fiscal policy to beat the effect of the financial depression [...] Well, Mr. Lang called on Mr. Scullin to support him and throw the British Garrison into the sea. Scullin could have, too, quite lawfully, under the ratified Statute of Westminster [...] At the time his, Scullin's, Federal Labor Party was collapsing around him. There was fighting in the streets of Sydney, a Fascist-type uprising [...] Scullin was deadly scared and deliberately let the Ratification slide, dodging the responsibility true nationhood would have left him with.[52]

For Herbert the situation was archetypal. An Australian patriot prevented from serving Australian interests because his action might hurt British banks. And prevented because an Australian Prime Minister, and a Labor one at that, preferred to maintain his own position at the cost of subservience to Britain rather than embark on the risky road of true independence. Nor is Scullin the only culprit. Delacy taxes Silver Tongue, as Menzies is called in the book, with his continuing failure to ratify the statute. Menzies is unrepentant:

'Where would ratification get us?'
'It would give us the independence that we only have
in token now.' [...]
'We can't afford to be independent. We've neither the
population nor the quality of people fit for it. We are still
colonial people. The Empire is our country.'

Menzies has no problem with what Delacy sees as the 'interference'
of Britain:

'What you call outside interference...where do you think
we'd be without it?'
'We would be independent...and by being so would
have the self-respect we utterly lack now as a Nation.'[53]

The problem is, *Poor Fellow My Country* suggests, that
ordinary Australians neither have, nor want, the kind of national self-
respect Delacy dreams of. If Australia's leaders have failed the test
of nationhood, so too have Australia's people. Menzies answers
Delacy's call for self-respect with: 'How many of our nine million
people do you reckon have any sense of what you call self respect?
[...] All the masses want is a home of some sort, a job, a little
pleasure'. 'You don't', responds Delacy, 'have a very high opinion of
the people you're responsible to'.[54] But neither does Delacy. After a
day spent sampling opinion on the Sydney ferries, he concludes
sadly that all the general populace 'wanted was security. What did it
matter who held the money, so long as they got their little whack?'[55]
Earlier he has agreed with Esk that Australians 'will sell out at any
price. They have no love of the soil. All they want is money, beer,
sport, a good time'. The people are no better than their leaders: the
leaders with their dream 'of personal power' and the 'vast majority' of
the people 'with no dream at all but of filling their bellies'.[56]

In the light of these views, it is surprising John Curtin is
treated so churlishly in *Poor Fellow My Country*. Why does Herbert
make so little of his patriotism? He mentions that Curtin 'was not
only frankly Anti-Imperialist, but during the Last Turn-out had been
jailed for so being'[57], but makes little of his refusal to kowtow to

COLONIALS AND CARPETBAGGERS

Britain when, with two divisions of the Australian Imperial Force sailing home for Australia, Churchill requested their diversion to Burma. Curtin's response was firm:

> From your telegram of February 22 it appears that you have diverted the convoy towards Rangoon and had treated our approval of this vital diversion as merely a matter of form. [...] Now you contemplate using the A.I.F. to save Burma. All this has been done, as in Greece, without adequate air support. We feel a primary obligation to save Australia [...] In the circumstances it is quite impossible to reverse a decision which we made with the utmost care and which we have affirmed and reaffirmed.[58]

Both the haughty tone and unyielding content of Curtin's refusal should have gladdened Herbert's heart, but it rates no more in *Poor Fellow My Country* than the statement that:

> Following [the announcement of the fall of Singapore], was a nasty hint from Storm-the-Barricades [Curtin] that, despite his insistence on having every Australian soldier home, Old Jack [Churchill] was covertly diverting the convoys already on their way, in a last desperate hope of bolstering the tumbling ruins of his Empire by submitting them to slaughter in Burma.[59]

Not only does this give Curtin no praise; it fails even to make clear that his actions have been both patriotically firm and successful. Far from praising Curtin, Herbert goes out of his way to ridicule him, mocking his rhetoric[60] and quoting with approval a British comment that he had 'the Mind of a Schoolboy'. Stranger still, Herbert makes no mention at all of Curtin's Minister for External Affairs, 'Doc' Evatt, who, in 1942, ratified the Statute of Westminster against fierce parliamentary opposition. Why is there no mention of this? Why, instead of portraying Evatt as a hero, does Herbert omit him altogether? The fact that he knew Evatt personally, and had solicited and received his help on more than one occasion, makes the omission even more churlish.[61]

One reason for the churlish treatment is found in 'the fact that Storm-the-barricades had fairly screamed for help from America within hours of the outbreak of the Pacific War'. The 'stupid bastard gets us free of British Imperialism, only to hand us over to the Yank', complains Delacy. 'I had a lingering hope that what looked like his Australianism would have brought us at last to stand on our own feet. Maybe the old leg-irons hang too heavily on us for us ever to be able to stand alone.'[62] Curtin saw the appeal to the United States as an assertion of independence from Britain. 'Australia looks to America', he said, 'free of any pangs as to our traditional links or kinship with the United Kingdom. [...] We know, too, that Australia can go, and Britain can still hold on. We are therefore determined that Australia shall not go'.[63] Herbert, judging Curtin's action with the benefit of hindsight, reads it not as an assertion of independence but as yet more subservience.

The final sign of how deeply rooted colonial attitudes are in Australia is the fact that their fiercest critic is himself tainted by them. 'The strength of your patriotism', Esk tells Delacy, 'is in the bitterness you feel about the general lack of true love of country in your compatriots'.[64] But it is a strange sort of patriotism that berates Australia as Delacy does. Australia, he says, is a 'lousy thing', a 'hateful community', 'bankrupt of anything but [...] stupidity, greed, guile, pettiness, cruelty'.[65] He attempts to justify his position by making a distinction between Australia and Australians. 'There is this kinship', he says, 'with one's country, if not with one's community'.[66] But the distinction is untenable and it is hard to see how, in his constant denigration of Australia, Delacy can lay claim to the patriotism he finds lacking in others. He is also equally implicated in subservience towards England. While always assuming the worst about Australians, he accepts without demur Esk's flattering account of British motives. 'We judge the world', says Esk, 'by ourselves... fair play and all that. It's our fair play and honesty of intention that gets us where we want to go'. Later, and with no hint of irony, Delacy tells Rifkah the British are 'so Decent, to put it as they do, about everything'.[67]

Delacy's blindness to his own failures in patriotism and sub-servience to the British adds the final ironic proof of how entrenched those flaws are in the Australian psyche. Whether Herbert was aware of the irony is another matter. On the evidence available, it does not seem so. Nowhere in the book is Delacy's scorn for Australia criticised or the complicit nature of his relationship with Esk questioned. Rather, in the picture he gives of Esk, the author reveals his own tendency to kowtow to the British. When, for instance, an Australian colonel orders troops to come to the aid of the police:

> Then the voice of General Esk was raised, in a tone never heard round these parts, cutting-sharp with power of personality and authority: 'Countermand that order, Colonel!'
>
> The Colonel swung on him, gaping. The General added: 'This is a civil disturbance. Get your men out of the way.'
>
> 'But...but, Sir, we've always helped the police in trouble...'
>
> 'I don't care what you've always done. It isn't a convict settlement any more. Countermand that order, man...or I'll do it for you, and relieve you of your command.'[68]

The implication is clear. It takes a real officer, a true-blue British officer, to stop the lousy colonials from behaving like lousy colonials.

Herbert's failure to recognise the flaws in Delacy's patriotism was another instance of the 'confessional' element making it hard for him to recognise in his fictional alter ego weaknesses he failed to recognise in himself. Like Delacy, Herbert was never backward in expressing both love for his country and scorn for his country-men. During his time in England, he yearned, he says, for 'Terra Australis, my brown land, my home-sweet-home', but, he con-tinues, 'my patriotism cooled off considerably after a spell back home in the unadulterated society of my countrymen'.[69] Both tone and content are pure Delacy. Pure Delacy, too, is the following des-cription of Herbert's meeting with the head of Collins Publishing, a British baronet:

When I contracted with Collins (Aust) I did not reckon on making myself available for what I called the Imperial Patronage of the reigning Sir William. Soon I was informed he would be visiting his Australian stable in 1975 and would be wanting to meet me. I kicked hard, declaring that I was no hack of his, that my contract was not with him but Collins (Aust). I have always avoided such people as the Absentee landlords who have always been the curse of my country.

Now Sir William was currently reading *Poor Fellow My Country*, and with gusto, according to reports, calling it one of the few masterpieces his house had published. I was informed that he wanted to meet me not as publisher but as admiring reader. So I had to concede or look a pig. However I did so only with the unequivocal proviso that I meet him as an enemy (no hand-shake) and leave it to him to make friends if he still wished it after hearing all I would have to tell him of how I feel about Absentee Landlords and Imperial Patronage. [...]

My war of independence—surely the first stand made in this craven country since Jack Lang—lasted 3 days— I guess I should express some kindly feeling for Sir William too (Il Padrone as I dubbed him, that being the name for the boss of the Mafia, which also calls itself a Family [...] a name that greatly tickled him, by the way). For he took it like the intelligent gentleman he is—as no Lousy Aussie publisher ever could.[70]

The similarity between this and Delacy's response to Esk is obvious: the ostentatious assertion of hostility to British hegemony followed by the rapid conversion and unabashed preference for British aristocrat over Lousy Aussie. It is one of the great ironies of *Poor Fellow My Country* that the attitudes not only of its main character but also of its author are the final shattering evidence of the colonialism against which both rail.

The picture *Poor Fellow My Country* gives of Australia is fiercely critical. Whether it is accurate or not is, strictly speaking, not a literary question, but it is one no Australian reader can ignore. Adrian Mitchell, writing in *The Oxford History of Australian Literature*, is in no doubt about the answer. 'The despondency at its core', he writes, 'suggests glowering prophetic vision grounded in the thirties, rather than in the observed reality of contemporary Australia. [...] Imaginatively [Herbert] is [...] stranded in attitudes, convictions and prejudices that are increasingly dated'.[71] Whether Mitchell is right is another question. Back in the seventies, when I first read the book, it did not seem so to me. Nor does it seem so now. On the contrary, recent events suggest that the picture the book gives of Australia is as relevant now as it ever was.

The legacy of our colonial past is still much as *Poor Fellow My Country* pictures it. How else to explain our Prime Minister's decision to mark the centenary of federation not by inviting foreign dignitaries to Australia but by leading a pilgrimage of Australian political leaders to visit the Queen in London? How else to explain the continued, passionate opposition to taking the Union Jack out of the Australian flag and abolishing the Queen's Birthday holiday? How else to explain the Australian people's decision to greet the new millennium by rejecting an independent republic in favour of continuing allegiance to the Queen of Britain? Nothing testifies to the continued relevance of *Poor Fellow My Country* more than that decision and how and why it was taken. When Alfie, in *Poor Fellow My Country*, rails against 'having to swear an oath of allegiance' to 'the bloody King of England', Frank replies, 'Probably most Australians feel that way about it...but don't think it matters'.[72] That attitude was well represented in the letters pages of Australian newspapers in the weeks leading up to the referendum. 'Why are we spending millions of dollars and all this time and effort on it. Will it shorten our hospital waiting times?'[73] asked one correspondent. 'The link with the British crown is a purely symbolic one and offers no impediment to the way we want to run our country'[74], argued another. In other letters, the colonial attitude was as strong as ever. 'A no vote', wrote one correspondent, 'would enable survivors of World War II [...] to enjoy our final few years living under a constitutional monarchy system for which we volunteered our services'.[75] Meanwhile, the leadership behaved as *Poor Fellow My Country* would predict. The Prime

Minister, preferring the security of the British connection to the uncharted waters of independence, cynically phrased the referendum question to ensure that republican fought republican and his (the minority) view prevailed. In similar, self-serving fashion, an ex-leader of the Labor Party, having some years earlier swallowed his republican principles sufficiently to accept the governor generalship, proceeded to swallow them even further in urging Australians to vote against the republic.

The sacking of Whitlam and the emergence of parties like 'One Nation' provide further testimony to the enduring relevance of *Poor Fellow My Country*. The similarities between One Nation and the novel's Free Australia party are many and obvious: the patriotic names, the strident nationalism, the racist scapegoating, the fragmenting into competing factions. The similarities between the sacking of Whitlam and the sacking of Lang are equally obvious. In the novel, Governor Game's dismissal of Lang is presented as evidence of Australian leaders serving the interests of Britain in order to serve their own interests. In 1974 Governor Kerr's dismissal of Whitlam was seen by many as evidence of Australian leaders serving the interests of the United States in order to serve their own. On this reading, America, disturbed at signs of independence in Whitlam's government, encouraged a self-serving coup by the opposition party.[76] Whatever the truth of America's involvement in the dismissal of Whitlam, signs of independence have been few and far between since his departure. Neo-colonial servility from both Labor and Liberal governments is again the order of the day: seen in the speedy commitment of Australian troops whenever America calls for support, the acceptance on Australian soil of secretive surveillance facilities controlled by America, and the speed with which, on every occasion, Australia hastens to toe the American diplomatic line. Malcolm Fraser, interviewed after a ceremony to mark the centenary of federation, bemoaned the fact that Australia was the only American ally to support President Bush's plan for a missile defence system. He hoped, he said, that Australia would one day become independent of America.[77] It was an ironic, iconic moment: on the centenary of federation an incumbent Liberal government criticised by a former Liberal Prime Minister for subservience to the same foreign power many believe helped him, thirty years earlier, to overthrow a duly constituted Australian Government.

The rejection of Whitlam in the election following his ousting further supports the picture given by *Poor Fellow My Country*. The electorate's unease with a government that placed political and social development before economic security matches the novel's picture of a people more interested in material well-being than the intangible benefits of asserting national identity. More recent elections have shown no change in the attitude of Australians to Prime Ministers with a vision encompassing something greater than economic well-being. Paul Keating, with his insistence on the republic, Aboriginal reconciliation and Australia's place in the world, became the most hated Prime Minister in recent history. In contrast, while they do not love him, Australians feel safe with Keating's successor, a man who opposes the republic and Aboriginal reconciliation, whose only 'vision' is to change the tax system and who judges every issue on the grounds of its benefits to the economy. In *Poor Fellow My Country* Delacy describes an Australian politician as someone who 'talked nationalism as if a nation were not a band of brothers bound by the mystery of earth-kinship but a limited company—The Commonwealth of Australia Inc'.[78] The description fits John Howard like a glove.

Further testimony to the relevance of *Poor Fellow My Country* can be found in the continuing debate over issues relating to Aboriginality and Australia's sense of self. A book published in 2000, for instance, was described as confronting the following questions:

> Can a white person, one born in Australia, ever belong here? We might be attached to the land, but can we ever really belong? Would a proper, formal and complete, honouring of the past; a full reconciliation between black and white alter white Australia's sense of belonging?[79]

The issues canvassed in *Poor Fellow My Country* are clearly still important and remain unresolved. Unlike Canada and New Zealand, no formal reconciliation with the Indigenous population has yet been achieved. The Prime Minister opposes any official apology, and polls show that a majority of Australians support his refusal.

The government's response to recommendations from the Human Rights Commission on the 'Stolen Generation' of Aboriginals removed from their families between 1910 and 1970 provides further evidence of continuing relevance. The commission recommended an official apology for 'gross violations of human rights'. The government's response came from its Minister for Aboriginal Affairs, a man whose similarity to *Poor Fellow My Country*'s Dr Cobbity is uncanny. Like Cobbity, Minister Herron seems to have been 'appointed to the job without the slightest knowledge of Aborigines'. Like Cobbity, he is a medical doctor, and for him too it seems 'the Aboriginal Problem's a Health Problem'.[80] Like Cobbity, he seems genuinely concerned to achieve improvements in the living conditions of Aboriginals but does so with all Cobbity's arrogant paternalism. His response to the recommendations was typically insensitive. He queried the number of children taken, quibbled over the term 'Stolen Generation', rejected any formal apology or compensation, and finally, as Cobbity would have been, was genuinely surprised that his response offended Aboriginals.[81]

Finally, and sadly, *Poor Fellow My Country* is undated in its pessimistic views on the future for Aboriginals who are unwilling or unable to 'assimilate'. In 1973, a year before *Poor Fellow My Country*'s publication, the Aboriginal leader Pat Dodson was involved in a study of Aboriginal living conditions in Australia. A quarter of a century later, in 2001, he was reported as saying, 'I think things have got worse. The social disintegration that appears to be going on, the family breakdown, the high levels of youth suicide, the health statistics…it's appalling'.[82] Statistical surveys paint a similarly depressing picture.[83] The case *Poor Fellow My Country* argues has yet to be proven wrong by events. Aboriginal communities that resist 'assimilation' continue to move, it seems, not towards 'integration' but 'disintegration', and continue to be blamed by whites for so doing.

The evidence cited is, of course, limited and subjective. This is not a sociological treatise and my intention has simply been to point to a few of the things that suggest that, though the externals of Australian society have changed since the thirties, the picture *Poor Fellow My Country* gives of that period embodies qualities that are as central to the Australian psyche now as they ever were. That is not to say the book gives a complete picture. For that, one must take *Capricornia* and *Poor Fellow My Country* together. Where *Poor Fellow My Country* deals with Australia's weaknesses, *Capricornia* deals with its strengths. Where *Poor Fellow My Country* deals with the ethos of that entity we call 'the nation', *Capricornia* deals with the spirit of the individuals who make up the nation. And that spirit is as evident in 2003 as it was in 1930.

It is one of the great ironies of Australia that, as a nation, it seems deficient in those very qualities individual Australians possess in delightful abundance. The nation that clings to its colonial past, is fearful of asserting its independence from the United States and seems to lack a clear sense of its own identity is peopled by individuals whose sturdy self-reliance and sense of self are unquestionable. The nation that supports the mean-spirited refugee and social welfare policies of a government like John Howard's is made up of individuals whose willingness to help others is surpassed by none. As anyone who lives in Australia can testify, there is still in Australians that sense of brotherhood Herbert celebrated in *Capricornia*. The codes of mateship remain strong and extend far beyond 'mates' to anyone who needs help. To give just one corroboratory incident from the many I and my family could cite after twenty-five years in Australia, I think of the time I bogged my vehicle by pulling off a dual carriageway onto a treacherously sandy verge. As I stood dithering, wondering what to do, up drove a battered ute and out stepped a laconic Aussie bloke: 'What's the problem, mate?' I showed him. 'No worries!' Within minutes, he'd towed me out. It turned out he'd seen me as he was travelling in the opposite direction up the dual carriageway and had had to drive some distance before a break allowed him to turn back and come to my rescue. Where else in the world would you find that? I've lived and worked in five countries and none of them comes close.

In *Poor Fellow My Country* praise for the Swagman spirit is rare[84] and descriptions of Australians behaving in a generous-spirited way are so infrequent, only the diligent researcher notices them.[85] For the most part, ordinary Australians are represented as loutish, mindless and mean-spirited. Only once does Herbert show an ordinary Aussie behaving like a good Capricornian. When he discovers Prindy with a gashed foot, Nugget Knowles proves both kind and competent. He applies a dirty but effective tourniquet and stitches the wound. He respects Aboriginal custom, responding to Prindy's request for a dressing of pipe clay with: 'Blackfeller fashion. That's good too'. He neither looks down on Aboriginals nor exploits them. He asks Nell to marry him and, when she demurs, refuses to use his position of power to pressure her. He is, as Queeny says, a 'properly goot man'.[86] However, having taken us briefly back into the world of *Capricornia*, where ordinary Australians had a nobility worth celebrating, Herbert turns his back again on that view of Australia and resumes the bitter, jaundiced picture he now has of his fellow countrymen. When we next see Nugget, he is portrayed as unflatteringly as his unlovely brother.[87]

The picture given of Australia in *Poor Fellow My Country* is not, then, the complete picture, nor is it an objective picture. It is Australia seen through one man's eyes, the account of a participant, not a historian. And if it catches important truths, that is partly because Herbert was himself so much an Australian that he shared, and understood from the inside, even the faults he attacked most bitterly. So much an Australian, too, that though his assessment of Australia's past and present was bitter and pessimistic, his view of its future was more equivocal. He pictures that future in the two stories that constitute the main plot of the book. One, the story of Jeremy Delacy, suggests the probable future, and its outcome is tragic. The other, the story of Prindy, points to an ideal future, and its outcome, while not happy, offers a kind of visionary hope. It is to the first of these stories we now turn.

CHAPTER 12

The Tragedy of Jeremy Delacy

ARISTOTLE described the tragic hero as 'good, though not preeminently just or virtuous'.[1] The description fits Delacy. With all his faults, his intentions are good. He seeks 'to learn to love [the land] enough to feel something of what those it was stolen from feel for it...so as not to die feeling like an alien and a thief'.[2] He does what he can to make up for the theft of Aboriginal land by holding Lily Lagoons 'in trust for the blacks who aren't, by law, allowed to hold it', and letting them 'use it as they like, make any demands on me that are within my capacity'.[3] Unlike most of his fellows, he takes the trouble to learn about Aboriginals. He understands their customs, acknowledges their 'special powers', and shows respect for their culture.[4] Aboriginals believe, for instance, that the *mangan* tree has 'the power to attract and spellbind lovers' and Delacy says, 'I accept that [...] as part of an environment I don't want to feel alien in'. Another tree 'reputed to have special powers' is the *kumbitji*, the ironwood tree. 'It's believed that if you sleep under one at night you won't ever wake up again', Delacy tells Bishoff, adding that he would never sleep under one because he'd 'feel [he] was flouting the conventions of the country' if he did so.[5]

But for all his well-meaning intentions, Delacy's life, as he himself says, 'isn't a story of achievement, but of utter failure'.[6] The reasons for that failure lie in his own character. He is the 'nark', the 'spoilsport', quick to criticise others but achieving little himself. He is more inclined to outbursts of anger than to doing anything useful. His response when Prindy is believed to have drowned trying to escape from the police is typical. 'I'm going to jam it down McCusky's throat till it chokes him', he rages. He continues with a dramatic promise to 'dedicate the rest of my life to breaking the power he and the rest of the bastards like him have over other human beings, just because they've been designated Protectors of Aborigines. [...] It's time', he says, 'a man did something real about it'.[7] He's quite right. It is time he did something 'real' about it. Instead, as all too often, his response is childish, self-indulgent and ineffective. First he visits the pub where McCusky and his friends are celebrating the birth of the Irish Republic and taunts them for accepting a Protestant as president of their 'Catholic State'. 'It's a loy', the enraged cry goes up as they move to eject him. Having stirred up the Irish, he visits the Scots who are celebrating New Year at McDodds's store. A few taunts about what the Irish intend doing to Presbyterians send them rampaging to the pub, where a battle between Irish and Scots ensues. All this seems very far from doing 'something real' about injustices perpetrated against Aboriginals. Delacy attempts to justify himself, saying, 'I never felt less like playing jokes in my life. But ridicule's necessary. It's the only criticism to get at fools with'.[8] It rings hollow. It's hard to see how stirring up the Scots and Irish provides any sort of criticism of Prindy's mistreatment. The truth is Delacy never does do anything very 'real' about anything. He rants and rages but when it comes to actually doing something, the most he ever achieves is futile gestures.

Even his activities at Lily Lagoons are an evasion of real responsibility, an 'escape', as Lydia says, 'from the realities of life'. His research at the end of the book into feral pigs is, says Alfie, like 'retreating into a laboratory...to find out what someone's dying of... and doing nothing about their dying'.[9] A man's maturity, Delacy himself says, 'should first be dedication to his community, his Nation, his Species', whereas he has dedicated himself only to 'odd things'—

'the crippled animals, the fossil humans, the land [...] laboriously remade pristine'. It is, by his own standards, not nearly enough. He is, he says, 'a disappointed man', his life 'negative' and Lily Lagoons merely the 'elaborate apparatus he had built up to keep the negation functioning to the limit of efficiency'.[10]

The word 'negative' becomes, as the book proceeds, more and more often associated with Delacy.[11] He is negative in his consistent refusal to accept responsibility. 'I don't lead any movement', he says. 'I'm a one-man band...the Scrub Bull.'[12] Though he allows Alfie to involve him in the Free Australia movement, he only plays at politics. Happy to complain about what is wrong, he makes no attempt to do what serious politicians must do: work hard and organise effectively. In the speech to inaugurate his breakaway political party, he admits he believes the cause already lost: '[I]t is too late, much too late, to realize the dream of *Australia Felix* [...] the rottenness the whole thing started with has become gangrenous, cancerous...is impossible to stop'.[13] Hardly the words to inspire a fledgling party! In Delacy, love-struck Alfie thought she had found a leader strong enough to make Free Australia a force in Australian politics. What she had actually found was a man doomed to failure in everything.

The least forgivable failure is his rejection of the opportunity to defend Australia during World War II. He is fierce in his criticism of politicians for not making defence of Australia their first priority, but when Esk puts him in charge of the army in northern Australia, Delacy accepts the position very reluctantly and, as with Free Australia, soon shows himself incapable of accepting the responsibility. Instead of helping Esk unify military opinion behind a strategy that would put Australian interests first, he makes that task impossible by grandstanding with a typically self-indulgent outburst of anger against the general who commanded his brother in World War I. It's another empty gesture, but this time one with serious consequences. Delacy, true to form, takes the easy way out and resigns the commission he never wanted, leaving Esk the impossible task of winning over the generals Delacy has so needlessly infuriated. With his plans in tatters and the northern command set to fall into the hands of Fabian Cootes, Esk taxes Delacy with responsibility for the debacle. Delacy attempts to evade responsibility, accusing Esk of being interested only in the British Commonwealth, about which, he says, 'I don't give a damn'. Nor, he continues, 'do the mob back there [...] The old bullying Empire...God Save the King and Bless the Lee-Endfield [sic] Rifle will do them'. Esk cuts through this self-serving reprise of the standard Delacy diatribe with a sharp 'You also evidently don't give a damn for your own country', pointing out that, with no effective defence of its own, the only alternatives left for Australia are 'to become part of the Japanese Empire or the U.S.A. or perhaps the U.S.S.R.'. With typical selfishness, Delacy replies that he himself has another alternative: 'to die fighting any bastard who tries to intrude on the bit of country I now consider I belong to'.[14]

It's the ultimate in negativity. Damn the rest of the country so long as Delacy can hold onto the piece he loves. And negativity, as events soon show, does not produce good outcomes. Having ceded power over northern Australia to Fabian Cootes, Delacy is unable to defend even that tiny part of it for which he has clear responsibility. It was he himself who had made his ability to defend Lily Lagoons a touchstone of success:

> [F]ailure to keep Prindy as a member of his household would be tantamount to failure of what he had given his life to. He had built Lily Lagoons as it was to stand as an example to the Nation of how honesty and wisdom could correct the hitherto accepted ravaging of the land and savaging of its owners. If McCusky could walk in with his hat over his eye and remove Prindy with the blessing of constituted authority, then he, Jeremy, must accept his enemies' evaluation of the place as nothing but a hideout for misfits and outlaws.[15]

Shorn of the power Esk offered him, Delacy can do nothing to protect Lily Lagoons when Cootes commandeers it, and forces Delacy and his family to leave. 'At long last', writes Herbert, 'the keep had been breached'[16] and Delacy has no-one to blame but himself. Had he not evaded the responsibility Esk offered, it would have been he, not Cootes, who controlled what happened—not only at Lily Lagoons but over the whole of northern Australia. Having failed to protect even Lily Lagoons, Delacy has no option but to retreat even further into useless, negative isolation. His plan to defend 'the bit of country I now consider I belong to' narrows down to a 'hideout' on the plateau where he can 'fight my own war'. The futility of the gesture is obvious even to him. 'My act of defiance', he says, 'is largely one of despair', and he refuses to let Ferris join him, saying Ferris's 'defiance must be positive'.[17]

Delacy's failure is reflected in the changing responses of even his greatest admirers. One by one, they see the feet of clay.[18] 'You seduced me', Alfie bitterly says at the end of the book, 'with your passionate talk of *Terra Australis* [...You] pushed me into war against your declared enemies [...] but when the war really started, you abandoned me'. Stung, Delacy responds, 'If you really believe I've let you down, you can join me now'. 'Join you in what?' she scornfully asks. 'Sitting round that cave of yours [...] till the Japs come and murder us.' She wants something more positive than that. When he tries to advise her as of old, she snaps, 'Don't tell me what to do...you who don't do anything'.[19] Rifkah, though less harsh in her judgment, is far too positive to blind herself for long to Delacy's limitations. When he can find nothing better to do than lament, 'Our cause is lost, of course. Our Arcady is soon to be raided by a rout of bully-boys. Our Arcadians will be scattered', she loses patience. 'Vot is zis Arcady?' she snaps. 'Zese pipple are human beings hanging onto zere own country. Many are sick pipple. Many are hungry pipple.'[20] While Delacy wallows in elegiac despair, Rifkah is rolling up her sleeves ready to do something.

The cruellest and most significant of Delacy's failures is his failure to achieve the one thing he has set his heart on: to be accepted by the land and its people. The closest he comes to that is the night he wakes in the bush to find an Aboriginal man of great 'beauty and nobility' looking down on him. Next day, Billy Brew tells Delacy the Aboriginals call such apparitions 'Yalmaru'. A Yalmaru, he says, is 'a familiar spirit that attaches itself to you through all your lives, to look out for you'. When his own Yalmaru appeared, says Brew, an Aboriginal friend told him that it 'belong to some old blackfeller before, finish now for good. He lonely. He grab 'old o' you. Now you all-same blackfeller...belong country'. Delacy is pleased. 'If I see things like a blackfellow,' he says, 'then I must belong like one'.[21] But he is wrong. The appearance of his Yalmaru, while heart-warming, does not ensure Delacy's acceptance. In this, too, as in so much else, he is a tragic failure.

The touchstone of Delacy's success in connecting with Australia is his relationship with Prindy. In this book, acceptance by Prindy signifies acceptance by Australia, and Prindy never does accept Delacy in the way Delacy wants—'as his grandsire, to love him as belonging to him'.[22] Herbert takes pains to make clear that Prindy never does accept him like that. When Delacy farewells him with '*Mummuk yawarra, Mora*', and Prindy answers '*Mummuk yawarra, Mullaka*', Herbert has McCusky ask him, 'What mean *Mora*?'

> The boy answered promptly, 'Dat-one gran'daddy cal-yem young feller belong o'him.'
> 'But you don't call him Gran'daddy, eh?'[23]

No, he doesn't. He calls him *Mullaka*, 'the boss', like any other Aboriginal would. For all his longing to be otherwise, Delacy knows that to Aboriginals, Prindy included, he is 'still alien [...] the *Mullaka*, the Boss'.[24] Prindy's unwillingness to acknowledge a close relationship with Delacy becomes even more significant in the light of his acceptance of such a relationship with Billy Brew, whom he calls *Kumija*, meaning 'Paternal Grandfather', and Barbu, whom he calls 'Papa'.[25] Cruellest cut of all, had Delacy but known it, Nugget Knowles, a man for whom he has nothing but scorn, has far more success than Delacy in winning Prindy's trust. When Delacy first attempts to engage Prindy in conversation, he is treated with wary caution and silence, hard though he tries to break the ice:

> Jeremy was the only one to speak, addressing Prindy: 'Well, young feller...have a good walkabout?' The grey eyes looking over a huge sandwich did not even blink. [...]
> As they drove off, Jeremy said to the boy beside him. 'By'n'by you got to learn to drive motor car.' The grey eyes met his. 'You like that?' No answer. [...]

[T]urning to the road with mouth pursed and brows rumpled [...] Jeremy said, 'I reckon we'll go straight back to Catfish, eh?' No answer. He added, 'We'll stop at the lagoons and get some geese. How are you on goose hunt, sonny?' Prindy smiled. [...]

As they sped on their way, Jeremy asked, 'You know that yarn about Old Crocodile been pull him down that goose, Nuttagul, Dream Time?' The boy nodded. 'All right...you tell-him-'bout.'

Prindy shook his head: 'Can't do it.'

'Wha'name?'

'That-one yarn no-more belong o'me.'

'I see. All right...tell-him 'bout one yarn belong o'you.'

But Prindy was silent.[26]

When Prindy meets Nugget he shows no such reticence. From the start, he responds in open, friendly fashion. Asked how he knows about pipe clay, 'Prindy started to tell of his *koornung* friend'. Asked 'Any good with a gun, young feller?' he replies, 'I goot wit' spear'.[27] Where Delacy struggles to get answers, Nugget is met with immediate trust and openness.

The one time Delacy does achieve a closer relationship with Prindy provides, ironically, further evidence of his failure. His influence on Prindy proves as negative as his influence on everything else. The problem is that, for all his stated belief in the value of Aboriginal culture, he is uneasy about Prindy's allegiance to that culture. '[H]e has to learn now', he says, 'that there are other ways of being free than with animal cunning and savage's magic'.

[W]hen I first heard him singing that song of his '*My Rown Road*' [...] I thought of how remarkable he was, in originality, intelligence...he with his background, intuitively seeking a way of life of his own. Now when I hear him playing it on his flute, I know it's in rebellion against what we're trying to do with him. You can teach him anything. [...] Yet all he's doing at Lily Lagoons is waiting for old Bobwirridirridi to turn up. [...] He doesn't give me

any credit for having cured him. [...] [H]e believes it was
the Pookarakka got him through, brought me to him, sent
me home with him...and, God help us, the same master-
mind will deal with Mick Cusky for him.[28]

Delacy's theory and practice are at odds. In theory he applauds
Prindy's allegiance to Aboriginal Australia and search for his own
way. In practice he is no better than any other coloniser—more
well-meaning than most, but just as convinced he knows what is best
for Prindy, and just as keen to impose that view on his young charge.

With great authorial tact, Herbert makes no overt comment
on the subtle changes in Prindy during the period of Delacy's
influence. He leaves it to readers to notice and interpret the fact that
the boy who previously acknowledged no authority save Bobwirridirridi's begins to look to Delacy for guidance in even the smallest
things.

[McCusky holds] his hand out to Prindy, saying '*Mummuk,
yawarra*, sonny...it's good to see you doing so well.'
Prindy looked at Jeremy, who nodded.[29]

At this point in the novel, Prindy loses, for a time, the unyielding
resistance to white influence he shares with Bobwirridirridi. He
becomes a pawn in Delacy's negative game. Dressed up like a
tailor's dummy, he is paraded about the town in order 'to rock 'em.
They saw you', crows Delacy, 'like a blackfellow before. Now it's
going to be as what to them's a gentleman'. When Prindy looks
alarmed, Delacy assures him, 'It's all right...I know you're a blackfellow first. I won't take you away from that. I only want to prove to
them that you and your people have as much dignity as they have'.
The gap between what Delacy professes and what he does yawns
wide. It needs no white finery to prove Prindy's dignity. That Delacy
thinks it does shows how far he is from understanding what it really
means 'being a blackfellow, first and last'. That Prindy, rather than
maintaining resistance to the empty game Delacy is playing, begins
to enjoy it emphasises the negative effect of Delacy's influence. 'It
was exciting', thinks Prindy, 'to walk the streets with that stance of

Nobleness and Excellence, beside the big man who carried those qualities so well, so that every head turned to look'.[30] Exciting! To walk tamely along, dolled up in European clothes, and showing off to the foolish and the ignorant. How have the mighty fallen. From the dark mysteries of Bobwirridirridi and Tchamala to this.

Significantly, this is the only section of the book in which we are given access to Prindy's thoughts. Elsewhere, even when Prindy wanders alone for a whole chapter, Herbert refuses even to guess at his thoughts and feelings, with the result that he remains inscrutable and mysterious and we never think of him as just another little boy. At this point, we do. Relationship with Delacy turns Prindy from a figure of enigmatic power into a normal little boy with a normal little boy's weaknesses. He 'titter[s]' behind Fay's 'ample back' when she swims and gets 'a disapproving look' from Rifkah. When Ferris is involved in conversation, 'Prindy, forgotten by Fergus, looked forlorn'.[31] Nowhere else does Prindy need the attention of white men. Nowhere else does he feel an emotion as feeble as 'forlorn'. Nowhere else does he show weakness of any sort. Here, he does:

> 'I can look out for [Rifkah], Mullaka.'
> 'No, son. She'd get sick. […] Trust me. […]'
> Prindy snivelled, 'I been promise I take her away if policeman come.'
> 'And I've promised to get her free again.'
> Unconvinced, Prindy dropped fair head to hands and wept. Stroking the head, and sounding close to tears himself, Jeremy muttered, 'D'you know…I've never seen you cry before.'[32]

No! And it is his fault he sees it now. It is his influence that has emasculated Prindy. But not for much longer. Once it is clear Delacy cannot fulfil his promises, his influence is over. Prindy once more goes his own independent way, no longer accepting any authority but Bobwirridirridi's. Meeting Delacy a little later, Prindy asks whether he has heard anything about Rifkah. When Delacy says, 'No…not yet', Prindy's expression 'changed to blankness, as if the man before him had suddenly ceased to exist'.[33]

Delacy loses Prindy's trust for the same reason he later causes Prindy's death. Both are the result of an irreconcilable conflict between Delacy's values and those of Aboriginal Australia. The conflict, over the efficacy of Tchamala's magical power, symbolises the difficulty of achieving a marriage between Aboriginal and Western cultures. It is easy enough for Delacy to avoid sleeping under the *kumbitji* tree and to pay lip service to the magic of the *mangan* tree. In similar fashion might he avoid walking under ladders and refuse to destroy a child's belief in Father Christmas. It is easy enough, also, to accept those aspects of Bobwirridirridi's magic that derive from powers Western civilisation understands: 'hypnotism, ventriloquism, sleight of hand' and 'trance states'.[34] But, for all his determination to accept the ways of the land, there is a point beyond which willpower cannot take you, and at that point Delacy inevitably stumbles. The point comes when he is asked to make a leap of faith too great for one brought up in the tradition of Western rationalism. He is too much the man of science to accept that Tchamala is more than myth, that he can and does intervene in human affairs. Respect for Aboriginal lore is not the same as belief in it, and when Rifkah's life is at stake it is too much to ask Delacy to trust in Tchamala.

Prindy, on the other hand, does trust Tchamala. It was Tchamala who kept him safe in the underground river and Tchamala who helped him free Rifkah. 'Old One been do it all right', he says. When Delacy insists Rifkah must return to the police because 'it's got to be done properly [...] white-feller way', he loses what influence he has achieved over Prindy. What is so 'proper', Prindy must think, about 'white-feller way' when it has proved singularly ineffective in helping Rifkah, while Tchamala's way has proved superbly successful. It's an impasse. To the white man, Prindy's success in effecting Rifkah's escape was the result of luck, not divine intervention, and Prindy must not be allowed to take her off into the bush. Without a belief in Tchamala, how can Delacy disregard the dangers? He knows Rifkah's 'feet'll turn septic', that 'she'll get a fever' and that if Prindy 'takes her into the Sandstone she'll die'.[35] All this he knows. But, just as certainly, Prindy knows that under the protection of Tchamala, none of these things will happen. Rifkah will not die. She will escape and be free. The conflict is irreconcilable. There can be no compromise between the two beliefs. It is no-one's fault. It is the way things are. And it leads ultimately, in the final scenes of Delacy's story, to disaster.

Those scenes begin with Delacy doing everything right. When Prindy and Savitra are set upon by a group of ceremonially painted Aboriginals, two of whom hustle Prindy away, Delacy behaves with absolute propriety. Savitra begs him to intervene but he knows this is 'blackfeller business' and refuses. Bobwirridirridi appears and, as tradition prescribes, asks for 'prejent [...] long o' bijnitch'. Delacy, as one of 'those formally responsible for a boy about to be initiated', is expected to 'pay those who gave their time and talent to it' and he willingly does so, happy to be accepted as part of the ancient tradition.[36]

The scene shifts to the Ring Place and the initiation ceremony, a long-drawn-out test of endurance. Hour after hour the ceremony proceeds until finally, the ritual circumcision complete, Bobwirridirridi presents the sacred *bidu-bidu* to Prindy. At last, it seems, the quest has ended in success. The initiation that has twice before been attempted and twice before failed has at last run its full course in accordance with tradition and all seems well. But all is not well. Back at Delacy's camp, Savitra slips surveillance and heads off in search of Prindy. She finds him in the middle of the Ring Place, his 'grey eyes wide with horror' because he knows what happens to women who intrude upon the ceremonies of the Snake Cult. He can do nothing to interfere with the ritual punishment that is immediately and brutally imposed: the knees and elbows broken one by one, the ritual rape, the breasts and genitalia cut off.

Meanwhile, back at the camp Savitra's absence has been discovered and her intentions guessed. And again, for all his lifetime's efforts to school himself to accept the right of Aboriginals to live as Aboriginals, Delacy finds he cannot leave them to do so. He must intervene, must, if necessary, exert the white man's power. If he can, he will stick to Aboriginal custom and 'buy her off'. But, in case that does not work, he takes his gun, saying, '[A]lthough I hate the idea, I might have to use it to come the whiteman over them'.[37] And so he sets off, following Savitra's tracks.

Suddenly Bobwirridirridi appears in full regalia. He greets Delacy in calm and friendly fashion, totally at ease. Delacy, tense

and nervous, asks about Savitra. Bobwirridirridi does not answer.
Delacy presses him, his voice 'hoarse with urgency', promising
Bobwirridirridi anything he wants. He offers a drink of brandy,
which is accepted politely. Keep the bottle, urges Delacy, and 'tell
him me which way that girl, eh?' It's time to end the skirmishing:

> The coals fixed the grey eyes again [...] The cackle was
> harsher: 'More-better you go back you camp, Mullaka.'
> 'Eh?' Jeremy looked at a loss, blinked hard.
> The old man pulled a spear from the bundle under his
> arm, not to point it, but to reverse it, dropping the butt-
> end to the ground, beginning to draw a line in the sand
> with it. Watching the procedure wide-eyed, Jeremy again
> said with a rush of speech, now with an hysterical note to
> it, 'I been do it good way long o' you. I been helip you
> from start. [...] I been 'shame for my rown countryman do
> it wrong thing long o' you...'
> The cackle cut in, harsher: 'You goot friendt, all right,
> Mullaka. Dat what for me talk goot-way long o' you now.
> I tell him you...more-better you go back long o' you
> camp.' The red eyes dropped to the spear in the sand.
> The skeleton figure began to back away, while the cackle
> went on: 'You savvy dat kind bijnitch, eh?' [38]

And, yes, Delacy does savvy that business. 'Such a line, drawn by
one who had the authority for it, was virtually limitless in the
direction in which it ran, and absolutely uncrossable for anyone who
saw it drawn.' The line drawn, Bobwirridirridi disappears, trusting
Delacy to follow tradition. It is a defining moment, a test of his
capacity to trust the Aboriginal way.

He fails the test, and who can blame him? After some
moments of worried indecision, he makes up his mind. 'No,' he says,
'damn me if I can allow it...bugger his line'. He steps over it and
heads for the Ring Place. Halfway there he catches what he thinks is
a glimpse of his Yalmaru. 'If it's you, old fellow,' he mutters, 'for
God's sake show me the right and proper thing to do. They have
their own way...but I have mine. I don't want to live out my life

regretting something I ought or ought not to have done'.[39] He continues on to the Ring Place, where he finds, to his horror, that, to expunge the desecration Savitra has caused, Prindy is undergoing 'a trial by ordeal'. At one end of the Ring stand the men of the Snake Cult, each armed with spear and woomera. At the other end, armed only with a boomerang, stands Prindy. As Delacy watches, a spear is hurled. Prindy's boomerang flashes down and deflects it. Another man steps forward. Another spear is hurled. Another deflection. But Prindy is clearly tiring and there are more men, more spears to come. Delacy cannot leave things be, cannot let tradition take its magical course, has to interfere. As the next spear is loosed he yells, 'Hey, Cut that out!' then watches in horror as, distracted by his shout, Prindy brings the defending boomerang up fractionally late and the spear finds its target.

Delacy leaps into the Ring, firing his gun. The spear throwers scatter and Bobwirridirridi materialises out of the scrub. 'What's matter you no-more look-out that boy?' Delacy yells furiously at him as he reaches Prindy and finds him at the point of death. As he bends over the boy he is shocked to feel pain in his own side. Bobwirridirridi has speared him! He can hardly believe it. 'What's matter with you?' he gasps. Bitterly Bobwirridirridi replies, 'You been kill-him my *Mekullikulli*, Whiteman'. 'Whiteman', now, not 'goot friendt'. By his actions Delacy has forfeited all claim to special status. Furious, Delacy meets blame with blame. 'You bastard…' he says, 'why you let that mob make boy stand-up?' Why, Bobwirridirridi rages back, did you 'bugger-him-up bijnitch?' Because, Delacy answers, the boy was too young. He could not survive such an onslaught. He not only could, replies Bobwirridirridi; he infallibly *would* have survived, if only the arrogant white man had not fatally breached the magical protection Bobwirridirridi had given him:

> The Pookarakka swung and reached for the painted boomerang, and seizing it, rose and lunged and shoved it before Jeremy's eyes, crying in the same tone, 'Nobody can beat him dat *Mahraghi*…spone you no come bugger-him-up!' […]

> [...] 'Me been tell him you right t'ing [...] No matter, you
> whiteman, you do it wrong t'ing...you come...finish
> *Mahraghi*...finish belong me *Mekullikulli!'*
> Jeremy breathed, 'Oh, Jesus Christ!'⁴⁰

There is no doubting the truth of what Bobwirridirridi says. Delacy
knows it and the reader knows it. The *Mahraghi*, the magic, would
indeed have protected Prindy if only Delacy had not buggered it up.
Bobwirridirridi did 'tell him right t'ing' and Delacy did 'do it wrong
t'ing' and in so doing ended the magic—and Prindy's life.

It's a marvellous climax, with all the bitter inevitability of great
tragedy. Had Delacy been able to take the step of faith needed to
trust in Bobwirridirridi's ancient power, Prindy would not have died.
But no white man, not even one as disposed to do so as Delacy,
could take that step. Bobwirridirridi's magic does have the power he
says it has, will protect Prindy if not weakened by the interference of
unbelievers. But Bobwirridirridi's magic lies at the other side of the
gulf between whites and Aboriginals. Delacy respects it but cannot
believe in it. He must therefore intervene, must follow the logic of
his white man's thinking, and, in so doing, must destroy Prindy and
the hopes that rest upon him. And were it all to be done again, there
could be no other conclusion.

It is when Bobwirridirridi 'knows he's beat', says Cahoon, that
he sings 'Poor Fellow My Country'.⁴¹ In calling the book *Poor Fellow
My Country* Herbert signals that he too is beat. He sees and feels
what is wrong. He cannot see what will put it right. He senses there
is no answer. He expresses these feelings through Alfie, who had
hoped her novel would 'rouse up [...] those who'll want to build a
True Commonwealth, not just exploit a lovely land and one another'.
She ends up thinking that Australians have 'no originality, no special
quality at all, nothing that'll be of any use to mankind...so no reason
to become but a dumping-ground for excess population not wanted
elsewhere, and a farm and a mine owned by outsiders to supply
outsiders first'. Her book, she says, should be 'finished...in a desert...
in despair'.⁴² The negativity of Delacy's life, the tragic inevitability of
his final actions, and the disastrous results of those actions are an
expression of Herbert's despair. Prindy's death is Delacy's final and

greatest failure. As the following chapter demonstrates, Prindy symbolises a 'New Australia', one grounded in its Aboriginal past, incorporating its migrant cultures and finding its own unique identity, its 'own road'. His death signifies allegorically the death of that hope. But though hope is gone, something still remains. Bleak though the reality is, it is still possible to dream. Through the story of Delacy, Herbert expressed the bleak reality. Through the story of Prindy, he pictured the dream.

CHAPTER 13

The Myth of Golden Prindy

TO express his dream for Australia, Herbert turned once again to the genre of high romance. This time, though, he had found an answer to the problem that had proved insuperable in *Soldiers' Women*: the problem of how to help his readers move with no sense of incongruity between the enchanted world of romance and the rational world of the novel. The answer was, in the event, simple. He changed the setting—from one in which the numinous was alien to one in which it was not. The world of wartime Sydney had not provided a credible setting for romance. The world of northern Australia did. Half of its population already lived in a world 'peopled by spirits' and 'controlled by magic'.[1] In their world, the world of traditional Aboriginality, the numinous and the mundane already coexisted without strain. It provided, therefore, a perfect setting for romance. All Herbert had to do was bring that world alive for readers.

He did so by using the techniques he discovered when writing *Seven Emus*. In *Poor Fellow My Country*, as in *Seven Emus*, he first taught his readers the numinous realities of the Aboriginal world as Aboriginal elders teach them—by telling stories of the Dreamtime.[2]

He then built acceptance of those realities through repetition. He tells, for instance, the story of the Waianga, the 'Spirits who built the clouds and sailed them hither and yon in accordance with Koonapippi's plan for replenishing the waters of the earth'. He describes how 'the Shade of Tchamala would sneak into the mountains and panic the sleepy Waianga into dropping their store of water so as to cause havoc'.[3] Having told the story once, he then proceeds to establish its relevance to the world of *Poor Fellow My Country* through frequent and increasingly elliptical references such as: 'That afternoon all the dust was settled and for days to come by a heavy downpour from that southward-drifting war between Old Tchamala and the Cloud Spirits'.[4] The matter-of-fact tone establishes the Waianga as real players in *Poor Fellow My Country*'s world and their battle as a recurring conflict between spirit powers. The frequency of the repetition and the modulation of tone soon carry readers to the point where the Dreamtime explanation seems as natural as the explanations of meteorological science. And so it is with the many other items of Aboriginal lore Herbert introduces in this way. It soon seems natural that when love is in the air the curlews, guardians of unborn baby spirits, go 'dancing along the dusty road ahead calling, *Kweeluk, Kweeluk!*'[5] We soon accept the pervasive presence of Tchamala in his many guises—as river, thunder and lightning, flood and storm, shark and crocodile, Rainbow Pool, Rainbow Head and Rainbow Reef. We soon come to expect the regular appearance in the night sky of that sly, mischief-making Dreamtime voyeur, Igulgul, the moon.

Aboriginal tradition gave Herbert a viable context for his romance, but it was to European tradition he turned for its characters and plot. Northrop Frye distinguishes six phases in the traditional romance plot and, as we shall see, each of these plays an important part in *Poor Fellow My Country*.[6] As for the characters, Frye's descriptions of the stock 'hero', 'heroine' and 'old wise man' of European romance fit Prindy, Rifkah and Bobwirridirridi exactly. The 'old wise man', for instance, was 'often a magician' who accepted 'mutilation or physical handicap [as] the price of unusual wisdom or power'.[7] Just so was it with Bobwirridirridi, whose stomach was eaten away by white man's arsenic just before Tchamala 'took him away up into the sky [...] and there gave him the powers of Boss Snake Man'.[8]

Rifkah's links with the traditional heroine of European romance are equally close. Frye describes the heroine thus:

> [T]he reward of the quest usually is or includes a bride. The bride-figure is ambiguous: her psychological connection with the mother in an Oedipus fantasy is more insistent than in comedy [...] she is, of course, often rescued from the unwelcome embraces of another and generally older male, or from giants or bandits or other usurpers. The removal of some stigma from the heroine figures prominently in romance as in comedy, and ranges from the 'loathly lady' theme of Chaucer's *Wife of Bath's Tale* to the forgiven harlot of the Book of Hosea.[9]

Rifkah's sexually 'ambiguous' status is clearly evident in Herbert's original plan to include a scene in which Prindy and Rifkah 'lie together [...] arms about each other, mother and son, lover and lover'.[10] In the event, he opted instead for having Rifkah play out the two roles with different heroes. As mother she suckles Prindy at 'her breast like a baby'.[11] As bride she is claimed by the surrogate hero, Glascock. The 'stigma' Rifkah carries is that of having prostituted herself for the communist cause.[12] She is indeed the 'forgiven harlot'. The giants and bandits she is rescued from are the Commonwealth police. The older suitor is Jeremy Delacy, who opposes Prindy's plans to rescue Rifkah.

Moving to the romance hero, we find that his roots, too, are firmly planted in the traditions of European romance. The hero of romance, says Frye, is 'superior in degree to other men and to his environment' and capable of 'prodigies of courage and endurance'.[13] So it is with Prindy. On one occasion, though chained on both sides to adults and dashed against a rock by the full force of a river in flood, he waits with no apparent discomfort until the men hanging from his arms are pulled off by the current, and then walks back unscathed to the horses. On another, he survives being swept over a waterfall and tumbled along an underground river for seven days. His capacity in the face of mental challenges is equally 'superior in degree'. In one week he develops from an illiterate child to one who knows 'every *Meta* in the bloomin' [dictionary], from *Metabasis* to *Metazoic*. In another, he moves from 'some conventional rudiments' of mathematics to 'squaring everything and extracting the roots, and proceeding to cubes'.[14]

It is not, however, through his superhuman powers that Prindy expresses Herbert's hopes for Australia. No longer does Herbert picture his romance hero facing social and political challenges and winning through against the odds. In contrast to Norman Shillingsworth, Prindy is not an important player in the everyday world of ordinary mortals: he has no measurable effect on anything in that world and avoids involvement as far as possible. Prindy demonstrates Herbert's hope for Australia not through what he does but through what he is.

The hope he represents is signalled in an opening scene that draws subtly upon the traditional imagery of the first phase of romance, 'the myth of the birth of the hero'. In this phase, says Frye, 'The infant hero is often placed in an ark or chest floating on the sea' and the 'mysterious infant life enclosed in a chest' is 'closely linked' with a 'treasure hoard'.[15] In the opening scene of *Poor Fellow My Country*, the hero is found fishing in a pool wholly enclosed by rocks. The 'treasure hoard' enclosed within these rocks includes: the pool itself, 'emerald, silver, blue-enamel, gold'; the fish, 'a golden flicker in the emerald depths'; and, above all, the hero, 'a hair-sheen of gold' on his skin, 'a glint of gold' in his curls and a 'golden-brown hand'.[16] The scene establishes, from the outset, Prindy's significance as a symbol of hope, since 'the real source of wealth' in such scenes, says Frye, is the 'potential fertility or new life' that the hero brings with him, thus ensuring 'the turning of the cycle from the wintry water of death to the reviving waters of life'.[17]

The new life promised in the birth of Prindy is a new Australia. To emphasise this, Herbert connects Prindy, by blood or marriage relationship, with all the races and groups he sees as significant in Australia. His biological father and mother are a white station manager and an Aboriginal servant. One of his grandmothers is a squattocratic grande dame; one of his great grandfathers, an ambitious Irish Catholic policeman. His stepfather is part-Aboriginal, part-Chinese. He is unofficially adopted by an Indian Hindu, unofficially married to a part-Aboriginal, part-Indian girl.

In addition to family relationships, there are a number of significant mentor relationships. The romance hero's 'true father', says Frye, 'is sometimes represented by a wise old man or teacher'. Prindy has many such wise old teachers. First, Bobwirridirridi teaches his 'neophyte' about 'their master, Tchamala'. Next, George teaches him bush lore. Then Barbu teaches him 'Hindu Myths and Legends'. Billy Brew follows with 'astronomical science and Greek mythology'. Next comes Delacy with maths and physics and finally Maryzic with Catholic theology.[18] Between them, these father figures represent the Aboriginal, European and Asian strands in Australian culture. By having Prindy accept each, for a time, as his guide, Herbert acknowledges the role each culture has to play in building a new Australia.

But though all have a part to play, there is no doubt who is most important. The one mentor whose authority Prindy accepts totally, and throughout the novel, is Bobwirridirridi. Herbert's dream is of a truly Australian Australia, and what better way to emphasise that than to show Prindy, courted by so many, maintaining throughout an unwavering allegiance to the old black witchdoctor, that powerful symbol of ancient Australia. The bond forged in the opening scene remains strong until severed by death. Even when whites seem most in control, Bobwirridirridi most powerless, it is in him alone Prindy trusts. And as it is significant that whites find him ugly and ridiculous, so it is significant that Prindy is never put off by his appearance. Bobwirridirridi is inextricably a part of the ancient land and culture of Australia and Prindy the golden will always embrace that ancient body no matter how emaciated, no matter how soiled and smelly:

> The old man, completely naked, was curled up to face the wall. When the guard lay a rough hand on a skeleton shoulder and jerked him round, he came as supinely as any dried-out black corpse [...]
> A claw came reaching. Prindy took it. The claw ran up the golden forearm. The skeleton strove to sit. The guard jerked it up. The skin-and-bone arms sought to embrace the golden vision. Prindy moved into them. The claws grasped and smoothed, smoothed and grasped. The clipped grey skull fell against the golden hair.[19]

As Bobwirridirridi is Prindy's spiritual father, so Rifkah is his spiritual mother. Bobwirridirridi tells Prindy that Rifkah could 'become his *Koyu*, or Mumma, if she let the Old One take a good look at her up through his hole in' the Rainbow Pool. A poor swimmer and desperately afraid, Rifkah nevertheless does what is asked of her, and swims to the centre of the pool. Back on the beach Prindy says, 'Now you properly my *Koyu*' and seals the relationship by sucking her breast 'blackfeller way'.[20] In the world of the novel, as we have seen, Rifkah signifies the model New Australian. In the world of romance, that significance is enriched by associating this best of newcomers with the mother goddess of Aboriginal mythology. Bobwirridirridi tells Prindy she is 'not just a whitewoman but a Shade of Koonapippi' and on two occasions Koonapippi appears to Rifkah, beckoning her and saying, 'I vont you. I vill show you ze vay'.[21] The relationship with Koonapippi is a sign of acceptance. In the world of the novel, Delacy, for all his efforts, is not accepted by the ancient land and culture of Australia. In the world of romance, Rifkah fares better.

Prindy's acceptance of Rifkah as surrogate mother and Bobwirridirridi as surrogate father signify the marriage between the best of the old and the best of the new that has produced, in Prindy, a new Australia. The progress of that new Australia is pictured allegorically through the central plot element of *Poor Fellow My Country*: the quest of the hero, Frye's third phase of romance. Prindy's quest is the traditional quest of young Aboriginal males who, following initiation, 'must go on the long journey called *Look Him Road*'.[22] Normally, the road is predetermined. 'Your Road is the way you must go through life as the reincarnation of a Dream Time ancestor.' Prindy is different. In the first chapter we find him singing, 'My Road. My Rown Road. I go look dat Road'.[23] His quest for a 'Dreaming Road' that is 'his own' signifies the search for a new Australian ethos grounded in, but not limited by, Australia's past.

Prindy's quest involves many journeys. With Bobwirridirridi he travels to the coast to view the works of Tchamala. With Nelyerri he travels to Palmeston. With George he treks through the bush. With Barbu he trades round the stations. He accompanies Esk on his review of coastal defences. He sails with Rifkah to Leopold Island.

On each journey he learns something about Australia. And as he learns, he sings. The night following his first plane flight, for instance, he sings in his sleep an 'imitation of the sound of aero engines in concert, rising and falling to make melody'.[24] It is all part of the quest. First he must discover, then he must sing into harmony all the disparate elements of Australia: old mixed with new, ugly with beautiful, white with black, nature with man. On the New Year's train trip to Palmeston, for instance, he finds music in everything:

> Kangaroos leaping up the hills, going for their lives because of the engine's *Boo-hoot, Boo-hoo-hoot!* Then clanging through winding granite cuttings, with the sweet wet smoke blotting out the dripping walls and filling the compartment till you coughed to the engine's laboured coughing: *Huff-huff-huff-huff-huff.*
>
> Music in it all to sing to: *Click-clack-click-clack, boo-hoo-hoot, Old-Man Kangaroo, doin' a scoot!...Roholing wheel, Sibilent night, All is fair, All is bright, Roholing whee-el, boo-hoot, a-click-clack* [...]
>
> The engine need not have stayed there while the prisoners were being transferred to the baggage compart-ment of the brake van, out of which a bunch of drunk navvies and their swags had been cleared; but it did, while its crew, in full voice sang *The Red Flag.* The navvies took up the song. Soon half the train was bawling it. [...]
>
> *Though cowards cringe, and traitors sneer, we'll keep the Red Flag flying here.*
>
> Prindy sang it softly to himself, not the words, but the lilt of it! *La-la-l'-la, la-la-l'-la, la-la-la-la-la-la-l'-la,* as he knelt staring out on the miles of sweet pickin' where the kangaroos, blue now, and some emus, and Lord Vaisey's bulls and cows and calves, and a small herd of buffalo, went racing from this hooting puffing smoking disturbing element of man [...]
>
> Piggy wasn't dead—not quite. Chas Chase, who had an ambulance certificate, gave the prognosis that replaced *The Red Flag* as the theme of the wheels when again they

got rolling: *'Poor Old Piggy...he won't see the New Year
in...won't see the New Year in... won't see the New Year
in.'* [...]
The murdered country fell behind. The drunks snored.
Grandfather Trotters stared and stared at his first glimpse
of eternity. All water now ran eastward. Prindy shifted to
that side to watch it vanish like swift-moving snakes into
the greenery. Now he was singing to the song of the
wheels: *He won't see the New Year in.*[25]

It's another superb piece of writing. The German Christmas celebrated at policeman Stunke's house the night before, Hannaford's
communist bravado, the alien, introduced animals and the sweet
familiarity of the Australian bush, the sordid revelry of whites, the
ancient joy of corroboree, the life of the land, the death of man—all
sung into harmony by the master of song.

In pursuit of his and Australia's 'rown road', Prindy must resist
the many false roads urged upon him. Nugget Knowles wants him to
become 'a crackerjack stockman', Kitty Windeyer 'a great composer',
Hannaford 'a big man [to] fight for your people', Cahoon the 'best
officer the country had ever seen'.[26] Each recognises the special
potential in Prindy, but each wants to develop it in ways that serve
their own interests. And Herbert's vision of Australia's 'rown road' is
one that leads beyond mere exploitation by sectional interests.

The attitudes of his black companions add further strands of
meaning to the allegory. They represent, on the one hand, the false
road of total rejection of Aboriginality; on the other, the dead-end of
allegiance to traditions that resist change. It is the women who, siren-
like, tempt Prindy to reject Aboriginal tradition altogether. Queeny
and Savitra mock that tradition; Nelyerri attacks it. All three are
involved in attempts to stop Prindy's initiation. The falseness of the
road they follow is shown by its disastrous results: their own and
Prindy's deaths. In contrast, King George's influence is, up to a point,
positive. There is much he can teach, and Prindy is a willing learner.
But George's road is not Prindy's. Though 'his being yearned for
Aboriginal community with his environment, rejecting the patent
empty alienness of the non-indigenous [...] blackman's rote had

limited the expression of his spirit', and it is with a sense of release that when George dies, Prindy finds himself once again 'free to follow his Rown Road'.[27] The road George represents is a road whose limitations Herbert explored in *Seven Emus*. The hallowed certainties of 'Blackman's rote' offer security in a dangerous world, but at the expense of innovation and progress. It is not the road for Prindy. He rejects the alien individualism of the non-Indigenous in favour of 'Aboriginal community with the environment', but his quest is for a way to achieve that community while at the same time forging a new destiny for Australia unhampered by the limiting rigidities of tradition. The road Prindy seeks is one that leads him back to the Dreamtime, thus giving him a firm base in the oldest, most Australian culture on the continent, while also leading forward into the future. In *Seven Emus* there is no such road. In *Poor Fellow My Country* the new road has been found. It is the road of Tchamala, and it is towards initiation into the cult of Tchamala that Prindy quests unswervingly throughout the book.

As one of the great gods of the Dreamtime, Tchamala anchors Prindy firmly in traditional Aboriginal culture, but as the great disrupter he points towards change and development. Herbert says as much when, after describing Tchamala as 'the Serpent, who sneaked into the paradise Koonapippi had created', he continues, 'Perhaps you need evil to give value to good, a sort of negative to positive to give potential, as in electrodynamics...otherwise you have inertia'.[28] Tchamala is negative to Koonapippi's positive. The initial creation of the world belongs to Koonapippi, but it is Tchamala's disruptiveness that encourages humans to change and develop. Like Nature in *Capricornia*, Tchamala challenges and invigorates humankind. By constantly stirring things up, he forces creatures out of the suffocating shelter of Koonapippi's protection. Koonapippi's enforcement of law leads to order, stability—and stagnation. Tchamala and Igulgul, 'given to encouraging the breaking of laws instead of ruthlessly enforcing them', lead to change.

As servants of Tchamala, Bobwirridirridi and Prindy, while connected to Aboriginal tradition, are also outsiders and thus open to changes that can rejuvenate the old way of life and fit it to cope with the new. Bobwirridirridi relishes the opportunity to fly a plane, 'cackling for joy' and doing it so well the pilot calls him 'a natural'. He is happy to use the magic of modern chemistry, 'coming back to camp one day with what he claimed to be a *Mawnyinga*, or Mosquito Shade' caught 'through the magic of that wondrous new insect repellant of the Yankees, Dimethyl Phthalate Cream'.[29] Prindy, too, while firm in his allegiance to traditional culture, is not limited by it. In contrast to Rifkah, who resists baptism passionately as a betrayal of Judaism, Prindy is happy to accept 'all such good stuff in the way of Bijnitch' when 'Old Tchamala was hunted out' by Maryzic's Catholic ceremonies.[30] Tchamala is in no way diminished by Prindy's enjoyment of Catholic ritual.

It would be a mistake, however, to see Tchamala's role as purely positive. His allegorical significance in *Poor Fellow My Country* is complex and includes positive and negative. He is both guardian and nemesis to Prindy, and symbolises both the potential for renewal and the inevitability of failure. To establish one aspect, Herbert draws upon Tchamala's place in Dreamtime mythology; to establish the other, he draws upon his connection with the monsters of European romance.

'The central form of quest-romance', says Frye, 'is the dragon-killing theme' often manifested in a plot involving a land 'laid waste by a sea-monster' that is sometimes 'identified' with 'Satan and the Edenic serpent'.[31] The connections between this tradition and Tchamala are clear. He, too, is a serpent. He, too, materialises as a watery monster: sometimes a crocodile, sometimes a shark. He, too, is linked with the devil: Herbert speaks of 'those masters of the Negative in Nature, the Old Ones, Satan, Ahriman, Tchamala'.[32] The word 'negative' is significant. The negativity of Tchamala's influence is seen in the change to Prindy's song following his introduction to the mysteries of Tchamala. '*Boss Tchamala by'n'by,*' Prindy now sings, '*Learn me kill him Whiteman die. Dat my Road, my proper road, my Rown Road*'.[33] This is clearly not the road to reconciliation and a new, cooperative future. Musing, during its composition, on how to end the novel, Herbert wrote, 'We have to see [Prindy] go out as a victim of what dominates it all, the power (perverse) the Rainbow Serpent'.[34] Prindy represents Herbert's dream of a new

Australia, but as the servant of Tchamala he also symbolises the tragic impossibility of that dream.[35] Tchamala, the master of change and symbol of new, hopeful directions for Australia, is also the lord of negativity and symbol of Australia's inevitable failure. Twice Prindy nearly dies in the river that is one of Tchamala's shades; the third time there is no escape, and Prindy's death at the hands of the god he serves symbolises the inevitability, as Herbert sees it, of the failure of his dream for Australia. The negative influence of the past is too powerful for the dream to become reality.

Nevertheless, though the quest is doomed to end in failure, Herbert's descriptions of it establish a sense of the idealised perfection he dreams of for Australia. When Prindy travels alone through the bush after the deaths of Nellie, Queeny and George, Herbert draws on the conventions of the second phase of romance, 'the innocent youth of the hero', to create a vision of what it is to live in harmony with one's environment. Frye describes the second phase as set in

> a pastoral and Arcadian world [...] full of glades, shaded valleys, murmuring brooks, the moon and other images closely linked with the female or maternal aspect of sexual imagery. Its heraldic colors are green and gold, traditionally the colors of vanishing youth.

Different though this world sounds from the Australian bush, it is what Herbert pictures at this point of the novel. 'Friendly or helping animals', Frye tells us, 'are conspicuous' in this world and the hero is often nurtured by animals and 'providential birds'.[36] So it is with Prindy:

> Indeed, the heading of the birds his way may have been more in the way of collaboration than coincidence [...] How could he find succour in that blasted land? Someone must show him. The parrots showed him the kapok trees he would otherwise have had to hunt for. The crested bell-birds showed him where the grasshoppers were lurking, ringing their tiny bells of voices. Crested

wedgebills [...] showed him pods opening to shed seeds
that made good nutty munching. Red quandong cherries
were the spotted bower-birds' offering.[37]

As Herbert would have been first to agree, the description of Prindy's
journey is not realistic. Few Australian writers spent more time alone
in the bush[38] and he knew its unforgiving nature. 'You've no idea
how hard it is', he once said, 'to get a feed in this wilderness of ours,
you've got to keep working all the time'.[39] The picture of the bush
given at this point of the novel is not, then, the result of ignorance
but of a writer using a particular genre to create the sense of a world
in which perfection is possible and the land, its animals and its
people live in harmony.

Later in the novel, Herbert places Rifkah too in this enchanted
world. Fleeing from the police, she is dropped from the train outside
Palmeston. The moment she is alone, the bush becomes for her too
a place where animals are friends and magic is in the air:

> Igulgul came out deliberately [...] because it must have
> been pretty scary to be suddenly alone at night in the
> bush for the first time [...] with all those things crowding
> round, scuffling, hopping, flapping, snuffling, croaking,
> squeaking, coming to look at one who with moon-
> pearly face and flaming hair—surely the Earth Mother,
> the Ol'Goomun-Ol'Goomun [...] come back to her
> children.

And so she sits, the Queen amid her creatures, as they come forward
to pay court: first Mininjorka the Bandicoot, then Murrimo the
possum, next Mudburrabah the Wildcat and finally

> three circling shadows that called their own names—
> Karra-Keera, Karra-Keera, Karra-Keera! Plovers they could
> rightly be called [...] The birds landed with the grace of
> sprites, to go trotting round and round the shining
> visitant, bobbing their wattled heads, still calling their
> names—Karra-Keera, Karra-Keera, Karra-Keera!

> But sight of old friends seemed only to stir up memories
> contrasting so sadly with present realities that the great
> eyes swam. Igulgul turned the tears to pearls as they
> streamed. Now there was sound all round like tiny
> clicking of tongues in sympathy, culminating in the distant
> cry of Kweeluks: Kwee-luk, Kweeee-luk, even the Mother
> of the Land is lost! We are all lost who are native to it by
> birth or love...Poor Fellow, Our Country.[40]

Lost she is, but only when forced back into a world where romance
has no place. Alone for a brief time in this moonlit dream world, she
is ringed with magic, at home in a better world than the one to
which she returns with the arrival of Clancy, whose apology for
leaving her in such a 'God-forsaken place' is full of unconscious
irony.

For Prindy there is no such breaking of the harmony of
romance. As he continues his journey, 'the mysterious rapport with
nature that so often marks the central figure of romance' becomes
even stronger.[41] A white dingo joins him:

> Now, dingoes like to attach themselves to solitary humans
> [...] He stayed with Prindy for quite a while [...] They
> shared the bustards and wallabies that one or other
> brought down [...] At night Prindy would [...] talk to him,
> sing to him. Wanjin never answered. Perhaps he expected
> Prindy to read his mind, too. Legend had it that the
> original Wanjin learnt to read others' minds from the
> Ol'Goomun [...] Wanjin always wanted to be somebody's
> dog; only he just couldn't take the servitude that goes
> with it. Prindy asked him, 'Wha' 'bout you be my properly
> dog, eh? You number-one hunter...me too. [...] Wha'
> 'bout it, eh, Wanjin?'
>
> It may have been that pressing; or Full Moon and a
> gathering of his clan for one of those dismal concerts they
> so love to indulge in [...]; or the simple fact that he had
> done his bit in bringing this golden child who seemed to
> be specially favoured by Ol'Goomun Nature through the

> wilderness for delivery of his destiny; but the night of the
> Full Moon he slipped away.[42]

This is Herbert at his best, holding the mysterious and the mundane
in easy balance, modulating smoothly between scientific statement
and Dreamtime legend. The dingo is simultaneously a dog obeying
normal biological drives and White Wanjin fulfilling Koonapippi's
behests. The cause of his leaving is both biologically natural and
divinely inspired. The magical world of romance and the everyday
world of the Australian bush co-exist without strain.

The section continues with 'the moon and other images
closely linked with the female or maternal aspect of sexual imagery'[43]
becoming ever more insistent:

> [W]ithin a short while there was his other friend of the
> long nights, Igulgul [...] gilding the higher tree-tops
> beyond the water-hole. Prindy sighed again, watched the
> gilding turn to silver, saw more and more of the trees, and
> then the stony way light up as a stage for the dancing
> black shadows of the windblown bushes on the rise.
> Prindy, naked as he was born, cuddled into the dusty
> warmth of his Mother Earth.[44]

He is roused by the sound of piping and, drawn like Shakespeare's
Ferdinand by 'musics' blown on the wind, is caught in a net set to
catch the Golden Finch. His captor, Barbu, seeing 'the golden head,
so golden to the magic touch of Igulgul', calls him 'a god from
Paradise...a lil golden god'. It is left to his prosaic little daughter, a
character who refuses to live in the charmed world of romance, to
tell him, 'Dat no god...dat Prindy Ah Loy'. Barbu rejects so mundane
a reality:

> [H]e stared and stared. So god-like was the figure in its
> slender beauty, all shiny gold of skin and towselled [sic]
> hair, so luminous of eye, so calm. He persisted, 'But if you
> are just colour poy...how come you 'ere...from desert...
> from novhere?' [...]

The little girl answered in that same dry tone, 'He
runned away from Compound.' [...]
'But t'at Compound two hunneret mile from 'ere...and
t'e vild, vild desert and t'e mountain in betveens. How
vone lil poy...if he not a god...if a god don't 'elp him...
Ho!' Barbu became all excitement again: 'I haf it...Mother
Shasti, Goddess of Children, haf bring him for you, my
daughter!'...
'Jitty Indian talk.'[45]

This passage again demonstrates Herbert's ability to hold real and
fabulous worlds in delicate balance. With one part of the mind we
see Barbu as his daughter sees him, and 'Jitty Indian talk' earths a
mood that would otherwise slip into sentimentality. With another
part we see the golden god Barbu sees. Choice is unnecessary: the
real world is indeed real and it is indeed marvellous, if only prosaic
little Australians like Savitra could learn to see it. Against the picture
given elsewhere of a land rejected and destroyed, romance here
offers a vision of pastoral harmony. Wonder can co-exist within the
day-to-day realities. The two are not incompatible. If only Australians
could learn to see the wonder of Australia, they might keep alive the
spirit needed to defeat sterile materialism.

Having used the motifs of the second phase to establish a
general sense of harmony, Herbert used those of the fourth to flesh
out the details of that harmony. 'A central image' of the fourth phase,
Frye tells us, 'is that of the beleaguered castle'.[46] It is an image
Herbert has used before. Black Adder and Red Ochre stations in
Capricornia and Seven Emus Station in *Seven Emus* are all
beleaguered castles built to defend those inside from the world
outside. Red Ochre is 'the Poundamore stronghold in Capricornia',
Black Adder 'the O'Cannon garrison' whose fall 'before the advance
of one Julius Derkouz' leads to the farewell, 'goodbye Black Adder,
fallen fort'.[47] In Lily Lagoons the association with the beleaguered
castle of traditional romance is made explicit, with Lydia calling it
'the Robber Baron's fastness' and Delacy calling it his 'keep'.[48]

'The central theme', Frye tells us, of the fourth phase of
romance is 'that of the maintaining of the integrity of the innocent

world against the assault of experience'.[49] To do that, characters retreat from the corruption of court and town into the country. Just so does Delacy retreat to Lily Lagoons, his 'refuge from a society that mostly sickens me'. Lily Lagoons offers sanctuary to 'all creatures needing it'. Its 'soft heartbeat', the generator, pulses gently on, *'Home, Home, home, a-home'*, testifying that all is well within the confines of the castle.[50] Echoes of that heartbeat can be heard in all that is good and life-affirming in *Poor Fellow My Country*: in Rifkah's courageous 'stroke, stroke, stroke' out into the 'pull, pull, pull' of the Rainbow Pool, in the 'Life, Life, *L'chaim*' that is 'God's True Purpose' for the world, in 'the blue, the blue, the blue' of the sky and 'the rain, the rain, the rain' of Rifkah's first love-tranced stay at Lily Lagoons, and finally in the 'love, love, love' of her idyll with Glascock on Leopold Island.[51]

The beleaguered castle is more than just an escape from the world; it stands as a model for the world to emulate. Lily Lagoons was created to stand 'as an example to the Nation of how honesty and wisdom could correct the hitherto accepted ravaging of the land and savaging of its owners'.[52] The beleaguered castle, in all Herbert's books, is a place where Aboriginal and Asian Australians have the same freedoms and opportunities as white Australians. Oscar Shillingsworth at Red Ochre, Tim O'Cannon at Black Adder and Bronco Jones at Seven Emus all establish fortresses whose economic strength will, they hope, ensure the security and freedom of half-caste children. Norman at Red Ochre establishes for a time a community in which white Australians 'can't talk bigfella whiteman' to half-caste and Chinese Australians.[53] Lily Lagoons is a place where Aboriginals are free to 'use [the land] as they like', a place where neither policeman nor bureaucrat can walk in and oppress them 'with the blessing of constituted authority'.[54]

Herbert's ideal Australia involves a community living in harmony and he finds symbols for that harmony in the homely ceremonials of eating and drinking. At Red Ochre the Chinese cook prepares a meal

> with so much cunning that the borderline between the tastes of Orient and Occident was not perceivable, so that Orientals and Occidentals were able with relish to make

inroads into one another's fare; and thus the twain were brought together for once at least.[55]

At Lily Lagoons the harmony between races appears in the Jewish meal requested by the white Australian Delacy, prepared in 'a state of religious ecstasy' by the European refugee Rifkah, and accepted as 'a new way to commune with Old Tchamala'[56] by Prindy, the Aboriginal Australian.

To intensify the sense of harmonious perfection, Herbert moves into the fifth phase of romance. Frye describes this phase as presenting a 'reflective, idyllic view of experience' through its picture of 'an erotic world' where 'true lovers are on top of a hierarchy of what might be called erotic imitations'.[57] The first of *Poor Fellow My Country*'s four love idylls, between Nugget Knowles and Nelyerri, is an 'erotic imitation' that functions, like the mechanicals in *A Midsummer Night's Dream*, as a comic counterpoint to the idyll of the 'true lovers', Rifkah and Delacy. Like Delacy, Nugget feels he is in an enchanted world. Like Delacy, he takes his maiden for long moonlit walks. Unlike Delacy, Nugget is mocked by the author who comments, 'such walking and talking would make anyone tired in a mile', and who has Queeny asking scornfully, 'Wha's matter dat Nugget…he calico-cock?'[58] Nonetheless, for all Herbert's mockery, even the 'erotic imitation' of a mechanical has in it something of the idealised perfection of this phase of romance. Nugget's behaviour towards Nelyerri is wholly admirable. He treats her with respect, seeks to marry her, knowing his family will scorn him for doing so, and is gentle and caring where all other men she has known have been rough and exploitative.

The idyllic view of experience found even at the level of the mechanicals intensifies when the scene shifts to lovers at the top of the hierarchy. For Delacy and Rifkah at Lily Lagoons:

> [It was] as if here in the flesh were something like what souls knew in the Nirvana. […] [W]hen Rifkah spoke of Jews it was concerning the lovely simple things of Jewish life: the festivals, the foods […] Never of the persecution. Jeremy talked of the Irish, or the lovely ritual of the

Catholic Church, but never of the meanness, the cruelty, the hypocrisy behind it all. He talked of the Aborigines, of their customs, their mythology, the perfection of their lives as children of Nature, not of the frightful reality of their dispossession. [...]

The walks usually lasted about an hour, perhaps as long as perfection can last.[59]

Through this idyll Herbert brings enchantment to the world of white Australia. Hitherto we have seen it only in the bush with Prindy. Now, with the enchanted walks and Shabbos rituals, the white station owner enters the world of romance. Unfortunately, he proves unable to live within that world. He has lived too long with failure, is too deeply imbued with negativity. Unable to protect the heroine from her enemies, he entrusts her to his son Clancy, and it is between him and Rifkah that the third idyll is played out. Once again it is an 'erotic imitation', but not this time a genial one. Clancy behaves at first very much like Nugget, full of respect and callow eagerness, but then he becomes greedy and the magic turns sinister as love turns to lust. A wild Dionysian bacchanal on the beach has a threatening feel to it. It is followed by Clancy's attempted rape and Rifkah's flight into a stormy sea.[60]

And so it is left to the last idyll to bring perfection. In a situation reminiscent of Shakespeare's final romance, Rifkah, Prindy and Savitra are caught in a tempest and thrown up on the shores of Leopold Island, where Rifkah finds love in the arms of Glascock the priest, while Prindy lies in the arms of his childish paramour, Savitra. Thus, through a process of displacement, are the romance hero and heroine joined in a love whose connections with medieval romance are at this point made explicit:

[S]o idyllic was the situation [...] that it might be said the place fairly cried out for comparison with some Happy Land of Legend. Yet where, in *all* legendry, was ever such a place of undiminishing love-enchantment? Even Avalon, that *Ocean Island* of mediaeval romance, said to be located, *Not Far This Side of Paradise*, suffered disillusion, bitterly.[61]

The final idyll is the most passionate expression of Herbert's hope for Australia. Prindy, symbol of all that is best in the old, and Rifkah, symbol of all that is best in the new, are here united. The disparity in age would have made Herbert's original plan to have Prindy and Rifkah 'under blankets in the sand, arms about each other, mother and son, lover and lover'[62] problematic. Leopold Island was the better option: with Herbert implying their union through a shared idyll in which each is paired with a partner of their own age, the resulting foursome bound together in a dream of love. The dream, unfortunately, is short-lived. The Japanese arrive; Glascock is butchered; the others flee; and the stage is set for the final attempt at initiation that ends in Prindy's death.

On one level, Prindy's death signifies the death of Herbert's hopes for a new Australia. On another, the level of myth, those hopes still survive. Myth, wrote Levi-Strauss, is 'the means by which a people succeed in moving themselves from a world of irreversible time into a synchronic world of ritual in which time is annihilated'[63], and it is through the mysterious timelessness of the myth of golden Prindy that, against all reason, hope is kept alive in *Poor Fellow My Country*. That hope derives partly from associations Herbert encourages us to make between the story of Prindy and traditional myths of renewal, and partly from the use of repetition.

In *Capricornia* Herbert used repetition to establish a sense of the timeless conditions of Capricornian life. In *Poor Fellow My Country* he uses it to establish a sense of the timelessness of Prindy's quest. Again and again Prindy sets out on his journey towards initiation. Again and again he is chased. Again and again he is captured and held in bondage. Again and again he escapes and sets out once more. Each time, once capture is complete, the quest for the moment impossible, Prindy accepts the position calmly. Questions are met with a wide-eyed stare and silence, but no rancour. When Cahoon, who has just caught and chained him, asks for a tune on the flute, 'Prindy obliged with some Indian music'. When, still chained, they meet Delacy, who asks about Prindy's pony, 'Prindy answered cheerily enough, "He all right, Mullaka."'[64] When Rifkah and Prindy are trapped by Sergeant Sims, and Sims asks, 'How you doing, young feller?' Prindy 'amiably' replies, 'All right, Sigs'.[65] Rifkah, meanwhile, is anything but amiable:

she bristles with resentment. Their different reactions point to a contrast between time-bound mortals and the timeless hero of myth. For Rifkah the capture puts an end to her joy in the arms of Glascock; for Prindy it is simply a pause in his march towards initiation. They may stop him a thousand times, he will wait a thousand times until the way is clear and then proceed on his quest again.

As in *Capricornia*, repetitive descriptive detail reinforces the sense of timelessness. At one point Prindy is hunted by what looked like 'shiny black devils'; at another by 'gleaming black riders'. At one point Barbu's 'long black claw' catches him; at another Jinbul's 'black claw' does the same.[66] Three times he begins his initiation rites, and three times the interference of outsiders disrupts those rites. In all three scenes, the trouble is caused by a half-caste woman. In all three, they are speared for their interference. In all three, Prindy is pictured 'staring'—'great-eyed' in one, eyes 'wide with horror' in another.[67] The repetitiveness of detail emphasises the fact that all these journeys, all these captures, all these attempts at initiation and all these disruptions are the same journey, the same capture, the same attempt, the same disruption. Prindy is the Australia of Herbert's dreams, the country that never was but always might be. Like the sun rising, travelling the sky and setting, day after day in timeless cycle, so Prindy travels, comes close to initiation, is captured and imprisoned, travels again. Prindy's quest has no beginning and no end; it is a quest in progress, never triumphantly achieved but never conclusively failing, implying perpetual possibility.

The sense of perpetual possibility is reinforced by the associations Herbert encourages readers to make between the death of Prindy and the myth, found in many cultures, of the god whose death brings renewal to the world. It is a myth played out twice in scenes involving Prindy, twice in scenes involving Rifkah, once in a scene involving both, and once in a bitter parody involving Delacy.

The first playing out of this myth begins when Prindy, pursued by police, finds his escape blocked by the river. A 'heavy silence' falls, except for

> the muffled thunder of the great water [...] sweeping to the suck of that mighty yellow serpent, the river. Prindy

rose as if the roar was a voice calling him, and ran straight
towards it [...] heading for that point where the
Pookarakka had tried to deliver himself into the hands of
the Master [...] just down there was a kind of hill of water,
sloping down to a wall of it; [...] it could be taken for a
great sucking mouth—the smooth slope the tongue, the
leaping watery wall the upper lip.

The tongue caught the two bobbing heads [...] The
maw opened to them. They vanished.[68]

The scene draws upon both pagan and Christian myth. On the one hand
Prindy is the drowned God of European spring rituals, a willing sacrifice
to the water, running 'straight towards it' there to 'deliver himself into the
hands of the Master'. On the other hand there are suggestions of 'Christ
crucified' as Herbert links Tchamala's kingdom with the hell of medieval
mystery plays through his choice of the word 'maw' and reference to a
'great sucking mouth'. It is, significantly, Christmas Day when Prindy
descends into the depths and 'dawn on New Year's Day' when he rises
again. The promise of renewal is apparent in 'a dawn so bright that the
birds seemed to be waking with especial joy to it'. After the willing
sacrifice comes the hope of the resurrection. Like Mary visiting the tomb
of Jesus, Delacy goes sorrowfully to the Rainbow Pool and there finds:

A small human thing, a skeleton almost, scarcely distin-
guishable from the rubbish in which, prone, it struggled
feebly in striving towards the approaching man, skinny
reaching arms, a death's head with gaping blackened
mouth, but life in the deep eye sockets, life blazing as the
sockets raised themselves to meet eyes of the same
intense grey. [...] Pus oozed from a score of lacerations,
and from cracked lips and nostrils. Even the marsh flies
left the thing alone.[69]

It's another marvellous piece of writing, full of rich ambiguity and
moving subtly between allegory and myth. Allegorically Prindy is 'the
oppressed Aboriginal', a Poor Tom figure whose degradation cries
shame upon the white world that has brought him to this 'basest

and most poorest shape'[70], but he is also, and paradoxically, 'the Aboriginal proud and dauntless', for it is no coincidence that 'death's head', 'blackened mouth' and eyes 'blazing' in 'deep eye sockets' bring to mind the repeated formulaic description of his defiant master, Bobwirridirridi. Meanwhile, from the perspective of myth, Prindy is Australia reborn, the risen saviour, back from the depths where for seven days he has been tested beyond the strength of ordinary men. Like Christ his body is torn and broken. Like Job even the flies shun his company. Yet from death cometh life: for in this death's head life 'blazes' as he strives towards the approaching Delacy.

Prindy's second ordeal replicates the first. It occurs at the same spot, and again he offers himself willingly to the river, pulling with him Jinbul and Cahoon, who are manacled to him, one on each side. As they are swept downriver they hear

> a sort of continuous hissing, but beyond it somewhere a growing roar [...] Jinbul, the grey-faced, accepting the inevitable, had sunken eyes only for what lay further ahead, a dark line, like a thin lip [...] Plainly it was a lip, quivering as if with suppressed laughter over the presumption of little men. [...] As the lip opened to reveal the maw, those on the extremities of the chain were swept around as if sucked from both sides, leaving the chosen one, the mid-link of this magic chain, to fetch up against what for a fact was a shelf of rock even if serving as a laughing lip.[71]

Again hell's 'maw' gapes. Again it sucks downward. But this time a rock saves Prindy—saves him while symbolically crucifying him, spreadeagled against the rock with, Christlike, a sinner on each side. When both bodies are wrenched from the manacles that hold them to him, the sun rises in a sign of renewal, and the resurrected saviour, 'hair now flying golden in the breeze', rises and sets off on his quest again.

In Rifkah's ordeals, references to water monsters become more insistent. In the first, the reef that shipwrecks her is the 'monstrous swimming length' of Tchamala; the crabs that nibble her are 'tiny monsters'. In the second, the storm is a 'monster advancing upon them' with 'monstrous gaping mouth [...] its top lip a great curl of blackest cloud, the boiling sea its gnashing teeth, its throat a grey void from which icy breath soon smote them'. Once again the imagery mixes pagan and Christian myth. The monstrous sea has the 'gaping mouth' of medieval representations of hell; it is a 'grey void'; it pours 'in a black stream downhill' and 'ran fire'. In the first scene Tchamala threatens to 'drag [Rifkah] down into luminescent chaos' and the crabs' mouths are 'gaping maws'. The Christ figure hinted at in Prindy's second ordeal is overtly signified in Rifkah's ordeals. In the first she hangs from the 'climbing-spikes' of a beacon in the Christ pose of traditional icons, 'head hung drooped over the shoulder of the loose-hanging arm'; in the second, Christlike, she calls out in her agony '*Lieber Gott...Lieber Gott*'.

It is at this point of both scenes that the difference between Rifkah and Prindy becomes clear. Prindy is the saviour figure, a willing sacrifice to the god he serves; Rifkah, the sacrificial victim bound to the rock and in despair until, miraculously, the saviour arrives. The sea-kweeluks in the first scene scream 'above the tumult of the waters: [...] *Somebody is lost!*' In the second scene Rifkah, 'in grey chaos, alone', is joined by a hammerhead shark whose 'great grey eye on a black stick' comes 'so close as fairly to stare into [her] soul'. It is the final test. After the dark night of the soul comes redemption, heralded by the sun and brought by the surrogate hero: in the first scene, as Glascock approached, 'the Sun broke through'; in the second, '[t]he Sun glinted' just before he appeared.[72]

Through Rifkah's ordeals, Herbert reinforces the myth of regeneration implicit in the story of Prindy. He uses Delacy's struggle in Sydney Harbour differently. Delacy's ordeal functions as a deliberate contrast to the trials of Prindy and Rifkah. Theirs take place in a world where myth is possible; his in a world that denies the numinous. Its similarities of detail—the wall he falls down, the near drowning, the threat of sharks—only emphasise its difference. In white, urban Australia there is no mystery left. The stress is on the rubbish that clogs the bay, the dirty water, the slimy rocks. 'A grey head floating amongst rotten cabbages and broken fruit cases.' Sharks are no longer shades of Tchamala but contemptible scavengers in 'waters [...] too befouled [...] to support any life but that which subsisted on filth'.[73] These waters are death-giving, not life-giving. The miraculous cycle of death unto life is absent; here is only death unto death, deadness all around. Jeremy emerges from the water into the final death of his hopes for Australia. The treatment he receives on Garden Island proves that arrogant colonial power is stronger than the spirit of Australian independence, and he can do nothing about it.

And so to the final scene of all, the last sacrifice. Prindy is dead and, with his death, romance and its possibilities seem to have died, too. Lily Lagoons has become a uranium mine. The rocks that covered Tchamala's river have been blasted away, disclosing the 'mysterious underground stream' that has been diverted

> to supply the great Uranium Treatment Plant set up on the site of Lily Lagoons Homestead. That meant the end of the Rainbow Pool, at least as the place of Moah it had been from the Beginning. Except during the Wet Season it was now dry

and used as a 'rubbish dump'. The Painted Caves are similarly despoiled by tourists, who 'identify themselves with the Dreamtime by making their own contributions to the paintings'. As for Rifkah, the romance heroine has become an 'old fogey', the 'withered spouse' of 'Lopsided Pat' Hannaford.[74]

With romance apparently dead, it seems fitting that the final scene is reminiscent of Delacy's ordeal in Sydney. In both, a man and a woman are surrounded by mobs mouthing catchcries. In both, the woman attracts the ire of the mob by trying to voice an Australian viewpoint. In both, the man is thrown down a wall into the water, and in both he is disabled and has difficulty swimming. If the final scene is less depressing, it is because, rejected though it is by most, the mystery, 'the Moah', has not yet been completely destroyed. As Hannaford is carried 'into the milky stream' that, twice earlier, took Prindy into its powerful embrace, Rifkah, knowing Pat cannot swim, slides in to help him. And so to the final paragraphs of the novel:

Her head came up like a bubble of dark blood above the milk. Pat was out in racing midstream now and well away. She struck out, was soon in the flood-race. Pat had vanished. But there ahead of her, retreating at the same swift rate as she advanced, was a strange sight—a quadrageminal pattern of four bubbles. She stared, stopped swimming, swept on.

Were the great eyes behind the flared nostrils really intense grey, or only appeared to be so upon the racing white water? Her mouth opened wide, to give forth a cry that rang to the very tops of the few remaining river trees: 'Prindy...Prindy...*Ngoornberri...ngungah...ngungahhhhh!*'

Down went the pattern of bubbles. Down went the copper head that looked like a bubble of blood. Nothing else for the gaping world to see. Only the *Moah* of the river to be sensed, by those with senses not yet too blunted by the jack-hammer logic of the *kuttabah* as still to be aware of the all-pervading *Mahraghi* of this ancient land, *Terra Australis del Espiritu Santo.*[75]

Thus finally does Rifkah re-enter the world of romance, taken by the hero whom death cannot conquer and who now appears as one of Tchamala's shades, the great crocodile. And thus it is that Prindy still lives on, the Australia of Herbert's dreaming, the myth more real than reality, the country that never was but always is, a perpetual possibility for those who, like Herbert, refuse to give up the dream of *Australia Felix.*

T. S. Eliot once wrote:

Time present and time past
Are both perhaps present in time future,
And time future contained in time past.
If all time is eternally present
All time is unredeemable.
What might have been is an abstraction
Remaining a perpetual possibility
Only in a world of speculation.[76]

One of Herbert's great achievements in *Poor Fellow My Country* was to find a way not only to record the brutal logic of 'time future contained in time past' but also to give a powerful sense of perpetual possibility to 'what might have been'. On one level, it is all too clear that the 'time present' of Cobbity, Cootes and McCusky and the 'time past' of Delacy's father and the Vaiseys will inevitably be 'present' in the 'time future' (our present) of the final depressing pages of the book. But romance allowed Herbert an escape from the historical tyranny of the novel and enabled him to give powerful life to 'a world of speculation' through the myth of Prindy, which shows 'what might have been' alongside what was and is; 'what might still be' alongside what perhaps must always be. But if *Poor Fellow My Country* is Herbert's *Tempest*, it is also his *King Lear*. If the hope of romance sustains us to the end, it is shot through with the sad inevitability of tragedy. Yes, the *Mahraghi* is still there, but no-one except Rifkah sees it. No-one understands. No-one cares. And therein lies for Herbert the tragedy of Australia.

APPENDIX

HERBERT'S SHORT STORIES

Early Stories and Novellas, 1925–27

'North of Capricorn' (AJ)
'The Unforgivable' (AJ)
'The Maniac and the Full Moon' (SN)
'The Atheist' (SW)
'The Man in the Moon's Story' (AJ)
'The Opportunity Chaser' (AJ)
'The Coming of Ezekiel Mort' (AJ)
'The Way of a Man' (AJ)
'The Sea Vultures' (novella) (*PALS*)
'Giants of Iron' (novella) (Un)
Untitled (novella) (Un)

Written in Northern Australia, 1928–29

'The Medicine' (AJ)
'The Long Arm' (AJ)
'The Other McLean' (AJ)
'The Rainmaker' (AJ)
'When an Irresistible Force' (AJ)
'Faint Heart' (AJ)
'The Beauty of Barbara' (NS)

Written in England

'Living Dangerously' (WWM)

Written after Returning from England, 1933–34

'Sounding Brass' (AJ)
'Sailor Bring Joy' (AJ)*
'Tale of a Woman's Love' (AJ)
'Misanthropy' (SS)

'The Widow McLean' (AJ)
'Machinations of a Jinx' (AJ)
'When No Man Pursueth' (SS)
'Shotgun Wedding' (Un)
'The Devil of Dollypot Reef' (AJ)
'The Best Laid Plans' (SS)
'Michaelos is a Miser' (AJ)
'Moonshine' (AJ)
'Look into My Eyes' (AJ)
'Miss Tanaka' (AJ)

Later Stories Published in *Larger Than Life*

'Sequel to a Song'**
'A.T.C. Barragoola'
'Keeping the Peace'
'Mercy Flight'
'Rocky the Rig'***
'The Flying Fat Boy'
'Come on Murri'
'An Eagle Called Ned Kelly'
'Femme Fatale'
'Rise and Fall of Jeremiah Stacey'
'Marrying Money'
'Once a Policeman…'
'Day of Shame'
'Kaijek the Songman'
'Last Toss'

*	A revised version of 'Living Dangerously'
**	A revised version of 'Machinations of a Jinx'
***	A revised version of 'Misanthropy'

Key to publications in which the stories were first printed
AJ   *Australian Journal*
NS   *Northern Standard*
SN   *Sunday News*
SS   *Sunday Sun*
SW   *Smith's Weekly*
Un   Unpublished
WWM   *Wild World Magazine*

NOTES

FL   Fryer Library, Queensland University
OUP   Oxford University Press
UQP   University of Queensland Press

A Partisan Introduction

1   Don Grant, 'Xavier Herbert's botch', *Overland*, 65, 1976, pp. 43–7.

2   Laurie Clancy, *Xavier Herbert*, Twayne Publishers, Boston, 1981, p. 132.

3   Herbert to Sadie Herbert, 28 September 1968, Box 48, FL Mss 83. 'People bore me. What dreadful bore [sic] practically all people are! All my life I've suffered with swelling of the feet thro' having to listen to people's dull, dull talk. You can hear anything the average person has to say on any subject in about 3 mins.'

4   Xavier Herbert, 'I sinned against syntax', *Meanjin*, 19(1), 1960, pp. 31–5. 'I couldn't copy anyone. To do so would be to betray unoriginality, the first attribute [sic] to literary distinction. So I invented a syntax of my own. I reckoned that that, if nothing else, would win me recognition for literary genius.'

5   William Blake, 'Proverbs of hell', *Poetry and Prose of William Blake*, Nonesuch Press, London, 1921, p. 183.

6   Arthur Miller, *Collected Plays*, Cresset Press, London, 1958, p. 33.

7   Herbert to Beatrice Davis, 31 May 1956, Box 26, FL Mss 83.

8   I have adopted the convention of enclosing in square brackets those ellipses that indicate my omission of text from the original.

9   Herbert to Sadie, 14 September 1968, Box 48, FL Mss 83.

10   Herbert to Sadie, 1 August 1974, Box 51, FL Mss 83.

11   Herbert to Sadie, 7 October 1968, Box 48, FL Mss 83.

12   Herbert to Sadie, 2 October 1968, Box 48, FL Mss 83.

13   Gore Vidal, *Matters of Fact and Fiction*, Vintage Books, USA, 1978, p. 74.

14   Robert Reid, '*Playboy* interview Xavier Herbert', *Australian Playboy*, June 1982, p. 135. '[I]t was a kind of trance thing, and I got so used to it that I would write solid for 16 hours.'

15   Northrop Frye, *Anatomy of Criticism*, Penguin, London, 1990, pp. 303–4.

16   ibid., p. 312.

17   To avoid confusion between Frye's specialised use of the word and its common usage, quotation marks are used for Frye's use of 'novel' throughout this introduction, and in subsequent chapters in places where there might otherwise be confusion between the two meanings of the word.

18   Adrian Mitchell, 'Fiction', in Leonie Kramer (ed.), *The Oxford History of Australian Literature*, OUP, Melbourne, 1981, pp. 123–6.

19   Frye, *Anatomy*, p. 308.

20   ibid., p. 305.

Chapter 1: An Apprenticeship in Popular Romance

1   This chapter owes much to the research of Russell McDougall, as a result of which all the early stories have been collected in a single volume. A chronological outline of those stories can be found in the Appendix.

2   'The staples of his literary diet were the cowboy/adventure fiction of Zane Grey, the "he-man" novels of Rex Beach, and the sado-masochistic fantasy of *The Sheik* by E. M. Hull' (Russell McDougall (ed.), *South of Capricornia*, OUP, Melbourne, 1990, p. 1). 'Like his mother, who was "a confirmed reader of tripe", he also enjoyed Edgar Wallace' (Frances de Groen, *Xavier Herbert*, UQP, St Lucia, 1998, p. 41).

3   Xavier Herbert, *Disturbing Element*, Fontana, Melbourne, 1976, p. 207.

4   McDougall, *South of Capricornia*, p. 31.

5   ibid., p. 3.

6   ibid., p. 176.

7   Northrop Frye, *Anatomy of Criticism*, Penguin, London, 1990, pp. 186–7.

8   'The Maniac and the Full Moon', 'The Atheist' and 'The Coming of Ezekiel Mort' (McDougall, *South of Capricornia*, pp. 49, 55, 101).

9   'The Opportunity Chaser', 'The Way of a Man', 'Giants of Iron', 'The Medicine', 'The Other McLean', 'The Rainmaker' (McDougall, *South of Capricornia*, pp. 84, 111, 182, 210, 242, 262).

10   Xavier Herbert, interviewed by Elizabeth Riddell, transcript, Box 60, FL Mss 83.

11   Xavier Herbert, *Capricornia*, Angus & Robertson, Melbourne, 1971, chs 11, 12.

12   Xavier Herbert, recorded conversation for the National Library, 13 December 1975, transcript, FL Mss 83.

13   Xavier Herbert, *Poor Fellow My Country*, Collins, Sydney, 1975, chs 7, 8.

14   Xavier Herbert, 'A Novelist's Responsibility to History', sound tape, Queensland University Library, 1976.

15   Xavier Herbert, *Soldiers' Women*, Fontana, Netley, 1978, pp. 82–3.

16   ibid., pp. 269–70.

17   Herbert, *Poor Fellow My Country*, pp. 1436–7.

18   McDougall, *South of Capricornia*, pp. 202, 254.

19   In the pre-*Capricornia*n stories there is one story about an ingenious trick ('The Coming of Ezekiel Mort', McDougall, *South of Capricornia*, p. 101); in the post-*Capricornia*n stories there are six ('The Devil of Dollypot Reef', McDougall, *South of Capricornia*, p. 462; 'The Best Laid Plans', 'Michaelos is a Miser', 'Moonshine', 'Look into My Eyes', 'Miss Tanaka', Xavier Herbert, *Larger than Life*, Fontana, Melbourne, 1976, pp. 102, 141, 180, 152, 169).

20   Herbert, *Soldiers' Women*, p. 216.
21   Herbert, *Poor Fellow My Country*, pp. 356–7.
22   McDougall, *South of Capricornia*, p. 293.
23   ibid., p. 37.
24   ibid., p. 2. 'His decision to become a doctor and move to Melbourne was precipitated primarily by an enthusiastic, chance encounter with *The History of Mr Polly*. Devouring this most popular of H.G. Wells' novels in a single afternoon, Herbert was so overwhelmed as to believe that he had been given his first real insight into life…'
25   ibid., p. 56.
26   ibid., p. 103.
27   ibid., p. 60. 'Under [Colin Wills's] tutelage, Herbert read seriously for the first time in his life—Huxley, Arnold Bennett, Sinclair Lewis, Dreiser, Thomas Mann, and others…'
28   ibid., p. 210. 'I met Dickens'— more particularly *Dombey and Son*— 'and…delighted in Dickens' style'.
29   ibid., p. 211.
30   ibid., p. 119.
31   ibid., p. 127.
32   ibid., p. 132.
33   ibid., pp. 318, 332.
34   ibid., p. 58.
35   ibid., pp. 263–4.

Chapter 2: The Great Leap Forward

1   Frances de Groen, *Xavier Herbert*, UQP, St Lucia, 1998, pp. 45–6.
2   Xavier Herbert, interviewed by Elizabeth Riddell, transcript, Box 60, FL Mss 83.
3   Robert Reid, '*Playboy* interview Xavier Herbert', *Australian Playboy*, June 1982, p. 135.
4   ibid. As Chapter 5 demonstrates, it is unwise to assume that Herbert's version of events is strictly accurate. Frances de Groen queries the timing he gives for the writing of *Capricornia*. Herbert said six weeks. De Groen says he had eighteen months in which he could have been working on it. She does not mention, or query, what he says about his mode of writing (de Groen, *Xavier Herbert*, p. 85). As Chapter 9 demonstrates, there is ample evidence that for *Poor Fellow My Country*, he adopted similarly 'ecstatic' writing strategies.
5   de Groen, *Xavier Herbert*, p. 91.
6   Xavier Herbert, *Capricornia*, Angus & Robertson, Melbourne, 1971, p. 204.
7   ibid., pp. 42–3.
8   ibid., p. 113.

9   ibid., pp. 60–1.

10   ibid., p. 31.

11   ibid., p. 125.

12   ibid., p. 118.

13   ibid., p. 1.

14   ibid., p. 365.

15   ibid., p. 172.

16   ibid., p. 431.

17   ibid., pp. 162, 158.

18   ibid., p. 161.

19   ibid., p. 469.

20   ibid., p. 202.

21   George Orwell, *Selected Writings*, Heinemann, London, 1958, pp. 147–8.

22   Herbert, *Capricornia*, p. 174.

23   ibid., p. 69.

24   ibid., pp. 127–8.

25   Gore Vidal, *Matters of Fact and Fiction*, Vintage, USA, 1978, p. 74. 'Absorbed by his subject, the genius is a natural innovator.'

26   Xavier Herbert, *Soldiers' Women*, Fontana, Netley, 1978, pp. 7–11.

27   ibid., pp. 32, 140.

28   Bruce Kawin, *Telling It Again and Again*, Cornell University Press, Ithaca, 1972, pp. 2–3.

29   ibid., p. 4.

30   Herbert, *Capricornia*, pp. 156, 373, 435–6.

31   ibid., pp. 111, 261.

32   ibid., chs 9, 10.

33   ibid., p. 256.

34   ibid., pp. 209–10.

35   ibid., pp. 225, 43.

36   Russell McDougall (ed.), *South of Capricornia*, OUP, Melbourne, 1990, pp. 263–4; Herbert, *Capricornia*, p. 68.

37   Herbert, *Capricornia*, pp. 59, 366, 373.

38   Xavier Herbert, *Poor Fellow My Country*, Collins, Sydney, 1975, pp. 215, 219.

39   Xavier Herbert, 'The agony and the joy', *Overland*, 50–51, Autumn 1972, pp. 65–8.

40   Herbert, *Capricornia*, p. 345.

41   ibid., p. 310.

42   ibid., pp. 6–7.

43   ibid., p. 8.

44   ibid., p. 17.

45   ibid., p. 24.

46   The word 'half-caste' poses problems for anyone who writes about Herbert. On the one hand, its racist connotations are offensive. On the

other hand, it is the word Herbert, being a man of his time, uses for a concept that is important in his novels. For a commentator, to use a less offensive synonym such as 'part-Aboriginal' would pose problems, leading to potentially confusing mismatches between quotations from Herbert using the word 'half-caste' and related commentary using the word 'part-Aboriginal'. This being so, the best option seems to be to stick to the word Herbert used while apologising for any offence this may cause.

47   See the comparisons between Lydia, Alfie and Rifkah discussed in Chapter 11; also the deliberately repetitive descriptions of the Beatrice River Races, through whose small differences of detail Herbert establishes a sense of the changes occurring from year to year in the political atmosphere of Australia.

48   Herbert, *Capricornia*, pp. 224, 258.

49   ibid., p. 328.

50   ibid., p. 497.

51   ibid., p. 509.

52   Northrop Frye, *Anatomy of Criticism*, Penguin, London, 1990, p. 304. 'A suggestion of allegory is constantly creeping in around its fringes.'

53   ibid., p. 312.

54   E. M. Forster, *Aspects of the Novel*, Penguin, Middlesex, 1962, p. 75. 'In their purest form [flat characters] are constructed round a single idea or quality.'

55   Herbert, *Capricornia*, pp. 502–4.

56   Frye, *Anatomy*, pp. 310–11.

57   Herbert, *Capricornia*, pp. 78–83.

58   ibid., pp. 185–7.

59   ibid., pp. 313–31.

Chapter 3: In Praise of the Swagman Spirit

1   Tom Inglis Moore, '*Capricornia*', *Australian Highway*, 20 March 1938, pp. 21–3.

2   Vincent Buckley, '*Capricornia*', *Meanjin*, 19(1), 1960, p. 23.

3   Xavier Herbert, 'As a prophet, the great satirist was a failure', *Sydney Morning Herald*, 10 January 1984, p. 7.

4   Xavier Herbert, *Capricornia*, Angus & Robertson, Melbourne, 1971, p. 143.

5   Herbert to Don Chipp, 9 July 1978, FL Mss 83.

6   Herbert, *Capricornia*, p. 460.

7   William Shakespeare, *King Lear*, act I, scene 2, line 128.

8   Herbert, *Capricornia*, p. 117.

9   ibid., p. 203.

10   *Murders:* Kurrinua, Jock Driver, Frank McLash, Cho See Kee, Con the Greek and 'A Jap'. *Deaths from youth and age:* Roger Shillingsworth,

Mollie O'Cannon, Margaret O'Cannon's baby, Oscar, Mrs O'Shay, Mr O'Hay. *Train deaths:* Ballest, O'Pick, Tim O'Cannon. *Sea deaths:* Krater, Maud O'Cannon.

11 Herbert, *Capricornia*, p. 510.
12 ibid., p. 295.
13 ibid., p. 236.
14 ibid., pp. 128–9.
15 Xavier Herbert, speech to Adelaide Arts Festival, March 1962, transcript, FL Mss 83.
16 Xavier Herbert, recorded conversation for the National Archives, 12 July 1961, transcript, FL Mss 83.
17 Herbert, *Capricornia*, p. 330.
18 ibid., p. 321.
19 ibid., p. 20.
20 ibid., pp. 319–21.
21 ibid., pp. 324–5.
22 ibid., p. 325.
23 ibid., p. 319.
24 ibid., p. 405.
25 ibid., p. 131.
26 ibid., p. 132.
27 ibid., pp. 235–6.
28 ibid., p. 325.
29 ibid., pp. 46–7.
30 ibid., p. 163.
31 ibid., p. 145.
32 ibid., p. 40.
33 Buckley, '*Capricornia*', p. 18.
34 Herbert, *Capricornia*, p. 403.
35 ibid., p. 127.
36 ibid., p. 321.
37 ibid., p. 21.
38 ibid., p. 130.
39 ibid., pp. 173, 151, 247.
40 ibid., p. 119.
41 ibid., p. 217.
42 ibid., p. 202.
43 Buckley, '*Capricornia*', p. 25.
44 Herbert, *Capricornia*, p. 14.
45 ibid., p. 244.
46 ibid., p. 321.
47 ibid., p. 93.

Chapter 4: Aboriginality as Subject, Symbol and Setting

1   Frances de Groen, *Xavier Herbert*, UQP, St Lucia, 1998, p. 171. 'During the remainder of 1957 he speedily reworked the 30,000-word 1942 version of "Seven Emus" into a 60,000-word novella.'

2   Herbert to Beatrice Davis, 14 April 1959, Box 26, FL Mss 83.

3   Herbert to Sadie Herbert, 27 October 1964, Box 44, FL Mss 83.

4   Xavier Herbert, *Capricornia*, Angus & Robertson, Melbourne, 1971, pp. 327–8.

5   ibid., p. 293.

6   ibid., pp. 328, 330.

7   ibid., p. 294.

8   ibid., p. 373. The other passage is the one describing Red Ochre Station after the death of Oscar Shillingsworth. 'The devil of the departed master was everywhere. It […] stole among the shadows, moaned in the nor'east wind, flew with the ragged clouds across the moon's dead face, wailed in the timber of the river—Kwee-luk!—Kwee-luk!—Kweeee—luk!—I am lost!'

9   ibid., p. 295.

10   ibid., p. 296.

11   ibid., p. 306.

12   ibid., p. 307.

13   ibid., p. 456.

14   ibid., p. 458.

15   Xavier Herbert, Notes for 'Yellow Fellow', Box 7a, FL Mss 83. *Chapter 2:* 'Blacks who killed Coles brought in, inquest and up to court. Little Parinti's experiences, the arrival, the compound, Clerk of courts and insignia. Jahligeeta asked to give evidence against her husband. Defence objects—judge says she has no legal standing and won't allow objection.' *Chapter 14:* 'V. J. White comes down and orders Parinti away as apprentice to Wyatt at 6 shillings a week. Duchess [i.e. Jahligeeta] is put in laundry and exploited.' *Chapter 20:* 'Duchess taken to hospital. Dr Fothergill won't touch a black. She is put in Asiatic ward. Dr Kirkland can't be found. Duchess bleeding to death. Duchess dies. Faith tries to get her buried at cemetery. Undertaker won't do it. Parinti arrives to find mother buried in tip.' *Chapter 21:* 'Dolly in family way. White orders Parinti to marry her. Tells him he'll give him a halfcaste house (describe slum).'

16   ibid. *Chapter 13:* 'Coming of girls from mission. Their arrest. Parinti fights a policeman.' *Chapter 18:* 'Parinti's band. Visit to Residency. Row with officers off warship. Gets locked up. Spectacular row—exposure of Abbott and wife. Band asked to come without Parinti. Parinti comes under influence liquor.' *Chapter 19:* 'Describe the road job and how halfcastes are robbed. Parinti makes trouble and forms halfcaste gang of his own and cuts out whitemen. Great trouble and job is closed down.' *Chapter 22:* 'Red

Anthony is going to contest seat at elections; Sol offers to secure him the halfcaste vote if he will promise to get them the right to drink. Red is elected. A number halfcaste[s] are given license to drink—refused full citizen rights. A grand party. Parinti and Sol lead a mob. Whites are beaten up. Sol and Parinti get jailed. Sol and Parinti make impassioned pleas in court.' *Chapter 24:* 'Formation of Euraustralian League. Parinti is made President. League broken up. Parinti leads deputation to Red, asking for justice. Red hunts them. Parinti threatens him. Red gives him in charge.' *Chapter 26:* 'League is made nation-wide. His father leads campaign against him—calling it an invasion—the bringing in of halfcastes. Parinti declares he will contest next elections.' *Chapter 27:* 'Envoys sent all over country to bring halfcastes in. A great campaign.' *Chapter 28:* 'Parinti elected. Anomaly of elected member of land unable to collect his salary or drink. Gets all citizen rights for himself and wife.'

17   Xavier Herbert, *Bulletin Literary Supplement*, 1 January 1983. In 1936 he founded a 'Euraustralian League' that failed because he realised Euraustralians could only advance in white society by rejecting their blackness. Xavier Herbert, recorded conversation for the National Library, 13 December 1975, transcript, FL Mss 83. He also 'went out into a tin and tantalite district […] to get the black miners' rights and get them to work for themselves. What I didn't realize was that the blacks don't like working for anybody even themselves, which is very wise'.

18   In the planning stages of his novels Herbert often gave different versions of a character's name. The 'Tony Lauma' mentioned here is clearly the same character as a 'Tommy Lamma' mentioned in his notes for Chapter 30.

19   Xavier Herbert, *Seven Emus*, Fontana, Melbourne, 1977, p. 106.

20   Herbert, *Poor Fellow My Country*, Collins, Sydney, 1975, p. 669.

21   Herbert, *Seven Emus*, pp. 91, 107.

22   The description given of Aboriginal cultures by Herbert was not a strictly accurate one. He was more interested in the symbolic significance of Aboriginal culture than its anthropological realities. Frances de Groen, for instance, points out that Herbert's 'use of Kunapipi and related Karawadi mythology' in *Poor Fellow My Country* is inaccurate (de Groen, *Xavier Herbert*, p. 210). Giving an accurate anthropological account of Aboriginals was not the main purpose. If it served the symbolic purpose better to change and falsify the anthropological facts, so be it.

23   Herbert, *Seven Emus*, p. 11.

24   ibid., pp. 85, 68.

25   ibid., pp. 20, 105.

26   ibid., pp. 63, 171.

27   ibid., pp. 20, 33.

28   ibid., p. 139.

29   ibid., p. 82.

30   ibid., pp. 73, 16.

31   ibid., pp. 119, 17.

32   Herbert, *Poor Fellow My Country*, p. 20. 'A bloody nutching', he has Delacy say in *Poor Fellow My Country*, 'is what the average white person is'.

33   Herbert, *Seven Emus*, p. 123.

34   ibid., p. 106.

35   ibid., pp. 56–7.

36   Herbert, *Poor Fellow My Country*, p. 755.

37   Herbert, *Seven Emus*, pp. 83–4.

38   ibid., pp. 84, 91.

39   ibid., pp. 60–1.

40   ibid., pp. 20, 83.

41   ibid., p. 66.

42   ibid., p. 120.

43   Xavier Herbert, 'A town like Elliott: "There is NO solution to the Aborigines' problem"', *Bulletin*, 31 March 1962, pp. 23–5.

44   Herbert, *Seven Emus*, p. 116.

45   ibid., pp. 113–14.

46   ibid., pp. 56–7.

47   ibid., pp. 46–7.

48   ibid., p. 83.

49   ibid., pp. 105–6.

50   ibid., p. 155.

51   ibid., p. 164.

52   ibid., pp. 56, 81, 90.

53   Herbert, 'The agony and the joy', *Overland*, 50–51, Autumn 1972, pp. 65–8.

Chapter 5: Confession and Psycho-sexual Theorising

1   Kathleen Herbert to Herbert, 30 July 1961, FL Mss 83. 'You were worried that you were unable to pick up the thread of writing again (how often you spoke of the One-book-Author).'

2   Northrop Frye, *Anatomy of Criticism*, Penguin, London, 1990, p. 307.

3   Tom Flynn and Stephen Maginnis, for instance, both railway workers, both married to Aboriginal women, are the real-life originals for Tim O'Cannon in *Capricornia* and Pat Hannaford in *Poor Fellow My Country*. Stephen's Aboriginal wife, Lucy, and her children, Val and Joe, also feature in both novels. On Stephen's death in a railway accident, Lucy, Val and Joe were forced by the authorities into the Aboriginal compound (see Frances de Groen, *Xavier Herbert*, UQP, St Lucia, 1998, p. 60). The event, and Herbert's anger at it, are reflected in the experiences of Constance and her daughter Tocky in *Capricornia*, and Nelly and her son Prindy in *Poor Fellow My Country*.

4   de Groen, *Xavier Herbert*, pp. 103–4 (Kahlin), 113–14 (Australia First), 131–4 (war experience).

5   Of the many incidents that have a real-life basis, an interesting one is the following recalled in a letter to his wife: 'Remember I was lying in a creek bed in the moonlight spending the previous night in a painted cave, and a huge Aboriginal man stood beside me, so vividly that I saw him even after I woke—the Kwinkin, as Percy called him' (Herbert to Sadie Herbert, 5 September 1968, Box 48, FL Mss 83). We see here the genesis of Delacy's Lamala experience and his subsequent talking it over with Billy Brew (Percy Trezise in real life).

6   de Groen, *Xavier Herbert*, pp. 271–2. The frequent references in this and other chapters to Frances de Groen's meticulously researched and beautifully written biography of Herbert testify to the great value I have found in her work.

7   Xavier Herbert, recorded conversation for the National Library, 13 December 1975, transcript, FL Mss 83.

8   de Groen, *Xavier Herbert*, pp. 33, 75, 86. 'Olive Drake [...] wrote to him condemning his portrait of her as Julie Cobb, a sexually experienced young girl whose "mistake" he aborts, and asking why he wished to hurt her with such "dreadful lies"' (p. 33). The accounts Herbert gives in autobiographical pieces of his time in England 'are significantly discrepant and patently unreliable' (p. 75). 'Herbert's account of his return to Australia was a complete fabrication, yet one which he assiduously revised and embroidered from 1933 right up to his death in 1984' (p. 86).

9   ibid., p. 202.

10   Xavier Herbert, *Disturbing Element*, Fontana, Melbourne, 1976, p. 19.

11   ibid., pp. 28, 27.

12   ibid., p. 42.

13   ibid., p. 21.

14   Herbert, *Seven Emus*, Fontana, Melbourne, 1977, p. 146.

15   Herbert, *Disturbing Element*, pp. 138–9. As he watches his brother go off to war: 'What was my beloved brother doing out there on the dark ocean [...] Surely not weeping like a sissy for me, as I, the hopeless sissy, wept for him'. When he cried at the death of his cat: 'Hopeless sissy I thought myself, as blinded with tears I pedalled my way to work'.

16   ibid., p. 246.

17   Herbert to Sadie, 10 August, 17 November 1968, Box 48, FL Mss 83. Herbert speaks of how he was 'the only man in Redlynch to stand up for two rounds' to a visiting professional boxer and how, though a 'Clumsy Ike and the Scariest of Cats', he took up flying in middle age and mastered it. That the flying was a test of manhood appears in the following. 'You have to be a man with Nev [Neville Mitchell—flying instructor] or receive his contempt. [...] Don't forget that taking the aeroplane was a training in moral strength.'

18	Herbert, *Disturbing Element*, p. 21. 'I have been preoccupied for most of my life with trying to overcome the cowardice I believed due to his malicious mishandling of me.'
19	ibid., p. 104.
20	Herbert to Sadie, 30 July 1974, Box 51, FL Mss 83.
21	Herbert, *Capricornia*, Angus & Robertson, Melbourne, 1971, p. 311.
22	Herbert, *Disturbing Element*, pp. 8–10.
23	ibid., p. 66.
24	ibid., pp. 11–12, 48.
25	Xavier Herbert, 'The Little Widow', Box 15, FL Mss 83, V/11/154.
26	Herbert, *Disturbing Element*, p. 62.
27	ibid., pp. 157–60. All the names Herbert uses in *Disturbing Element* are pseudonyms.
28	de Groen, *Xavier Herbert*, p. 32. Herbert, *Disturbing Element*, pp. 202, 206. He 'became a joke' and showed 'utter lack of pride' complaining to 'mutual acquaintances' that 'she was spurning me, who loved her with my life'.
29	Herbert, *Disturbing Element*, p. 104.
30	de Groen, *Xavier Herbert*, p. 33. 'The portrait of the artist as a successful young rake becomes even more doubtful if external evidence is also taken into account.'
31	Herbert, *Disturbing Element*, pp. 161–3, 166.
32	ibid., pp. 183–9.
33	ibid., pp. 191, 193.
34	ibid., p. 202.
35	de Groen, *Xavier Herbert*, p. 190.
36	Herbert, *Disturbing Element*, p. 174.
37	ibid., p. 204.
38	Herbert to Sadie, 14 August 1968, Box 48, FL Mss 83.
39	Herbert, *Disturbing Element*, pp. 202, 212, 104.
40	ibid., p. 104.
41	Herbert, 'The Little Widow', pp. IV/22/119, III/10/31.
42	Xavier Herbert, 'I sinned against syntax', *Meanjin*, 19(1), 1960, pp. 31–5.
43	Herbert, *Disturbing Element*, p. 123.
44	ibid., pp. 225–6.
45	Xavier Herbert, *Soldiers' Women*, Fontana, Netley, 1978, p. 56.
46	de Groen, *Xavier Herbert*, pp. 79, 196.
47	Xavier Herbert, speech to Adelaide Arts Festival, March 1962, transcript, FL Mss 83.
48	Herbert to Hergenhan, 2 October, undated and 19 February 1971, Box 8, FL Mss 203. Herbert 'was afraid return to Pharmacy would ruin [his] development as a writer [and] Sadie knew this and accepted it. It proves her great nurturing talent'. 'She's very jealous of the scripts, even of the rubbish I've written in the drafting. She'd save every scrap if she could.'

'When doubtful letters arrive, my wife reads them first to save me involvement in what could be emotional waste of time.'

49   In an interview for Queensland University, Sadie said she didn't have time to read much. She had read 'a good book when in hospital' (Sadie Herbert, taped interview, University of Queensland Library, Audio Visual Collection, 1976, tape 2). Her love of the radio appears in the following from Herbert's Literary Log. He wanted her to come with him to visit a friend on Friday. 'She promptly said she couldn't because "My Word Session" (BBC 30 mins) on radio. I'd already cancelled invitations for her to go on Sat night (pictures) and Sun (radio play)' (Xavier Herbert, Literary Log, 1 October 1965, Boxes 1–3, FL Mss 83).

50   Sadie's opinion of 'The Little Widow' is a case in point. Sadie 'liked "LW" above all else I've written, except for odd bits of it. But she is no better judge than I' (Herbert to Beatrice Davis, 11 March 1959, Box 26, FL Mss 83). 'The Little Widow is a very interesting piece of work and must be published someday to show Xavier's character' (Sadie to H. L. White, 7 August 1963, FL Mss 83).

51   de Groen, *Xavier Herbert*, p. 199.

52   Herbert to Hergenhan, 13 November 1970, Box 8, FL Mss 203.

53   Herbert to Sadie, 26 October 1968, Box 48, FL Mss 83.

54   Herbert to Sadie, 7 July 1973, Box 50, FL Mss 83.

55   de Groen, *Xavier Herbert*, pp. 262–3.

56   Herbert to Sadie, 11 August 1968, Box 48, FL Mss 83.

57   Herbert to Beatrice Davis, 31 May 1956, Box 26, FL Mss 83. 'The allegory won't change the behaviour of mankind but it will prepare the way for preaching the doctrine of sexual sublimation as the means of Man's attainment to the fullness of his powers, to his Salvation, his enthronement as a god.'

58   de Groen, *Xavier Herbert*, p. 151. 'As Kevin Green has demonstrated, Herbert borrowed almost verbatim from [*The Science of Life* by H. G. Wells, J. S. Huxley and G. P. Wells] for the lecture on evolutionary progress and ethical development delivered in *Soldiers' Women* by authorial alter-ego Lieutenant Colonel Leon.'

59   Herbert, *Soldiers' Women*, p. 13.

60   ibid., pp. 369–70.

61   ibid., p. 125.

62   ibid., p. 368.

63   ibid., p. 401.

64   ibid., p. 237.

65   ibid., p. 145.

66   ibid., p. 266. '[Pudsey] slept, while the moon, who should be her patroness and renew her for positivity every twenty-eight days, was chased down the western sky by those enemies who had doomed her and her like to the negatives: the Scorpion, the Wolf, and the Crow.'

67   ibid., p. 344.
68   ibid., p. 191.
69   ibid., p. 281.
70   ibid., p. 392.
71   ibid.
72   ibid., p. 265.
73   ibid.
74   ibid., p. 87.
75   ibid., p. 392.
76   ibid., p. 288.
77   Herbert to Sadie, 11 October 1968, Box 48, FL Mss 83.
78   Herbert to Beatrice Davis, 1 May 1956, Box 26, FL Mss 83.
79   Herbert, *Soldiers' Women*, p. 371.
80   ibid., pp. 101–2.
81   ibid., p. 125.
82   ibid., p. 77.
83   ibid., pp. 246–7.
84   ibid., p. 136.
85   ibid., pp. 189, 90, 362.
86   ibid., pp. 389, 391.
87   ibid., pp. 288, 409, 362, 371.
88   Xavier Herbert, *Poor Fellow My Country*, Collins, Sydney, 1975, p. 888.
89   ibid., p. 157.
90   ibid., pp. 158, 160, 166.
91   ibid., pp. 488, 751, 764.
92   ibid., pp. 547, 115, 738, 925.
93   ibid., p. 925.
94   Herbert, *Capricornia*, p. 17.
95   ibid., p. 313.
96   Herbert, *Poor Fellow My Country*, pp. 49, 410, 439.
97   Herbert to Sadie, 1 October 1968, Box 48, FL Mss 83.
98   Herbert, *Poor Fellow My Country*, pp. 140, 1282, 867–8.
99   ibid., p. 1296.
100   ibid., pp. 548, 284, 547.
101   ibid., p. 554.
102   Herbert, *Disturbing Element*, p. 217.
103   Herbert, *Poor Fellow My Country*, p. 1314.
104   Herbert, *Capricornia*, p. 384.

Chapter 6: Confession and the Construction of Character

1   Xavier Herbert, speech to the Conference of the Society of Hospital Pharmacists, October 1963, transcript, FL Mss 83.
2   Herbert to Laurie Hergenhan, undated, Box 8, FL Mss 203.

3   Herbert to Sadie Herbert, 1 October 1968, Box 48, FL Mss 83.

4   The names Barbara, Anne and Carol are pseudonyms.

5   Herbert to Sadie, 7 November 1968, Box 48, FL Mss 83.

6   Herbert to Sadie, 8, 10 November 1968, Box 48, FL Mss 83.

7   Herbert to Sadie, 28 September 1968, Box 48, FL Mss 83. 'I'm not really friendly with Bruce, nor he with me. [...] Perhaps it's the intelligence of the man that counts. Yes, that's it. Poor Bruce is only a little nit-wit. It's the nit-wits who have to put on the front to compensate, and coming into contact with someone who is not taken in, are uncomfortable. This Superintendent here, Hadlow, although an exceedingly pleasant man, *avoids* me. Of course he's a nit-wit.'

8   Herbert to Sadie, 7 November 1968, Box 48, FL Mss 83.

9   Herbert to Sadie, 28 September 1968, Box 48, FL Mss 83.

10   Herbert, recorded conversation for the National Library, 13 December 1975, transcript, FL Mss 83.

11   Xavier Herbert, 'Bang goes my O.B.E.!', *Bulletin*, 22 February 1961, p. 52.

12   Herbert, recorded conversation for the National Library. 'If I've got any talent at all it's that of perspicacity.'

13   Xavier Herbert, speech given at a farewell luncheon, sound tape, Queensland University Library, 1976.

14   Herbert to Sadie, 14 September 1968, Box 48, FL Mss 83.

15   Xavier Herbert, *Poor Fellow My Country*, Collins, Sydney, 1975, pp. 236, 523.

16   ibid., pp. 537, 923.

17   ibid., pp. 157, 1177.

18   Xavier Herbert, *Soldiers' Women*, Fontana, Netley, 1978, p. 101.

19   ibid., pp. 222–3.

20   ibid., p. 119.

21   ibid., p. 205.

22   Xavier Herbert, *Seven Emus*, Fontana, Melbourne, 1977, p. 22.

23   Herbert, *Soldiers' Women*, p. 186.

24   Herbert, *Poor Fellow My Country*, p. 1153.

25   Accosted by an arrogant soldier she despises, 'Fay was panting, but evidently striving to be calm'. Athol, as he begs Pudsey to stay with him, 'clung with hands, panting' (Herbert, *Soldiers' Women*, pp. 225, 182). Delacy is frequently 'heaving with feeling' and 'fighting for breath'. Clancy, his desire for Rifkah urgent, 'let her go, panting' and after attempting to rape her is 'panting now, perhaps from anger, or guilt'. Alfie, when Fay McFee insists on publishing a story about her, 'panted, "There's such a thing as libel."' (Herbert, *Poor Fellow My Country*, pp. 139, 1271, 939, 983, 345).

26   Athol, with 'face flaming and jerking', asks Pudsey what her intentions are and then, his hopes fulfilled, flies to get a taxi, 'perhaps to hide the sudden flaming and jerking of his cheek' (Herbert, *Soldiers' Women*,

pp. 182, 185). Excitement sets a young man's 'lovely hazel eyes flaming with excitement that in a moment also set his features jerking madly' (Xavier Herbert, 'The Little Widow', Box 15, FL Mss 83, p. IV/34/131). 'Poor Darcy's face was jerking as he flogged the starter.' Rifkah kisses Jeremy's 'slightly jerking cheek'. Willy Ah Loy's face is 'quivering in that Aboriginal way under deep stress' (Herbert, *Poor Fellow My Country*, pp. 896, 1005, 197).

27   In passionate defence of Rifkah, Jeremy is 'crimson and strangling for speech'. Angry at his treatment by a station boss, he 'husks at him' (Herbert, *Poor Fellow My Country*, pp. 902, 1016).

28   'Mrs Pewsey puckered up her little witch's face, perhaps not nearly so much in hostility as in sudden grief' (Herbert, *Soldiers' Women*, p. 98). Saddened, Clancy watches his father leave 'with face puckered like a wilful but unhappy boy'. Willy Ah Loy's face is 'puckered as with misery' and Green Ant's 'old mouth puckered' when disappointed in his desire to avoid trouble (Herbert, *Poor Fellow My Country*, pp. 189, 196, 198).

29   Rifkah's eyes 'rolled slightly' when Clancy tells her they are to marry; Glascock's are 'goggling' when he finds Rifkah naked; Fay's are 'popping with excitement' when she thinks of a plan to catch her enemy out (Herbert, *Poor Fellow My Country*, pp. 938, 950, 350).

30   When Nelly Ah Loy 'shrieked into his face, [Willy] blinked' (Herbert, *Poor Fellow My Country*, p. 195).

31   Selina has brown eyes, Rosa 'sunstone-brown', Madeleine 'taffy-brown', Fortitude 'brown dog's eyes' (Herbert, *Soldiers' Women*, pp. 72, 10, 196, 112). Rifkah has 'hazel eyes' (Herbert, *Poor Fellow My Country*, p. 679). Sadie had 'fine hazel eyes' (de Groen, *Xavier Herbert*, p. 79).

32   Herbert, *Soldiers' Women*, p. 124. A similar slip occurs in *Poor Fellow My Country* at the point when Dr Cobbity, normally blue-eyed, is acting the larrikin. As Cobbity baits Delacy his 'green eyes twinkled'. Once again Herbert unconsciously changes eye colour to suit behaviour (Herbert, *Poor Fellow My Country*, p. 575).

33   Herbert, *Poor Fellow My Country*, pp. 472, 1138.

34   Herbert, *Soldiers' Women*, p. 127.

35   Sadie Herbert, taped interview, University of Queensland Library, Audio Visual Collection, tape 3.

36   E. M. Forster, *Aspects of the Novel*, Penguin, Middlesex, 1962, p. 75.

37   Among the many characters based on real life are: The Bloke and The Chief based on Stephensen and Miles of the Australia First party; Cobbity and McCusky based on S. A. Cook, Protector of Aborigines, and Vin White, Cook's assistant; Bickering and Maryzic based on Judge Wells and Bishop Gsell; Glascock and Cootes based on Father McGrath and Bill Stanner (Betty Candy, 'The Historicity of *Poor Fellow My Country*', unpublished thesis, Macarthur Institute of Higher Education, 1986, pp. 40, 43, 45, 99, 118).

38 Herbert, *Poor Fellow My Country*, p. 292. Herbert took from his memories of these people only what he wanted. The resultant portraits may or may not be historically accurate. In this case it wasn't. Judge Wells, unlike Bickering, was not at all sympathetic to Aboriginals, 'repeatedly bemoaning the fact that he could not flog Aborigines', and strongly opposed to granting them any civil rights (Timothy Hall, *Darwin 1942: Australia's Darkest Hour*, Methuen, Sydney, 1980, p. 121).

39 Candy, 'The Historicity of *Poor Fellow My Country*', p. 82, explores the links between The Bloke and P. R. Stephensen. Relations between Herbert and Stephensen, amicable in the beginning, deteriorated over the years until Herbert was referring to him as 'the most infamous Australian since Ned Kelly' (Herbert, 'The Facts of the Publication of *Capricornia*', FL Mss 83).

40 Candy, 'The Historicity of *Poor Fellow My Country*', p. 34.

41 ibid., p. 35.

42 Herbert, *Poor Fellow My Country*, p. 1333.

43 ibid., p. 1350.

44 Whereas the book tells us Cootes is a 'cheat' 'knowing nothing about Aborigines' in comparison to Delacy, 'the only man who does know anything' (Herbert, *Poor Fellow My Country*, p. 767), Allan Ashbolt, who also served in the North Australia Observer Unit, says Stanner far outstripped Herbert in knowledge of Aboriginals. Whereas the book pictures Cootes as a weakling and a coward, Ashbolt says 'Stanner was physically much tougher than Xavier imagined' (Allan Ashbolt, 'Bushrangers who watched and waited for invaders', *Sydney Morning Herald*, 26 April 1986).

45 Northrop Frye, *Anatomy of Criticism*, Penguin, London, 1990, p. 308.

46 Herbert, *Soldiers' Women*, pp. 7, 9.

47 ibid., pp. 8, 11.

48 ibid., p. 47.

49 ibid., pp. 105–6.

50 Herbert, recorded conversation for the National Archives, 12 July 1961, transcript, FL Mss 83. They were not, he said, 'taken from life' but 'synthesised from all sorts of ladies I have known'.

51 Herbert, *Soldiers' Women*, p. 55.

52 ibid., p. 234.

53 Herbert to Sadie, 11 September 1968, Box 48, FL Mss 83.

54 Xavier Herbert, *Disturbing Element*, Fontana, Melbourne, 1976, pp. 157–8, 190. Clancy's relationship with his mother reflects Herbert's with his mother. In Clancy's brief relationship with Rifkah, we see the same mixture of cloying sentimentality and crude sexuality that appears in Herbert's early sexual experiences.

55 Candy, 'The Historicity of *Poor Fellow My Country*', pp. 88–91.

56 Herbert, *Poor Fellow My Country*, pp. 285, 337, 1082, 632, 1179–80. Alfie's appointment as Protector of Aborigines (p. 285), her kindly treatment of

her charges and her loss of the job a few months later (p. 337) replicate Herbert's experience in 1935 as Temporary Superintendent of the Kahlin Aboriginal Compound. cf. 'We were too good for them—I used to take them in the truck to the pictures every Wednesday. Xavier made toilets for them—got water to bath in. That's why we got thrown out' (Sadie Herbert, taped interview, tape 1). Like Herbert, Alfie's writing career begins with popular journalism. Like *Capricornia*, her first book deals with the 'treatment of the Aborigines' (p. 1082), is published with the help of the Free Australia movement (p. 616) and wins the Sesquicentenary Literary Competition (p. 632). Her second book, like *Poor Fellow My Country*, is written to show 'the filthy thing' of Australian subservience, and 'bring it out in words that'll be bayonets to stab the Britishist bastards to the heart' (pp. 1179–80).

57   Herbert to Sadie, 14 August, 16 March 1968, Box 48, FL Mss 83.

58   Edward Kynaston, 'Flawed achievement', *Overland*, 62, Spring 1975, pp. 76–8.

59   Xavier Herbert, 'Little Foxes', unpublished ms, Box 60, FL Mss 83. '[Kynaston] says I created in Jeremy a man who is "a romantic idealist [...] pedantic and pompous, an inverted racist, sexist, mercilessly selfish, hopelessly, thoughtless self-deluding old hypocrite" which I did deliberately.'

60   Herbert, *Poor Fellow My Country*, pp. 546, 1176–7. When, for instance, Delacy refuses to help Alfie with her second novel, she complains he becomes 'negative [...] as soon as something positive's put to you'. The only other weakness commented upon, just once and very briefly, is his pomposity. When Delacy says of the main character of Alfie's second book, 'You make your Belamy a bit of a pontificator' and calls him 'a bit of a stuffed shirt', she replies, 'He's you of course', and laughs at him for being 'Charles Belamy to perfection'. This brief mockery is the only time Herbert distances himself sufficiently from one of his own weaknesses to see it in the character he has created.

61   Herbert's sexism, selfishness and self-delusion are examined in Chapter 5. His racism can be seen both in his letters and his novels. Ironically, the man who was so passionate in attacking racism directed at Aboriginals was himself thoroughly racist in his assessment of 'foreigners'. He speaks, for instance, of 'believing Germans to be deceitful people' (Herbert to Sadie, 22 June 1973, Box 50, FL Mss 83) and of hating his neighbours' 'filthy dago unconcern for other people' (Herbert to Sadie, 25 June 1973, Box 50, FL Mss 83). Elsewhere he describes a Sydney park as 'full of wops and Huns and all sorts of odd animals' (Herbert to Sadie, 13 July 1974, Box 51, FL Mss 83) and casually tells Sadie, 'You couldn't trust [a Chinaman], nor would a chinaman be clean' (Herbert to Sadie, 1 October 1968, Box 48, FL Mss 83). The same casual racism appears in the novel itself in generalisations such as 'the Russian, being naturally stupid and

brutish, is the arch-enemy of the clever Jew' (*Poor Fellow My Country*, p. 659).

62   '[Delacy's] first quality is his perception. His tragedy is due to it—just as my own would be tragic but for the talent I have to sublimate it into art' (Herbert to Sadie, 14 September 1968, Box 48, FL Mss 83). 'He has the same passion as I, but without the means to express it. He is a strong brave man. But he is limited by not have [sic] a means again of fulfilling himself in strength and courage' (Herbert to Sadie, 20 March 1968, Box 48, FL Mss 83).

63   Herbert to Hergenhan, 13 November 1970, Box 8, FL Mss 203.

64   Herbert, *Poor Fellow My Country*, p. 553.

65   ibid., p. 1282.

66   ibid.

67   ibid., p. 1283.

68   ibid.

69   ibid., p. 1294.

70   Herbert to Sadie, 15 November 1968, Box 48, FL Mss 83.

71   Herbert, *Poor Fellow My Country*, pp. 509–13.

72   ibid., pp. 151, 160, 175, 533. Lydia, seduced by 'the deep male music of his voice' and his 'craggy manly beauty' (p. 151), 'wants to make love' to him (p. 160). Bridie, whom he has known from the cradle, seduces him because her husband is impotent, she is desperate for a baby and she has 'always loved' Delacy (p. 175).

73   ibid., p. 1158. 'The look of appeal returned. "Will you go and see her while you're down? [...] The baby's yours, Jeremy [...] Will you Jeremy... please!"'

74   ibid., p. 1057. 'You were made for one another...my little girl and you [...] You are what she would've liked me to be [...] I've never had your masculine strength and integrity.'

75   ibid., p. 1254.

76   ibid., pp. 1112, 1162.

77   ibid., pp. 1020, 1059–61.

78   Herbert to Don Chipp, 9 July 1978, FL Mss 83. His desire for political influence is seen in a letter to the leader of the newly formed Democrats: 'After listening to you the other day I thought there may be some hope in what you have started [...] What I would like best would be to meet you with a group of your Party and express my own ideas—which are idealistic, of course, as they must be—and see how they go over. Would you be interested? I do have a very large following of true patriots. I have been called "The Greatest Australian of All" [...] I will be happy to leap into it with you, if I find I can trust you as a true Australian'.

Chapter 7: Didacticism and the Role of Romance

1   Herbert to Beatrice Davis, 31 May 1956, Box 26, FL Mss 83.

2   Herbert to Sadie Herbert, 14 September 1968, Box 48, FL Mss 83.

3   Xavier Herbert, 'Suggested blurb for *Poor Fellow My Country*', Box 60, FL Mss 83.

4   Herbert to Sadie, 6 September 1968, Box 48, FL Mss 83.

5   Herbert to Sadie, 1 September 1968, Box 48, FL Mss 83.

6   Describing a chance meeting with a priest: 'We had quite a talk—about Jews, Catholics and sex. I did most of it. He was evidently very interested' (Herbert to Sadie, 25 September 1968, Box 48, FL Mss 83). Describing a conversation with Dr Laurie Hergenhan: 'I also told him the meaning of the dream. He went red and was so upset that I had to pat his back and explain that *everybody* is a chook in dreams. Oh that did flatten him. I had to give him ½ hrs lecture on the Psychopathology of everyday life to put him right' (Herbert to Sadie, 21 July 1974, Box 51, FL Mss 83).

7   Xavier Herbert, *Poor Fellow My Country*, Collins, Sydney, 1975, pp. 611, 1076, 286.

8   Herbert to Sadie, 29 August 1968, Box 48, FL Mss 83.

9   Herbert to Sadie, 23 July 1974, Box 51, FL Mss 83.

10   A further example is: 'Speaking of fused participles, I discovered one in P. White's latest THE VIVISECTOR. I must write to his publishers about it. [...] The writer who betrays to me the fact that he is ignorant of the F.P. falls terribly from grace in my estimation' (Herbert to Laurie Hergenhan, 10 March 1970, Box 8, FL Mss 203).

11   Herbert to Sadie, 28 June 1973, 4 July 1973, Box 50, FL Mss 83.

12   Herbert, recorded conversation for the National Library, 13 December 1975, transcript, FL Mss 83.

13   ibid.

14   Xavier Herbert, 'Australia—in the Crystal Ball', Box 20, FL Mss 83.

15   Northrop Frye, *Anatomy of Criticism*, Penguin, London, 1990, p. 312. 'The digressing narrative, the catalogues, the stylizing of character along "humor" lines, the symposium discussions, and the constant ridicule of philosophers and pedantic critics are all features that belong to the anatomy.'

16   Xavier Herbert, *Capricornia*, Angus & Robertson, Melbourne, 1971, p. 124.

17   Xavier Herbert, *Soldiers' Women*, Fontana, Netley, 1978, pp. 178, 287.

18   ibid., p. 330.

19   ibid., pp. 203, 228, 97–8, 99.

20   Gavin Casey, 'The Red Page—Book of the Year, 1961', *Bulletin*, 30 December 1961, p. 33.

21   Beatrice Davis, suggestions on *Soldiers' Women*, note referring to page 646, Box 26A, FL Mss 83.

22   Xavier Herbert, 'The Little Widow', Box 15, FL Mss 83, pp. V/60/203, V/63/205.

23   Gillian Beer, *The Romance*, Methuen, London, 1970, p. 26.
24   Xavier Herbert, *Larger than Life*, Fontana, Melbourne, 1976, p. x.
25   Herbert to Sadie, 7 November 1968, Box 48, and 10 July 1974, Box 51, FL Mss 83.
26   Herbert, recorded conversation for the National Library.
27   Herbert to Sadie, 28 July 1974, Box 51, FL Mss 83.
28   Herbert to Sadie, 27 July 1974, Box 51, FL Mss 83.
29   Herbert to Sadie, 31 July 1974, Box 51, FL Mss 83.
30   Herbert to Sadie, 4, 6 November 1968, Box 48, FL Mss 83.
31   Herbert, *Capricornia*, p. 237.
32   Herbert, *Poor Fellow My Country*, p. 1086.
33   ibid., p. 1008.
34   Beatrice Davis, suggestions on *Soldiers' Women*, note referring to pages 504–5.
35   Herbert, *Soldiers' Women*, p. 25.
36   Frye, *Anatomy*, p. 200. 'The heraldic colors [of the second phase of romance] are green and gold.'
37   Herbert, *Soldiers' Women*, pp. 40–1.
38   ibid., p. 44. 'Taffy was waiting for her in the boudoir. As she doffed the bathrobe she asked him what she should wear this golden day. He did not answer, but only stared at the breathtaking landscape of her nakedness, and when she began to hide it, turned away.'
39   ibid., pp. 391–2.
40   Beer, *The Romance*, p. 8.
41   Herbert, *Soldiers' Women*, pp. 358, 198, 320.
42   ibid., pp. 100–3.
43   ibid., p. 133.
44   ibid., p. 316.
45   ibid., p. 221.
46   T. S. Eliot, 'Whispers of immortality', *Selected Poems*, Faber, London, 1954, p. 42: 'Webster was much possessed by death/And saw the skull beneath the skin'.
47   Herbert, *Soldiers' Women*, pp. 138, 264.
48   Herbert to Hergenhan, 2 November 1970, Box 8, FL Mss 203.
49   Herbert, *Soldiers' Women*, p. 197.
50   ibid., pp. 329, 335, 269.
51   ibid., p. 288.
52   ibid., p. 292.
53   ibid., pp. 412–13.

Chapter 8: Curiouser and Curiouser: The Style Thickens

1   Xavier Herbert, 'I sinned against syntax', *Meanjin*, 19(1), 1960, pp. 31–5.
2   ibid.

3   Xavier Herbert, *Seven Emus*, Angus & Robertson, Melbourne, 1959, pp. 27–8.
4   Herbert, 'I sinned against syntax'.
5   Herbert to Laurie Hergenhan, 28 November 1970, Box 8, FL Mss 203.
6   Beatrice Davis to Herbert, 16 December 1959, Box 26, FL Mss 203.
7   Xavier Herbert, 'The Little Widow', Box 15, FL Mss 83, p. III/10/31.
8   Xavier Herbert, *Capricornia*, Angus & Robertson, Melbourne, 1971, p. 101.
9   ibid.
10   ibid., p. 297.
11   ibid., p. 9.
12   Xavier Herbert, *Seven Emus*, Fontana, Melbourne, 1977, pp. 45, 89.
13   Alexander Pope, *Selected Poems of Pope*, Hutchinson Educational, London, 1964, p. 37. Belinda's toilette in 'The Rape of the Lock', Canto One, lines 121–48, provides a direct comparison with this passage from *Soldiers' Women*.
14   Xavier Herbert, *Soldiers' Women*, Fontana, Netley, 1978, p. 99.
15   ibid., p. 175.
16   Frances de Groen, *Xavier Herbert*, UQP, St Lucia, 1998, p. 122.
17   Xavier Herbert, *Poor Fellow My Country*, Collins, Sydney, 1975, pp. 241–2.
18   ibid., p. 12.
19   Xavier Herbert, *Disturbing Element*, Fontana, Melbourne, 1976, pp. 64, 89, 90.
20   Xavier Herbert, 'Schooldays', typescript, FL Mss 83.
21   Herbert, *Disturbing Element*, p. 243.
22   ibid., pp. 115, 118, 144, 154.
23   Herbert, 'I sinned against syntax', pp. 31–5.
24   ibid.
25   Herbert to Hergenhan, 10 October 1970, Box 8, FL Mss 203.
26   Following the publication of *Soldiers' Women*, for instance, he appeared on a chat show with an academic from Melbourne University and sounded him out on the possibility of a Melbourne doctorate. Subsequently, on a trip to Perth he met the head of Adult Education and sought his help in acquiring a Western Australian one (Herbert to Hergenhan, 18 October 1970, Box 8, FL Mss 203). Returning home, he sent letters to his publisher pressing him to follow up these leads. The publisher tactfully replied that he felt 'an honorary D.Litt of Melbourne would [...] be particularly hard to come by' (A. Fabinyi to Herbert, 10 September 1963, FL Mss 83). Herbert persisted—but unsuccessfully. In a later letter he was gently but firmly told by a managerial assistant, 'With regard to the D.Litt at Melbourne University we are unfortunately not in a position to get this moving' (M. Sayers to Herbert, 23 September 1963, FL Mss 83).
27   Herbert to Manning Clark, 17 February 1980, FL Mss 83.

28   Herbert to Patrick White, 4 April 1979, drafted but not sent, Box 33, FL Mss 83.

29   White to Herbert, 13 July 1975, FL Mss 203.

30   Herbert to White, 12 April 1976, Box 11, FL Mss 203.

31   ibid.

32   Herbert to White, 4 April 1979.

33   Herbert, *Disturbing Element*, p. 19.

34   ibid., pp. 121, 155. He got his first job by 'crawling' to a man who scorned his application. As a young man, he accepted humiliation as the price of entry into the 'enchanted circle' of a middle-class friend. Later in life, he is happy to grovel to placate a woman he has offended: 'I was humble. [...] I keep muttering that I have nothing to say except that I want to shoot myself, I'm so sorry' (Herbert to Sadie Herbert, 12 November 1968, Box 48, FL Mss 83).

35   Herbert to Sadie, 1 October 1968, Box 48, FL Mss 83.

36   Herbert to Davis, 11 March 1959, Box 26, FL Mss 203.

37   Herbert to Davis, 14 April 1959, Box 26, FL Mss 203. 'There was the confidence shaking I suffered due to the non-acceptance of the style I had with so much labour developed. [...] I was convinced I'd have to abandon it. Not an easy thing to do after a labor of 20 years.'

38   Davis to Herbert, 9 March 1959, Box 26, FL Mss 203.

39   Herbert to Davis, 11 March 1959, Box 26, FL Mss 203.

40   Tom Inglis Moore to Herbert, 10 June 1959, Box 31, FL Mss 83.

41   Hugh Atkinson to Herbert, undated letter, Box 31, FL Mss 83.

42   Alan Rein to Herbert, 24 September 1974, FL Mss 83. Herbert to Alan Rein, 28 September 1974, FL Mss 83. Alan Rein, the Collins executive responsible for the publication of *Poor Fellow My Country*, experienced Herbert's touchiness when, in a friendly fashion, he made suggestions on a few minor details. A Jew himself, Rein pointed out that the Jewish characters, being German, would not have spoken Yiddish, and that Rifkah, having a non-Jewish mother, would not have learned Jewish tradition. There was not a breath of criticism. They were simply helpful suggestions on matters of fact. But that did not prevent the storm breaking over his head. 'Your letter', Herbert replied, 'distressed me deeply. An author of any standing is particularly irritated by being told on the eve of publication how he should have done the job. [...] You must know that a ban was put on all comment to me till this work is published'.

43   Davis to Herbert, 17 March 1956, Box 26, FL Mss 83. 'I saw the pattern and the purpose: to show [...] sexuality at its worst and at its best [...] and to express a philosophy of the ideal in love [...] brilliant observation, vivid and vital writing [...] but too much of everything, the lesson repeated ad nauseam, over-writing and caricature [...] I have enough imagination to be acutely conscious that every manuscript represents a human being,

and this makes the job more difficult even when I do not know the authors. With you it's gone beyond this. I think the emotion, the sense of life and destiny, you have conveyed to me in writing of your opus has intimidated and embarrassed me.'

44   Davis to Herbert, 20 March 1956, Box 26, FL Mss 203.
45   Herbert to Davis, 1 May 1956, Box 26, FL Mss 203.
46   de Groen, *Xavier Herbert*, p. 244. 'Herbert's cruel public snubbing of Beatrice Davis whom he refused to invite to any of the celebratory functions' during the launching of *Poor Fellow My Country*.
47   Frances de Groen & Laurie Hergenhan (eds), *Xavier Herbert Letters*, UQP, St Lucia, 2002, p. 435.
48   Davis to Herbert, 13 March 1959, Box 26, FL Mss 83.

Chapter 9: The Rule of Old Zave

1   Xavier Herbert, Literary Log, 23 August 1965, Box 3, FL Mss 83.
2   Herbert, Literary Log, 25 September 1965, Box 3, FL Mss 83.
3   As editor of *Australian Literary Studies*, Hergenhan had asked Herbert's permission to publish a speech Herbert had given at the 1962 Adelaide Arts Festival. Herbert was more than pleased to have the speech given the attention he believed it deserved, and friendly relations between the two men were established and grew.
4   Herbert to Laurie Hergenhan, 28 November 1970, Box 8, FL Mss 203.
5   Herbert to Hergenhan, 6 June 1971, Box 8, FL Mss 203.
6   Herbert to Sadie Herbert, 20 June 1973, Box 50, FL Mss 83.
7   Herbert to Sadie, 16 October 1968, Box 48, FL Mss 83.
8   Herbert to Dr H. A. Copeman, 29 November 1978, FL Mss 203.
9   Herbert, Literary Log, 26 August 1965, Box 3, FL Mss 83.
10   Herbert to Sadie, 17 June 1966, Box 46, FL Mss 83.
11   Herbert to Hergenhan, 10 March 1970, FL Mss 203.
12   Herbert to Sadie, 20 September 1968, Box 48, FL Mss 83.
13   Herbert to Sadie, 20 March 1968, Box 48, FL Mss 83.
14   Herbert to Sadie, 4 October 1968, Box 48, FL Mss 83.
15   Herbert to Sadie, 10 August 1968, Box 48, FL Mss 83.
16   Herbert to Sadie, 6 March 1968, Box 48, FL Mss 83.
17   Herbert to Sadie, 12 September 1968, Box 48, FL Mss 83.
18   Xavier Herbert, 'My road to Ruhen', *Observer*, 24 December 1960, pp. 4–6.
19   Herbert to Sadie, 12 October 1968, Box 48, FL Mss 83.
20   Herbert to Sadie, 26 March 1968, Box 48, FL Mss 83.
21   Herbert to Sadie, 11 September 1968, Box 48, FL Mss 83.
22   Herbert to Sadie, 21 May 1966, Box 46, FL Mss 83.
23   Herbert to Sadie, 27 September 1968, Box 48, FL Mss 83.
24   Herbert to Sadie, 11 September 1968, Box 48, FL Mss 83.

25   Herbert to Sadie, 16 September 1968, Box 48, FL Mss 83.

26   Herbert to Sadie, 28 September 1968, Box 48, FL Mss 83.

27   Herbert to Sadie, 20 October 1968, Box 48, FL Mss 83. He calculates here that more than '44 busy days' and 'no less than 122 pages of draft or 18,300 words' have been wasted on one such wrong turning.

28   Herbert to Sadie, 14 September 1968, Box 48, FL Mss 83.

29   I can think of only one significant instance of character inconsistency: the mismatch between the generous-spirited Nugget Knowles who looks after Prindy and Nelyerri in Chapter 7 and the mean-spirited Nugget of the remainder of the book. As for incredibility, there is remarkably little. It strains credulity, it is true, when Rifkah, who fears horses, becomes a good enough jockey to win the big race. And it strains credulity when Kitty Windeyer, who loves Prindy, betrays him to Alfie, whom she hardly knows. But these are rare lapses.

30   T. S. Eliot, *The Sacred Wood*, Methuen, London, 1932, pp. 55, 58.

31   While the writing routine for *Capricornia* was different in detail, it was the same in involving an outpouring of ideas under conditions in which the control of the conscious mind was weakened. 'I discovered a method where I worked 32 hours straight, and slept 16. Sometimes I went to 38 hours—after that I would flake right out. Now, it was a kind of trance thing, and I got so used to it that I would write solid for 16 hours— actually, I would re-write what I had written the night before [...] and then on the following night, I would do a new draft, at which time I was sort of insane, and it all would pour out of me. Finally I would have to go to bed to sleep for 16 hours or so, and when I woke up it was like a torrent, a river running out of my head' (Robert Reid, '*Playboy* interview Xavier Herbert', *Australian Playboy*, June 1982, p. 135).

32   Herbert to Sadie, 10 March 1968, Box 48, FL Mss 83.

33   Herbert to Sadie, 14 September 1968, Box 48, FL Mss 83.

34   Herbert to Sadie, 4 September 1968, Box 48, FL Mss 83.

35   Herbert to Sadie, 8 October 1968, Box 48, FL Mss 83.

36   Herbert to Sadie, 27 September 1968, Box 48, FL Mss 83.

37   Herbert to Sadie, 4 September 1968, Box 48, FL Mss 83.

38   Herbert to Sadie, 24 October 1968, Box 48, FL Mss 83. 'I used to dream a lot about a huge serpent in a hole in the ground [...] What occurred [to] me all of a sudden was that I've had this idea of the Rainbow Serpent working in me for a long while.'

39   Herbert to Sadie, 27 September 1968, Box 48, FL Mss 83.

40   Darcy is the name Herbert is using at this point of the writing for the character called Jeremy Delacy in the published novel.

41   Herbert to Sadie, 6 October 1968, Box 48, FL Mss 83.

42   Xavier Herbert, *Soldiers' Women*, Fontana, Netley, 1978, p. 405. For example, to emphasise the unnaturalness of a mother's use of her son for vicarious achievement Herbert has Fortitude's pregnant girlfriend, Lolly,

behave in a wholly incredible fashion. Lolly detests Mrs La Plante and is at first, credibly, determined not to let her have anything to do with the baby. Then, in a complete about-face, she decides to give her custody of the child. Given her feelings about Mrs La Plante, there is no credibility to Lolly's action; it is a case of the author unable to resist giving one last Gothic turn of the screw to emphasise the unnaturalness of dominating motherhood. As she touches Lolly's pregnant belly, Mrs La Plante cries out, 'Praise be to God who hath restored to me my holy mission…to mould a man…to make a man!'

43   Herbert to Sadie, 23 March 1968, Box 48, FL Mss 83.
44   E. M. Forster, *Aspects of the Novel*, Penguin, Middlesex, 1962, p. 140.
45   Herbert to Sadie, 10 October 1968, Box 48, FL Mss 83.
46   Herbert to Sadie, 11 October 1968, Box 48, FL Mss 83.
47   Herbert to Sadie, 11 September 1968, Box 48, FL Mss 83.

Chapter 10: An Anatomy of Australia

1   Northrop Frye, *Anatomy of Criticism*, Penguin, London, 1990, pp. 308–9.
2   ibid., p. 309.
3   Xavier Herbert, *Poor Fellow My Country*, Collins, Sydney, 1975, pp. 890, 1021. For example, (*Hoff*) 'You can never destroy humanness…but you moost check it to fight vot is bad in humanity. Communism is ze cold hard fight against ze inhuman, so zat true humanness vill at last prevail.' (*Ferris*) 'Who's running the place? Here's the Commos, telling the police what to do, under Lord Vaisey's orders […] There's bloody Catholic Action can get Rifkah citizenship with a flick of the finger. And old Whiskers, with his *Pax Britannica*, organizing us for a war with people who could be our best friends. I ask you…what chance have dinky-di Aussies got…except through this Free Australia thing….'
4   ibid., pp. 75, 249, 368. The first we hear of the policy is when McCusky tells Delacy he is taking all part-Aboriginal children to 'an institution being built down in the centre' (p. 75). The grief of Aboriginal parents is seen in Nelyerri (p. 249). The callousness of the responsible authorities appears in McCusky's 'Now listen Nelly, that boy's going away […] and if you give any trouble, you'll be going back to jail. You'll get your boy back soon. Soon he'll be a man, with a good job […] Now shut up!' (p. 368).
5   ibid., pp. 1012–14. Beaten up by communist meatworkers for his supposed connection with the fascists of Free Australia, Delacy is run out of town by police in order to avoid conflict that would threaten the profits of British beef barons.
6   ibid., pp. 909, 995.
7   Frye, *Anatomy*, pp. 309, 39.
8   Herbert, *Poor Fellow My Country*, pp. 136, 330, 298–9.
9   ibid., pp. 1213, 707.

10   ibid., p. 325.

11   ibid., p. 675.

12   Frye, *Anatomy*, p. 310.

13   A discussion between Jeremy and Bishoff, for instance, takes up twenty-four of the first forty-eight pages, while thirty-six pages of the next hundred are devoted to one between Jeremy and Lydia. That adds up to sixty pages of the first one hundred and fifty.

14   Herbert, *Poor Fellow My Country*, pp. 21–57.

15   The first section runs from pages 21 to 27, at which point there is a break of nearly a page during which the two men meet and chat with Nelly and Ah Loy. The second section, from pages 28 to 39, concludes with another resting point as they 'were coming up to the front of the house' and Jeremy suggests they 'go in and have a drink' before continuing their walk. The third section, which runs from pages 40 to 47, is followed by a longer break in which much happens. Martin sneaks out for an assignation with his mistress. Bobwirridirridi tries to blackmail him and is whipped for his pains. Delacy and Bishoff come out to see what is happening and Delacy stops the whipping. Martin goes to bed and Delacy and Bishoff resume their discussion, which runs from pages 52 to 57, where it finally ends.

16   ibid., pp. 23–5. The first section, for instance, begins with them 'passing out through the gate of the garden'. Half a page later we are told, 'they passed the big low batten-walled harness shed'. Three-quarters of a page later, 'they were passing the dark kitchen'. Half a page later, 'they were nearing the garden gate'. And so on.

17   Frye, *Anatomy*, pp. 311, 312.

18   He begins on page 28 with 'It happened a good while back' and ends on page 47 with Bobwirridirridi's capture.

19   Herbert, *Poor Fellow My Country*, p. 39.

20   ibid., pp. 40–1.

21   ibid., p. 210.

22   ibid., pp. 15, 24, 157, 476, 70, 535.

23   ibid., pp. 81–2.

24   ibid., pp. 271, 305, 784.

25   The digressions in *Les Miserables* dealing with the history, geography and culture of France are longer and even less tied to the narrative than Herbert's digressions. cf. descriptions of the year 1817, the battle of Waterloo, and the geography of the Paris sewers (Victor Hugo, *Les Miserables*, Penguin, Middlesex, 1982, pp. 119–23, 279–324, 1061–75).

26   Herbert, *Poor Fellow My Country*, pp. 1156–7.

27   Frye, *Anatomy*, p. 308.

28   Herbert, *Poor Fellow My Country*, pp. 31, 42, 125. Delacy gives chapter and verse on civil rights abuses stretching from first contact to the present day. Having taken their land, early pastoralists, he says, 'dispersed' tribes

thought to be spearing cattle, poisoned them with arsenic left in flour bags and imposed an unwritten law against Aboriginals travelling over stock runs. At the same time, white miners were driving Aboriginals off their traditional land, prostituting their women, and killing those who gave any trouble. '[T]here were a number shot, women mostly, for giving the whitemen who used them Gonorrhoea they'd contracted from other whitemen! [...] one of the methods was to quietly murder any woman known to be infected. The official one was to put the suspects on the chain and march them up to the Railhead and dump them in the Aboriginal Compound at Port Palmeston.'

29   ibid., p. 22.
30   ibid., p. 568.
31   ibid., pp. 184, 223, 245, 75.
32   Xavier Herbert, 'A town like Elliott: "There is NO solution to the Aborigines' problem"', *Bulletin*, 31 March 1962, pp. 23–5.
33   Herbert, *Poor Fellow My Country*, p. 937.
34   ibid., p. 736.
35   ibid., p. 368.
36   ibid., p. 1457.
37   ibid., p. 1453. Having 'regard for the *kuttabah*'s economics' and enjoying possession of 'fine clothes, radios, guitars, motor-cars'.
38   ibid., p. 1462.
39   ibid., p. 1453.
40   ibid., p. 1455.
41   Kylie Tennant, 'How wrong is Xavier Herbert—a place like Tranby', *Bulletin*, 14 April 1962, pp. 26–7. Herbert's views were misunderstood when he first expressed them, as the response of Kylie Tennant to 'A town like Elliott' demonstrates: 'Our state and federal government departments are being persuaded by the success of co-operatives in other countries among primitive people and are coming to study this other alternative to the "swift extinction" or "assimilation by scattering" which was offered in the nineteenth century where Mr Herbert still lurks'.
42   Herbert, *Poor Fellow My Country*, p. 30.
43   ibid., pp. 58–61.
44   ibid., p. 62.
45   ibid., pp. 258, 261.
46   ibid., pp. 1461–2.
47   Herbert, 'A town like Elliott', pp. 23–5.
48   Herbert, *Poor Fellow My Country*, p. 1456.
49   ibid., p. 1034.
50   ibid., p. 30. In 1978 Herbert published a declaration in which he voices the same views. 'Until we give back to the Blackman just a bit of the land that was his, and give it without provisos, without strings to snatch it back [...] until we do that, we shall remain what we have always been

so far, a people without integrity, not a nation, but a community of thieves' (Xavier Herbert, 'Declaration by Xavier Herbert', April 1978, FL Mss 83).

Chapter 11: Colonials and Carpetbaggers

1 Xavier Herbert, *Poor Fellow My Country*, Collins, Sydney, 1975, p. 1355.

2 ibid., p. 1039.

3 ibid., p. 1081.

4 ibid., pp. 181–2.

5 ibid., p. 587.

6 ibid., p. 20.

7 T. S. Eliot, 'The waste land', *Selected Poems*, Faber, London, 1954, p. 57. The intention and method are the same. Both Eliot and Herbert juxtapose pictures of a tawdry present against the cultural riches of the past in order to criticise the fractured state of present culture. Both use scenes of booze-induced fellowship to represent the present. The tone of the ending of both is similar.

8 Herbert, *Poor Fellow My Country*, pp. 222–7.

9 ibid., pp. 235, 215–16.

10 ibid. *Fishing:* catfish (p. 11). *Hunting:* geese (p. 187), mud crabs (p. 339), duck (p. 386), lorikeets (p. 458). *Gathering:* stick egg galls (p. 389), cycad nuts (p. 425), honey (p. 607), turtle eggs (p. 329).

11 ibid., p. 10.

12 ibid., p. 9.

13 Herbert to Sadie Herbert, 3 October 1968, Box 48, FL Mss 83.

14 Herbert, *Poor Fellow My Country*, pp. 94–107, 485–510. Both pester him into taking them to visit Lily Lagoons. Both attempt to join him on his post-race drinking binge. On race day, though clearly unwelcome, Alfie insists on being one of the Lily Lagoons stable party, and spends the day frantically seeking attention.

15 ibid., p. 503. Lydia is provocatively rude to her hostess. She drives off with a married man with no concern for his, his wife's or his community's moral sensibilities. Alfie shows no concern for the proprieties of this society. 'There were numerous sharp glances. Alfie ignored them, looked about her boldly, followed Darcy to the door of the Scales Shed.'

16 ibid., pp. 680–1.

17 ibid., p. 127.

18 ibid., p. 688.

19 ibid., pp. 505, 543.

20 ibid., p. 554.

21 ibid., p. 142.

22 ibid., pp. 544–5.

23 ibid., p. 545.

24   ibid., p. 759.
25   ibid., p. 760.
26   ibid., p. 141.
27   ibid., p. 870.
28   ibid., pp. 578–9.
29   ibid., p. 219. 'Piggy's face, mostly purple before, with grog […] lay grey-faced, with slatey eyes half-open […] Prindy, on being told that it was his grandfather, gave […] one of those blank grey glances […].'
30   ibid., p. 319.
31   ibid., pp. 427, 428–9, 430, 434.
32   ibid., p. 1029.
33   ibid., p. 560.
34   ibid., p. 410.
35   ibid., p. 439.
36   ibid., p. 1063.
37   ibid., pp. 1237–8.
38   ibid., p. 24.
39   ibid., p. 669.
40   ibid., p. 24.
41   ibid., pp. 53–4.
42   ibid., p. 1166.
43   ibid., pp. 655, 660.
44   ibid., p. 95.
45   ibid., pp. 1395, 1021.
46   ibid., pp. 28, 119.
47   ibid., p. 1259. He describes the aftermath of the campaign in Greece thus: 'Tubby was still being reported as alive and kicking, mostly in news from luxurious Cairo, while most of Our Boys who had fought the Greek Campaign remained listed as Missing. The General wasn't kicking about the monstrous failure of the AIF in Greece. He was concentrated now on Churchill's latest game with the Knife, and was greatly angered by what he called the Callous Indifference of the Majority of the Australian People. He wanted more men—more and more men. […] He particularly wanted the Gallant Awstralians in it. You could always count on them'. Herbert's bitter mockery is an expression of his anger both at the British for using Australia to further their own ends and at Australian leaders who, far from resisting, fell over backwards to help them.
48   ibid., p. 772.
49   ibid., p. 1266.
50   Xavier Herbert, 'Declaration in Support of Labour', December 1975, FL Mss 83.
51   Herbert, *Poor Fellow My Country*, pp. 80, 98.
52   ibid., pp. 660–1.
53   ibid., pp. 1062–3.

54   ibid.
55   ibid., p. 1052.
56   ibid., pp. 666, 1081.
57   ibid., p. 1264.
58   Irene Dowsing, *Curtin of Australia*, Acacia Press, Blackburn, n.d., p. 124.
59   Herbert, *Poor Fellow My Country*, p. 1329.
60   ibid., p. 1264. 'It was a fact that the new Prime Minister's every utterance (and he made a lot these days, new as he was to having control of the National Broadcasting System) did sound rather like Storm the Barricades! But it could have been due less to intensity of feeling than to training in some Labor Debating School.'
61   Frances de Groen, *Xavier Herbert*, UQP, St Lucia, 1998, pp. 122, 131, 136, 142. Evatt was a fellow member of the Fellowship of Australian Writers. Herbert asked for and got help from him in getting into the army. At war's end, Evatt helped him get early discharge from the army.
62   Herbert, *Poor Fellow My Country*, pp. 1265–6.
63   Dowsing, *Curtin of Australia*, p. 110.
64   Herbert, *Poor Fellow My Country*, p. 667.
65   ibid., pp. 1035, 663, 531.
66   ibid., p. 1395.
67   ibid., pp. 662, 1115.
68   ibid., p. 697.
69   Xavier Herbert, 'Bang goes my O.B.E.!', *Bulletin*, 22 February 1961, p. 52.
70   Xavier Herbert, 'Untitled', Box 60, FL Mss 83.
71   Adrian Mitchell, 'Fiction', in Leonie Kramer (ed.), *The Oxford History of Australian Literature*, OUP, Melbourne, 1981, p. 126.
72   Herbert, *Poor Fellow My Country*, p. 333.
73   David Kingsbury, 'Letters to the editor', *The West Australian*, Perth, 30 October 1999.
74   F. J. Higgins, 'Letters to the editor', *The West Australian*, Perth, 1 November 1999.
75   John Lane, 'Letters to the editor', *The West Australian*, Perth, 1 November 1999.
76   <www.cia.com.au/vic/cia.html>. *Watching Brief*, Public Radio News Service, Melbourne, October–November 1988.
77   *Interview with Malcolm Fraser*, ABC Radio, 10 May 2001.
78   Herbert, *Poor Fellow My Country*, pp. 1031–2.
79   Peter Read, *Belonging: Australians, Place and Aboriginal Ownership*, summarised for *Late Night Live*, 2 August 2000, ABC web site, <www.abc.net.au/m/talks/lnl.html>.
80   Herbert, *Poor Fellow My Country*, p. 74.
81   Mark Ludlow, 'In a bind over ties', *The Sunday Times*, Perth, 9 April 2000, p. 46. 'The Human Rights and Equal Opportunity Commission heard estimates between 10% and 30% of Aboriginal children were taken. The

Howard Government disputes the number. [...] It says it was never more than 10%. [...] The Government estimates that the number [...] "forcibly or wrongly removed" may be as low as 1%. The Government says "there was never a generation of stolen Aboriginal children".'

82   '27 year journey returns to the same point', *The West Australian*, Perth, 19 August 2000, p. 13.

83   Max Brown, 'On the spot', *The Sunday Times*, Perth, 26 March 2000. The article lists the following statistics. Indigenous men and women are dying twenty years earlier than other Australians. Indigenous adults suffer the highest rates of imprisonment, at twenty-two times the non-Indigenous rate, despite representing just 2 per cent of the population. Twenty-three per cent of Aboriginals are unemployed, compared with 9 per cent of other Australians. Aboriginal children are up to eight times more likely to be abused and neglected and four times more likely to be in care. Eleven per cent of Indigenous people have post-school qualifications, compared with 31 per cent of other Australians. The same article points out that the federal government has spent '$14 billion on Aboriginal affairs in the past decade'.

84   Herbert, *Poor Fellow My Country*, p. 1259. The capacity of Australian soldiers to survive after a defeat in Europe elicits a reference to the 'individualism and resourcefulness [...] (which is perhaps the only Australian characteristic Worth a Dump)'.

85   ibid., p. 786. One such rare description is the following. 'There was no doubt about a general sympathy for Jews suffering under Hitler. That was shown readily enough to Kurt and Rifkah, when at the siding people off the train they didn't even know nodded in a way to indicate their feelings, and some went so far as to address them: "Things gettin' pretty crook for your mob over the other side. Sumpin ought to be done to stop them square-'ead bastards."'

86   ibid., p. 394.

87   ibid., p. 519. 'It was Nobby Knowles: "We'll get you Delacy...just you wait!" [...] Nugget Knowles had his say: "We'll get you all right, Delacy...just you wait!" Jeremy said, "Sounds like there's no such thing as a Knowles' mind."'

Chapter 12: The Tragedy of Jeremy Delacy

1   Aristotle, *The Poetics*, Heinemann, London, 1927, p. 47, ch. 13, verse 5.

2   Xavier Herbert, *Poor Fellow My Country*, Collins, Sydney, 1975, p. 99.

3   ibid., p. 1035.

4   ibid., pp. 187, 34. Delacy understands that 'storytelling is a matter of trade, like everything else' and that when he asks Prindy for a 'yarn belong to you' he must pay for that yarn with a 'present' (p. 187). 'I've known 'em', Delacy tells Bishoff, 'to tell of something happening a hundred miles

away in a place and to people they haven't seen in months...and sure enough, the news turns up eventually' (p. 34).
5 ibid., p. 25.
6 ibid., p. 531.
7 ibid., p. 615.
8 ibid., p. 623.
9 ibid., pp. 127, 1211.
10 ibid., pp. 531–2.
11 ibid., pp. 555, 1228. Alfie says: '[Delacy] only fights them for the sake of it. Negative, as I've said all along' (p. 555). 'Yes...that's what Jeremy Delacy was chiefly renowned for when I first met him...making fools of people. [...] It's a negative thing' (p. 1228).
12 ibid., p. 48.
13 ibid., p. 1074.
14 ibid., p. 1171.
15 ibid., p. 630.
16 ibid., p. 1297.
17 ibid., pp. 1272–3.
18 ibid., p. 1233. Lydia's disillusion is expressed in a bitter letter blaming Delacy for the 'futile death of my gallant, talented and noble father'.
19 ibid., pp. 1391–2, 1400.
20 ibid., p. 1280.
21 ibid., pp. 1097–8.
22 ibid., p. 761.
23 ibid., p. 575.
24 ibid., p. 737.
25 ibid., pp. 596, 600.
26 ibid., p. 186.
27 ibid., pp. 395, 403.
28 ibid., p. 631.
29 ibid., p. 643.
30 ibid., p. 644.
31 ibid., pp. 872, 847.
32 ibid., p. 907.
33 ibid., p. 973.
34 ibid., p. 22.
35 ibid., pp. 911–12.
36 ibid., pp. 1424–6.
37 ibid., p. 1438.
38 ibid., p. 1440.
39 ibid., p. 1441.
40 ibid., p. 1443.
41 ibid., p. 205.
42 ibid., pp. 1184–5.

Chapter 13: The Myth of Golden Prindy

1   Xavier Herbert, *Poor Fellow My Country*, Collins, Sydney, 1975, p. 36.
2   ibid., pp. 190, 418, 12, 181, 388, 710, 892, 870. There are stories about the origin of the world, rivers, rain and storms, porcupines, mountains, parrots, pigeons, butcher birds, kingfishers, kookaburras, geese, flowers and many more.
3   ibid., p. 190.
4   ibid., p. 594.
5   ibid., pp. 704, 175. When Bridie and Delacy make love, 'The Moon went down. The kweeluks found a baby spirit wandering, danced around it in the starlight, calling, calling: *Kweeluk...kweeluk...*' (p. 175).
6   Northrop Frye, *Anatomy of Criticism*, Penguin, London, 1990, pp. 198–203. Frye describes the six phases as follows: 'the myth of the birth of the hero', 'the innocent youth of the hero', 'the quest', 'maintaining the innocent world against the assault of experience', 'a reflective, idyllic view of experience' and the 'movement from active to contemplative adventure'. The presence of the first five phases is demonstrated in this chapter. The 'central image [is] that of the old man in the tower, the lonely hermit absorbed in occult or magical studies'. This phase is seen in Delacy's retreat at the end of the book, which was dealt with in Chapter 12.
7   Frye, *Anatomy*, pp. 195, 193.
8   Herbert, *Poor Fellow My Country*, p. 32.
9   Frye, *Anatomy*, p. 193.
10   Herbert to Sadie Herbert, 4 September 1968, Box 48, FL Mss 83.
11   Herbert, *Poor Fellow My Country*, p. 776.
12   ibid., p. 883.
13   Frye, *Anatomy*, p. 33.
14   Herbert, *Poor Fellow My Country*, pp. 619, 636.
15   Frye, *Anatomy*, p. 198.
16   Herbert, *Poor Fellow My Country*, pp. 9–10.
17   Frye, *Anatomy*, pp. 198–9.
18   Herbert, *Poor Fellow My Country*, pp. 181, 477, 594, 1008.
19   ibid., p. 1133.
20   ibid., pp. 775–6.
21   ibid., pp. 775, 1105–6.
22   ibid., p. 1426.
23   ibid., p. 26.
24   ibid., p. 747.
25   ibid., pp. 216–20.
26   ibid., pp. 399, 267, 600, 970.
27   ibid., pp. 464–5.
28   ibid., pp. 35–6.
29   ibid., p. 1417.
30   ibid., p. 996.

31	Frye, *Anatomy*, p. 189.
32	Herbert, *Poor Fellow My Country*, p. 1450.
33	ibid., p. 190.
34	Herbert to Sadie, 6 October 1968, Box 48, FL Mss 83.
35	Herbert to Sadie, 11 September 1968, Box 48, FL Mss 83. Herbert describes Prindy as 'the prepubital [sic] boy who is the symbol of the tragedy of the Australian Dream'.
36	Frye, *Anatomy*, pp. 200, 196, 199.
37	Herbert, *Poor Fellow My Country*, p. 465.
38	Frances de Groen, *Xavier Herbert*, UQP, St Lucia, 1998, p. 149. Herbert used to 'wander off into the rainforest for days on end, sometimes getting lost and having to follow creeks to reach home'.
39	Robert Reid, '*Playboy* interview Xavier Herbert', *Australian Playboy*, June 1982, p. 38.
40	Herbert, *Poor Fellow My Country*, pp. 920–1.
41	Frye, *Anatomy*, p. 197.
42	Herbert, *Poor Fellow My Country*, p. 466.
43	Frye, *Anatomy*, p. 200.
44	Herbert, *Poor Fellow My Country*, p. 467.
45	ibid., pp. 470–2.
46	Frye, *Anatomy*, p. 201.
47	Xavier Herbert, *Capricornia*, Angus & Robertson, Melbourne, 1971, pp. 45, 199.
48	Herbert, *Poor Fellow My Country*, p. 120.
49	Frye, *Anatomy*, p. 201.
50	Herbert, *Poor Fellow My Country*, pp. 120, 44, 63.
51	ibid., pp. 776, 804, 805, 826, 869, 1325.
52	ibid., p. 630.
53	Herbert, *Capricornia*, p. 414.
54	Herbert, *Poor Fellow My Country*, pp. 1035, 630.
55	Herbert, *Capricornia*, pp. 408–9.
56	Herbert, *Poor Fellow My Country*, p. 712.
57	Frye, *Anatomy*, p. 202.
58	Herbert, *Poor Fellow My Country*, p. 407.
59	ibid., pp. 704–5.
60	ibid., pp. 942–6.
61	ibid., p. 1325.
62	Herbert to Sadie, 4 September 1968, Box 48, FL Mss 83.
63	M. E. Novak, *Realism, Myth and History in Defoe's Fiction*, University of Nebraska Press, Lincoln, 1983, p. 43.
64	Herbert, *Poor Fellow My Country*, pp. 560, 562.
65	ibid., p. 1331.
66	ibid., pp. 204, 609, 469, 968.
67	ibid., pp. 198–9, 460–1, 1435–7.

68   ibid., pp. 610–11.
69   ibid., p. 624.
70   Shakespeare, *King Lear*, act II, scene 3, line 7.
71   Herbert, *Poor Fellow My Country*, p. 979.
72   ibid., pp. 947–50, 1320–1.
73   ibid., pp. 1190–1.
74   ibid., pp. 1452–3, 1456.
75   ibid., p. 1463.
76   T. S. Eliot, *The Four Quartets*, Faber, London, 2000, p. 3.

SELECT BIBLIOGRAPHY

I have limited this bibliography to works I have referred to in the book, and other works that I have read and that may, therefore, have influenced my thinking. Those interested in a comprehensive bibliography will find one in:

Sansome, David, *Xavier Herbert a Bibliography*, Occasional Papers No. 6, Northern Territory Library Service, Darwin, 1988.

FL   Fryer Library, Queensland University
OUP   Oxford University Press
UQP   University of Queensland Press

WORKS BY XAVIER HERBERT

Novels

(The editions cited are those referred to in this book)
Herbert, Xavier, *Capricornia*, Angus & Robertson, Melbourne, 1971 (1938).
—— *Seven Emus*, Fontana, Melbourne, 1977 (1959).
—— *Soldiers' Women*, Fontana, Netley, 1978 (1961).
—— *Poor Fellow My Country*, Collins, Sydney, 1975.

Unpublished Novels

Herbert, Xavier, Notes for 'Yellow Fellow', Box 7a, FL Mss 83.
—— 'The Little Widow', Box 15, FL Mss 83.

Autobiography

Herbert, Xavier, *Disturbing Element*, Fontana, Melbourne, 1976 (1963).

Short Stories

Herbert, Xavier, *Larger Than Life*, Fontana, Melbourne, 1976 (1963).
McDougall, Russell (ed.), *South of Capricornia*, OUP, Melbourne, 1990.

Articles and Other Shorter Pieces

Herbert, Xavier, 'I sinned against syntax', *Meanjin*, 19(1), 1960, pp. 31–5.

—— 'My road to Ruhen', *Observer*, Sydney, 24 December 1960, pp. 4–6.

—— 'Bang goes my O.B.E.!', *Bulletin*, 22 February 1961, p. 52.

—— 'How *Capricornia* was made', *Bulletin*, 8 March 1961, pp. 51–2.

—— 'Herbert's retort to Stephensen', *Bulletin*, 29 March 1961, p. 52.

—— 'Tom Flynn of Rum Jungle', *Bulletin*, 31 March 1962, p. 12.

—— 'A town like Elliott: "There is NO solution to the Aborigines' problem"', *Bulletin*, 31 March 1962, pp. 23–5.

—— 'May his spirit not be disturbed by hacks', *Tribune*, 5 June 1967, p. 5.

—— 'The agony and the joy', *Overland*, 50–51, Autumn 1972, pp. 65–8.

—— 'Declaration in Support of Labour', December 1975, FL Mss 83.

—— 'Declaration by Xavier Herbert', April 1978, FL Mss 83.

—— 'As a prophet, the great satirist was a failure', *Sydney Morning Herald*, 10 January 1984, p. 7.

—— 'Australia—in the Crystal Ball', Box 20, FL Mss 83.

—— 'Minjie Meanjin', Box 20, FL Mss 83.

—— 'Little Foxes', unpublished, Box 60, FL Mss 83.

Interviews and Speeches

Herbert, Xavier, recorded conversation for the National Archives, 12 July 1961, transcript, FL Mss 83.

—— recorded conversation for the National Library, 13 December 1975, transcript, FL Mss 83.

—— interview with Hazel de Berg, transcript, National Library of Australia Mss 888.

—— interview with Elizabeth Riddell, transcript, Box 60, FL Mss 83.

—— speech to Adelaide Arts Festival, March 1962, transcript, FL Mss 83.

—— speech to the Conference of the Society of Hospital Pharmacists, October 1963, transcript, FL Mss 83.

—— speech entitled 'A Novelist's Responsibility to History', sound tape, Queensland University Library, 1976.

—— speech given at a farewell luncheon, sound tape, Queensland University Library, 1976.

Reid, Robert, '*Playboy* interview Xavier Herbert', *Australian Playboy*, June 1982, pp. 33–9, 129–36.

WORKS BY OTHER WRITERS

Books

Beer, Gillian, *The Romance*, Methuen, London, 1970.

Clancy, Laurie, *Xavier Herbert*, Twayne, Boston, 1981.

de Groen, Frances, *Xavier Herbert*, UQP, St Lucia, 1998.

de Groen, Frances & Laurie Hergenhan (eds), *Xavier Herbert Letters*, UQP, St Lucia, 2002.

Dowsing, Irene, *Curtin of Australia*, Acacia Press, Blackburn, n.d.

Forster, E. M., *Aspects of the Novel*, Penguin, Middlesex, 1962.

Frye, Northrop, *Anatomy of Criticism*, Penguin, London, 1990.

Hassall, Anthony J. (ed.), *The Making of Xavier Herbert's* Poor Fellow My Country, Foundation for Australian Literary Studies, Townsville, 1988.

Healy, J. J., *Literature and the Aborigine in Australia 1770–1975*, UQP, St Lucia, 1978.

Hesseltine, Harry, *Xavier Herbert*, OUP, Melbourne, 1973.

Kawin, Bruce, *Telling It Again and Again*, Cornell University Press, Ithaca, 1972.

McLaren, John, *Herbert's* Capricornia *and* Poor Fellow My Country, Shillington House, Melbourne, 1981.

Vidal, Gore, *Matters of Fact and Fiction*, Vintage, USA, 1978.

Walker, Richard & Helen, *Curtin's Cowboys: Australia's Secret Bush Commandos*, Allen & Unwin, Sydney, 1986.

Articles and Other Shorter Pieces

Buckley, Vincent, '*Capricornia*', *Meanjin*, 19(1), 1960, pp. 13–30.

Casey, Gavin, 'The Red Page—Book of the Year, 1961', *Bulletin*, 30 December 1961, p. 33.

Clancy, Laurie, 'The design of *Capricornia*', *Meanjin*, 34(2), June 1975, pp. 150–6.

—— '*Poor Fellow My Country*: Herbert's masterpiece?', *Southerly*, 37(2), June 1977, pp. 163–75.

Daniel, Helen, 'Outsiders and society: *Poor Fellow My Country*', *Westerly*, 23(4), December 1978, pp. 37–47.

Dunstan, Keith, 'Xavier (Alfred Francis) Herbert', *Ratbags*, Golden Press, Sydney, 1979, pp. 133–45.

Grant, Don, 'Xavier Herbert's botch', *Overland*, 65, 1976, pp. 43–7.

Green, Kevin, 'Xavier Herbert, H. G. Wells and J. S. Huxley: Unexpected British connections', *Australian Literary Studies*, 12(1), May 1985, pp. 47–64.

Healy, J. J., 'Review of *Xavier Herbert* by Laurie Clancy', *Australian Literary Studies*, 10(4), October 1982, pp. 535–41.

Hergenhan, Laurie, 'An Australian tragedy: Xavier Herbert's *Poor Fellow My Country*', *Quadrant*, 21(2), 1977, pp. 62–70.

—— 'Rebuttal, a defence of Xavier Herbert's *Poor Fellow My Country*', *Overland*, 67, 1977, pp. 41–2.

Hesseltine, Harry, 'A fiction chronicle', *Meanjin*, 20(4), 1961, pp. 474, 478–9, 481.

—— 'Xavier Herbert's magnum opus', *Meanjin*, 34(2), June 1975, pp. 133–6.

—— 'Xavier Herbert', *Australian Literary Studies*, 12(1), May 1985, pp. 91–3.

Jeffery, P. W., '*Soldiers' Women*', *Overland*, 22 December 1961, pp. 50–1.

Kelly, David, 'Landscape in *Poor Fellow My Country*', *Overland*, 67, 1977, pp. 43–6.

Kiernan, Brian, 'Xavier Herbert: *Capricornia*', *Australian Literary Studies*, 4(4), October 1970, pp. 360–70.

Kynaston, Edward, 'Flawed achievement', *Overland*, 62, Spring 1975, pp. 76–8.

McQueen, Humphrey, '*Poor Fellow My Country*', *Arena*, 41, 1976, pp. 79–91.

Mitchell, Adrian, 'Fiction', in Leonie Kramer (ed.), *The Oxford History of Australian Literature*, OUP, Melbourne, 1981.

Moore, Tom Inglis, '*Capricornia*', *Australian Highway*, 20 March 1938, pp. 21–3.

—— 'The cry of the crow: Sombreness in Australian literature', *Meanjin*, 30(1), March 1971, pp. 5–26.

Prideaux, Helen, 'The experimental novel in Australia, part 1', *Prospect*, 3(2), 1960, pp. 13–14, 16.

Stephensen, P. R., 'How I edited *Capricornia*', *Bulletin*, 15 March 1961, pp. 33–4.

Stow, Randolph, 'Epic of Capricorn', *Times Literary Supplement*, 9 April 1976, p. 417.

Unpublished Theses

Airs, Roslyn, 'The Geography of *Poor Fellow My Country*', Macarthur Institute of Higher Education, 1986.

Candy, Betty, 'The Historicity of *Poor Fellow My Country*', Macarthur Institute of Higher Education, 1986.

Eurell, Louise, 'Xavier Herbert's Use of Aboriginal Mythology', Macarthur Institute of Higher Education, 1986.

Ikin, Van, 'Australian Political Novelists', University of Sydney, 1980.

Munro, Craig, 'Inky Stephensen, Xavier Herbert and *Capricornia*: The Facts about a Long Fiction', University of Queensland, 1977.

Interviews

Sadie Herbert, taped interview, University of Queensland Library, Audio Visual Collection, 1976.

INDEX